Geoffrey Hill's later work

Manchester University Press

Geoffrey Hill's later work
Radiance of apprehension

Alex Wylie

Manchester University Press

Copyright © Alex Wylie 2019

The right of Alex Wylie to be identified as the author of this work has been asserted by him in accordance with the Copyright, Designs and Patents Act 1988.

Published by Manchester University Press
Oxford Road, Manchester M13 9PL
www.manchesteruniversitypress.co.uk

British Library Cataloguing-in-Publication Data
A catalogue record for this book is available from the British Library

ISBN 978 1 5261 2494 4 hardback
ISBN 978 1 5261 6022 2 paperback

First published 2019

The publisher has no responsibility for the persistence or accuracy of URLs for any external or third-party internet websites referred to in this book, and does not guarantee that any content on such websites is, or will remain, accurate or appropriate.

Typeset by Newgen Publishing UK

To my parents,
and my sister

Contents

List of abbreviations   ix

1. 'A theory of energy'   1
2. A postscript on modernist poetics?   20
3. 'Turbulently at rest': order and anarchy in the later work   47
4. 'There are no demons': faith and metaphysical desire   77
5. 'Bless hierarchy': the cultural politics of Hill's later work   112
6. 'A calling for England': Hill and the political imagination   142

References   175
Index   183

Abbreviations

ATdT	*Al Tempo de' Tremuoti*
BH	*Broken Hierarchies: Poems 1952–2012*
C	*Clavics*
CCW	*Collected Critical Writings*
EoV	*Expostulations on the Volcano*
HOLC	*Hymns to Our Lady of Chartres*
L	*Ludo*
LIV	*Liber Illustrium Virorum*
O	*Oraclau	Oracles*
OB	*Odi Barbare*
OS	*The Orchards of Syon*
SC	*Scenes from Comus*
SS	*Speech! Speech!*
TCP	*A Treatise of Civil Power*
ToL	*The Triumph of Love*
WT	*Without Title*

Chapter 1

'A theory of energy'

If Geoffrey Hill's poetry has ever been at odds with prevailing literary tastes, fashions, and commitments, then his later work, both in poetry and criticism, is increasingly open about this being at odds. This later work is often a self-referential examination of just what it is that makes it so at odds with its surrounding literary and political culture, embracing that sense of "cultural recalcitrance"[1] – though certainly not entirely without caveat or regret. This strong sense of eccentricity, a favourite word of the later Hill's, arises both from his developments of New Critical and modernist beliefs, an investment bound to put him at bay among the postmodernist culture of the late-twentieth and early-twenty-first centuries, and from his acute sense of poetry being by nature political and historical, a sense which, as he saw it, made him a natural antagonist of the culture in which this late poetry takes, or does not take, its place. However, as widely acclaimed poet and critic, one of the most written-about of the last few decades in the English language, as well as fulfilling the role of Oxford Professor of Poetry in this period – not to mention being knighted in 2012 – Hill's self-presentation as an isolated and derided figure demands some explanation – which is one element of this book's general approach. Geoffrey Hill was routinely described as 'the greatest living poet in English'[2] and variants thereof, and so he had a formidable reputation as a poet – though it was, rather, his reputation as a formidable poet which made him, as he saw it, a decidedly minority figure in broadly cultural terms.

I categorise Geoffrey Hill's later work as roughly a twenty-year period, from around 1996 (the year of 'Dividing Legacies', an essay on T.S. Eliot which I see as inaugurating this later phase) to 2016, the year of his death at the age of eighty-four, in which Hill published his last piece, 'Mightier and Darker', an essay-review on Charles

Williams in the *Times Literary Supplement*.³ This body of work incorporates poetry, literary-critical essays, and Oxford Professor of Poetry lectures, and I draw here on unpublished material housed in the Brotherton Library at the University of Leeds which is dated to this period. Hill's later work is a distinct phase, though there are continuations and reminiscences of his earlier work within it; the period is distinguished not least by the stunning prolificity which it exhibits, Hill producing thirteen new books of poetry between roughly 1996 (*Canaan*, which is not figured here, was published in this year) and 2012; two books of critical essays; and fifteen Oxford Professor of Poetry lectures between 2010 and 2015. Hill had previously published six books of poetry and two books of criticism between 1959 and 1996.

The criticism of this later period may appear daunting to new readers of his work. It is deeply invested in philosophical perspectives, to the extent that one might categorise much of Hill's later work in criticism as 'philosophy of literature': personally, however, I feel that such a categorisation would detract from the available dimensions of literary criticism. Hill's criticism is philosophical, and his later poetry and criticism are a working through – not necessarily a working *out of* – various intellectual, moral, and psychological concerns. On that point, I would claim that the interdependence of the intellectual, the moral, and the psychological – that is, the emotional, the deeply personal – is necessary to writing of real importance: in a work of art, the 'problem' which the piece embodies is both a 'problem' in an existential sense and as intellectual and moral puzzlement. This sense of the problematic certainly drives Hill's later output, copious and challenging as it is: and a remark about poetry of the Movement of the 1950s, including such poets as Philip Larkin (a favourite *bête noire*) and Kingsley Amis, against which his early work (particularly his first collection, *For the Unfallen*, of 1959) took its directions, sums up this crucial aspect of his later work: "when you have techne without crisis, the result is poetry similar to that written by the Movement poets of the 1950s".⁴ Reading through the two new books of criticism in the *Collected Critical Writings*, and the thirteen books of poetry (to date) in this later period, one is constantly reminded that 'crisis' harks back to the Greek word *krinein*, to decide or judge: it is a word that holds in a single thought perplexity and resolution.⁵

Throughout the criticism of this later period, certain fundamental problems are being worried away at: one of the most fundamental of these being, precisely, *being*. Hill's obsession with being begins in his criticism as early as 1975, in the essay 'Perplexed Persistence: The Exemplary Failure of T.H. Green', being figured here as "that which points beyond the data":

> The difference between Kant and the Victorian students of Kant in England may well turn on a difference of emphasis concerning that which "points beyond the data". In Kant this is a "common element" existing as "a logical presupposition, a purely formal implication"; in Sidgwick and Green that which points beyond the data is more often a pious wish. Pious wishes are of course wholly valid, unless they are presented as logical presuppositions and purely formal implications. It is then that they cease to be "that which points beyond the data" and become the "ultimate vague reasons" which Whitehead has so precisely described. (*Collected Critical Writings* [*henceforth CCW*] 113)

I wish to begin my exploration of Hill's later work by remarking on his perplexed fascination with being; and to begin with that sentence, which might stand over much of the energy and drive of the later poetry: "Pious wishes are of course wholly valid, unless they are presented as logical presuppositions and purely formal implications." Along with Hill's perplexed concern with being, or "that which points beyond the data", goes an ethical self-recognition that one's own desires, or "pious wishes", cannot fail to orientate one's most "purely formal" interests. In other words, you cannot wish being into being, as it were, but to try to do so is more than understandable, provided you *recognise* that you are indeed doing this – and this sort of self-recognition is the crucial task of the writer, in Hill's view. In the words of F.H. Bradley, a philosopher central to Hill's later approach, the task is "to get within the judgement the condition of the judgement" (*CCW* 566). And in another relatively early essay, 'Our Word Is Our Bond' (1983), Hill writes (quoting T.H. Green again) "to place ourselves 'outside the process by which our knowledge is developed' is to conceive of an untenable 'ecstasy', whereas to recognize our being within the process is to accept our true condition" (*CCW* 158).

This apprehension, taken largely from F.H. Bradley also, is a crucial dynamo of Hill's later work, as it is one of its central themes. To what extent Hill is successful in this ethical task is debatable; indeed, the extent to which this scrutiny of self-recognition is ultimately a counsel of perfection is also up for debate, and, indeed, has been and is being debated.

Peter Robinson has recently expressed scepticism on this point. "Bradley", writes Robinson, "allows that 'the more the conditions of your assertion are included in your assertion, so much the truer and less erroneous does your judgement become'. But, he adds, 'can the conditions of judgement ever be made complete and comprised within the judgement? In my opinion this is impossible.' What Hill takes as a prerequisite for probity is – given the singular complexity and extent of the world when contrasted with (for instance) the limits of an individual's senses – exactly what Bradley believes to be impossible".[6] This is an important counter-argument, which actually draws attention to another essential element of Hill's later approach. Along with the obsessed concern for being in Hill's later work goes an enthusiastic commitment to what he calls 'eros' (*CCW* 571 *et al.*) – that is, an existentialist sense of *becoming* alongside the desire for being. It is this sense of eros, of becoming, which Hill takes from F.H. Bradley, that drives Hill's sense of "a theory of energy" which his later work explores and embodies. (The erotic sense being that the exploration *is* the embodiment.)

As early as the 1970s, then, Hill displays an interest in nineteenth-century British Idealism (philosophers like F.H. Bradley and T.H. Green), its exemplary failures and pious wishes. In part, this interest is part of an ongoing engagement with nineteenth-century British literary and intellectual culture, but it also represents an interest in being and its failure, whether exemplary or not, in an era of philosophical and economic materialism. If "Metaphysics remain | in common language something of a joke" (*BH* 490) then perhaps it is their embattled, derided nature which is of a kind with Hill's sense of being at bay; or perhaps an engagement with metaphysics in the present era demands an *un*common language. In short, the British Idealists such as Sigdwick and Green, here, and most emphatically F.H. Bradley, are important to Hill's later work, as is the tension between the "purely formal" and the "pious wish": or, put in starker terms, the objective and the subjective. Indeed, one of the major figures in Hill's later criticism, with whom Hill has a fraught and evolving relationship, is John Ruskin, a figure also piously wishing and asserting the purely formal, according to Hill's overall analysis – it is Ruskin's term "intrinsic value" which is a point of crux for Hill's later writings about poetry and being. 'Intrinsic value' is a term which evokes being, the essence, the thing-in-itself, just as it evokes the a-historical New Critical poem by which Hill is tempted.[7] "'Intrinsic value', as Ruskin uses it, is emphatic but not precise; though its power of emphasis is due in great part to its capacity to *suggest* precision" (*CCW* 388). This theme runs throughout Hill's later criticism, and is, in no small part, a worried vigilance over his own suggestions of precision: in the words of F.H. Bradley – that philosopher so crucial to Hill's later approach – "illusions begotten on the brain by the wish of the heart".[8]

Hill's critique of T.S. Eliot

A major point of departure for Hill's later work is his critique of T.S. Eliot. Bradley is readily associated with Eliot – who wrote his doctoral dissertation on the philosopher, and who published the essay 'Francis Herbert Bradley' in the *Times Literary Supplement* in 1927 – but Hill's later period is driven by his reading of Bradley. Indeed, Hill's critique of Eliot is driven in no small part by his interpretation of Bradley *contra* Eliot. However, Eliot's theory of impersonality, and his example as poet-critic, is a pervasive element in Hill's overall development as poet and critic. Hill's divergence from Eliot is begun to be spelled out explicitly in 1996, in what I take to be the beginning of Hill's later period, in the essay 'Dividing Legacies', a direction traced further yet in the later essays 'Eros in F.H. Bradley and T.S. Eliot' and 'Word Value in F.H. Bradley and T.S. Eliot', two essays included in *Alienated Majesty* in the *Collected Critical Writings* (2008), which were originally delivered as lectures at Cambridge University in January 2005.

Hill's critique of Eliot centres on Eliot's increasingly pragmatic view of poetry, which Hill sees as a dereliction ("Yeats died and Eliot abdicated", as he remarks [*CCW* 579]), but it is also about the different use to which the two poet-critics put their readings of F.H. Bradley. This critique should not be thought of as an all-out rejection of Eliot and his poetics: rather, it is an exploration and development of Eliot's ideas *beyond* Eliot, as the New Criticism in the mid-twentieth century was, including the work of such American poets and poet-critics as Allen Tate, John Crowe Ransom, and Richard Eberhart, for instance, figures hugely influential on Hill's early work. It is a correction rather than an outright repudiation, though Hill often comes out quite strongly against Eliot in the essays of *Alienated Majesty*. Hill's later work, too, is broadly New Critical in its allegiances, both proclaimed and tacit; though these allegiances can be quite overtly stated, as in one Oxford Professor of Poetry lecture, for instance, in which Hill quotes with heartfelt approval ("My God, if only I could have written that!") R.P. Blackmur's definition of poetry, that it is "language so twisted and posed in a form that it not only expresses the matter in hand but adds to the stock of available reality".[9]

The critique of Eliot's pragmatism implies another of the central concepts of Hill's later thought, namely intrinsic value. In 'Translating Value', the first essay in *Inventions of Value* (one of the two collections of later essays first published in *Collected Critical Writings* in 2008) Hill quotes what A.C. Bradley (F.H.'s brother) calls in 'Poetry for Poetry's Sake' the 'ulterior' values of poetry. These ulterior values are precisely what Eliot comes to espouse in his increasingly 'public' selfhood, according to Hill: that is, a selfhood whose emphasis is increasingly on the personality condemned in Eliot's early, seminal criticism. Eliot's abdication, as Hill presents it (*CCW* 579) speaks to a betrayal of high modernist values and anticipates the postmodernist cult of personality in which Hill finds himself stranded. "Such a distinction between self and personality – one in which priority is given to self – is now infrequently and insufficiently made", Hill claims in 'Alienated Majesty: Ralph W. Emerson', for example (*CCW* 496).

Hill describes the last chapter of Eliot's *The Use of Poetry and the Use of Criticism* (1933) as a "threnos" (*CCW* 563); that is, the declaration of Eliot's abdication, as it were, an unwitting elegy for the writer's own integrity. However, earlier in that book (originally delivered as a lecture series) Eliot also remarks:

When a poet deliberately restricts his public by his choice of style of writing or of subject-matter, this is a special situation demanding explanation and extenuation, but I doubt that this ever happens. It is one thing to write in a style which is already popular, and another to hope that one's writing may eventually become popular. From one point of view, the poet aspires to the condition of the music-hall comedian.[10]

This is roughly the opposite of Hill's approach in his later work. Eliot's passage is a strangely dissonant echo of the "music-hall theory of life"[11] dismissed by Bradley in 'Pleasure for Pleasure's Sake', the chapter on hedonism in *Ethical Studies* (1876); and it is indicative of Eliot's confusion around the notion of pleasure, according to Hill's claim. Indeed, the dissonance of this echo goes some way to illustrating Eliot's parting from Bradleian ideals. Eliot goes on: "Being incapable of altering his wares to suit a prevailing taste, if there be any, he naturally desires a state of society in which they may become popular, and in which his own talents will be put to the best use. He is accordingly interested in the *use* of poetry." The worldly interestedness of Eliot's position here is variously rejected in Hill's later essays; for instance, in the approbatory quotation of Ralph Waldo Emerson's "Genius is power; Talent is applicability" (*CCW* 530), which stands as a corrective to Eliot's sense of "his own talents [being] put to the best use".

It is Eliot's turning from power in this Romantic sense to that of power as social influence – the applicability of the music-hall comedian – which is a crux of Hill's contention. In 'Dividing Legacies' (1996), Hill identifies this turn for the first time, commandeering the terms 'pitch' and 'tone' to do it: "It was the pitch of *Prufrock and Other Observations* that disturbed and alienated readers; it was the tone of *Four Quartets* that assuaged and consoled them" (*CCW* 377). Pitch describes the commitment to immediate context, to the weight, history, and relations of words, what Hill calls (among other things) "word value" (*CCW* 532–547, 'Word Value in F.H. Bradley and T.S. Eliot', *et al.*); tone describes the attitude of a piece, 'attitude' in the senses both of message and of posture – its social applicability. Eliot's deterioration from pitch to tone is one from selfhood, which in Hill's thought is concurrent with language and history, to personality – playing the public persona, echoing national sentiment, and so on. Hill's own commitment to "immediate context" and "pitch" is simultaneously a commitment to the self over the personality, which is at the same time a commitment to Emerson's 'genius' over 'talent' (remembering that 'genius' comes from a word meaning 'spirit').

In the preface to the 1928 edition of *The Sacred Wood*, Eliot describes poetry as "a superior amusement" in a passage singled out for particular opprobrium in 'Eros in F.H. Bradley and T.S. Eliot' (*CCW* 555). Hill claims this is modelled on a passage from Bradley's *Essays on Truth and Reality* but is "markedly inferior to Bradley's" (*CCW* 555). Hill's contention to this general position is the following:

> Even if you say "superior amusement" only to save yourself from calling it something worse, you have unnecessarily given hostages to "the Pragmatist", who was suspected by Bradley of believing that the world of art belongs to the region of the worthless-in-itself.
>
> That body of opinion which focuses on, solidifies around, the sense of an object "worthless-in-itself" is a power with which you cannot compromise; the price exacted by your recalcitrance is that of alienation. (*CCW* 556)

Hill's later work is self-consciously pitched against this very "body of opinion" – and this commitment to being pitched *against* (a sense which ghosts his conception of "pitch") radically informs his reading of Eliot. In fact, the whole character of contemporary culture and society as Hill sees it is that which has solidified around the notion of the "worthless-in-itself": that is, the culture of commodity, in which value only exists in exchange, a contemporary situation in various places called "plutocratic anarchy", adapting William Morris's label "anarchical Plutocracy".[12] Eliot, in other words, compromises with this "body of opinion" which Hill sees as antagonistic to intrinsic value, the so-called "worthless-in-itself". Personality is to self what exchange value is to intrinsic value. "Eliot, once the enemy of personality", writes Hill, "has swung the weight of his own elderly personality in support of that very concept or entity" (*CCW* 554). In Hill's view, this is the nature of Eliot's decline from the pitch of *Prufrock* to the tone of *Four Quartets*. The younger Eliot, Hill claims, is all about "eros and alienation" (*CCW* 556): eros being, in Hill's terms, the "way of apprehension, a syntax of becoming" (*CCW* 534) which he finds in Eliot's early work, and which he associates explicitly with Bradley's thought and style; "alienation" referring to work which has "disturbed and alienated readers" and to the process by which the writer becomes alienated from the work, this latter a seminal concept of Eliot's in 'Tradition and the Individual Talent', in fact, to which Hill is utterly committed.

The passage previously quoted is notable for Hill's use of the word 'alienation', which can modulate its meaning rather confusingly in his later criticism, sometimes morphing its meaning from passage to passage. Sometimes alienation is a good thing, sometimes it is not. As poet of "eros and alienation", Eliot is being praised; the fact that *Prufrock and Other Observations* "disturbed and alienated" its readers is commendable; here, "the price exacted by your recalcitrance is that of alienation". Thus, the price one pays for not compromising with that "body of opinion" of the "worthless-in-itself" is alienation in an approbatory sense, the position in which Hill seems to find himself; however, it becomes apparent that Eliot is alienated by *not* doing this, and therefore alienated from his own earlier convictions, then; so that Eliot's later alienation is a form of dishonesty, or 'selling out', to use an appropriately plutocratic phrase. "He alienated himself more and more from immediate context while ingratiating himself more and more with generalized assumptions of, and about, pleasure" (*CCW* 557). In other words, Eliot's business is less and less to do with the being of the poem as a construct of words, and more to do with the business of being a public figure. This attitude permeates Hill's entire outlook on the 'purpose' of true art, its aversions to 'applicability', its value-in-itself; in an interview with *The Paris Review* in 1999, speaking of a book of reproductions of paintings by Anselm Kiefer, he remarked, "I have to say that I'm less gripped by them in this reduced form than I was with their actual presence. This may well be attributed to the judgment of the artist. There's no reason why a work should accommodate itself to the kind of reproduction and reduction that our methods of communication and circulation require".[13] Eliot's later poetry in Hill's view is certainly an example of "reduced form".

And it is "the judgement of the artist", and indeed the very nature of judgement, with which Hill is intimately concerned in the later work. In its Bradleian sense, judgement is an act which goes *beyond* itself while *remaining* itself – a typically Bradleian paradox; and indeed, this is an operative element of "Bradley's eros" (*CCW* 571). That is, judgement produces truth, which is necessarily a transcendent category, but that very judgement issues from a subject which is inescapably part of a world. As such, Bradley sees judgement as both transcendent and contingent in a way which appeals hugely to Hill. In *Essays on Truth and Logic*, Bradley spells out his theory of judgement:

> The "this" of feeling ... everywhere, I agree, is positive and unique. But when, passing beyond mere feeling, you have before you what you call "matter of fact" the case forthwith is altered. The uniqueness has now to be made "objective". It has to be contained within the judgement and has to qualify the content of your truth. (*CCW* 561)

This must be seen against Eliot's 'turn' from his earlier to his later phases (which happens much earlier on than Hill's), which, I would claim, happens even earlier than the preface to the 1928 edition of *The Sacred Wood*, though for slightly different reasons than Hill argues. It seems to me that the 'turn' in Eliot's work away from Bradley begins in earnest in 'The Function of Criticism' (1923) and centres on his new term 'orthodoxy' which supplants the more Bradleian 'tradition' of 'Tradition and the Individual Talent'. This term issues in the same essay in the famous description of criticism as "the common pursuit of true judgement".[14] Orthodoxy implies conformity to an objective standard; tradition, both etymologically and as Eliot defines it in the essay, implies a mutual conditioning, in this case between the new artwork and cultural tradition (or by implication between subjective and objective). Bradley might well say to this, with Hill's approval, that "you have failed to get within the judgement the condition of the judgement"; that is, there is too great a gulf between, on the one hand, the subjective applicability of Eliot's public persona, and the objectivism of orthodoxy and "true judgement". "Judgement proper", writes Bradley, "is the act which refers an ideal content (recognised as such) to a reality beyond the act".[15] And there is thus certainly evidence that Hill's reading of Bradley goes back at least to the 1970s: in 'A Short History of British India (II)', in the sequence 'An Apology for the Revival of Christian Architecture in England', included in 1978's *Tenebrae*, "There is a greeting | Beyond the act" (*Broken Hierarchies* [henceforth *BH*] 127), directly echoing Bradley's definition of judgement; and in 1977's 'Poetry as "Menace" and "Atonement"', "From the depths of the self, we rise to a concurrence with that which is not-self" (*CCW* 4) which is what one might call a more general 'Bradleyism'.[16] It is echoed also in that reference to Sigwick and Green, the "pious wish" for "that which points beyond the data".

The yearning from *within* the data for that which is *beyond* the data is characteristic of what Hill calls 'eros' in 'Eros in F.H. Bradley and T.S. Eliot': "If unspecified, unbounded yearning is one of the energies of eros, then 'somehow' is part of the erotic language" (*CCW* 549). In a rather crucial way, then, Hill's later work is driven by an obsession with this "yearning" as well as with the "unspecified" and "unbounded" which is the object of the yearning. Hill's obsessive fascination with intrinsic value should be seen within this context of eros, which is akin to what the post-Heideggerian philosopher Emmanuel Levinas called "metaphysical desire":

> The metaphysical desire does not long to return, for it is desire for a land not of our birth, for a land foreign to every nature, which has not been our fatherland and to which we shall never betake ourselves ... It is a desire that cannot be satisfied.[17]

Levinas's metaphysical desire is a desire *for* the metaphysical: it is the nature of this desire which is eros in Hill's sense. Levinas's phrase here recalls Hill's "metaphysical fantasy" ('Our Word Is Our Bond', *CCW* 157) (quoting J.L. Austin) and "metaphysical fancy" ('The Tartar's Bow and the Bow of Ulysses', *CCW* 200). The desire for the metaphysical is always in some sense a fantasy or fancy in Hill's work, and this is a major trope of the later poetry. Hill's sense of eros, then, is not simply an impulse of energy defined impressionistically as vital or 'erotic', a new vitality arising from personal circumstances or even the advent of antidepressants – not merely this, anyway. It is the 'somehow-ness' of Bradley, and the "unspecified, unbounded" energy in its interrelations with the specified and bounded which drive the later poetry and provides its intellectual scaffolding. The "freedom and power" (*CCW* 126) of the creative imagination is its simultaneously grasping its boundedness and unboundedness. To put it another way, the imagination's power resides in the recognition of its constraint and powerlessness. Or as Hill puts it, "There is something in constraint which frees the mind, and something in freedom which constrains it" (*CCW* 573). In other words, 'eros', that which points beyond the data, as Hill defines it, is nothing without its material, the "semantic field" (*CCW* 571).

Intrinsic value is by definition "beyond the data". It is a translation, into a value-term, of the Kantian thing-in-itself, the *ding an sich*.[18] Bradley himself expresses scepticism about the thing-in-itself, in *The Principles of Logic*, a work to which Hill refers in 'Eros in F.H. Bradley and T.S. Eliot':

> We must remember that, even if we are able to assert about such a subject as Things-in-themselves, we must always be on our guard against an error. We may be affirming about the meaning of a word, or about a mere idea in our heads, and may confuse these facts with another type of fact.[19]

Also, "Things-in-themselves are not anything at all in the real world, though, considered as illusions, they no doubt have qualities".[20] Hill is also deeply invested in the qualities of illusions. He approaches this question explicitly for the first time in the essay 'Translating Value', though the concern is discernible in much of his earlier work also: "it took rather longer than I care to admit before I was prepared to concede that Ruskin's 'intrinsic value' does not guarantee, or even have a direct relation to, the presence of intrinsic value. The phrase is at best a promissory note, at worst a semantic relic to ward off the evil eye of commodity" (*CCW* 383). I would claim that a comprehensive view of Hill's approach to this problem must take account of this Bradleian ambiguity – though whether or not one considers this a valid position or not is another matter.

As Hill remarked in an interview of 2011, "There is a largely unknown order of human beings who believe in that impossible thing: intrinsic value. One must work as if intrinsic value were a reality, even though I myself know no way of demonstrating its real existence".[21] This "largely unknown order of human beings" is a markedly less afflated version of Shelley's "unacknowledged legislators", and of the imaginative elite – perhaps, indeed, an imaginary elite. Hill's intrinsic value here recalls the Absolute, which Bradley characterised as indescribable, even ineffable. Hill's belief in the impossible is more like an impossible belief: it is a kind of sceptical faith which, again, is very Bradleian, but which he has evinced at least since an interview of 1983 in which he spoke of his work as a "heretic's dream of salvation expressed in the images of the orthodoxy from which he is excommunicate".[22] One of the articles of the faith from which Hill is excommunicate is, in his later work, intrinsic value.

As Hill writes in 'Eros in F.H. Bradley and T.S. Eliot' in a discussion of Eliot's review of the 1927 reprint of Bradley's *Ethical Studies*: "There is a stratum of Bradley's style, which makes it peculiarly what it is, and in which Eliot shows no interest" (*CCW* 550). This element is the 'somehow-ness' of Bradley's style, what Hill calls its 'eros'. This eros of style is an eros of ethos, also, and Hill goes on to quote a passage from Bradley's *Ethical Studies* which encapsulates this: "The artist and poet, however obscurely, do feel and believe that beauty, where it is not seen, yet somehow and somewhere is and is real; though not as a mere idea in people's heads, nor yet as anything in the visible world" (*CCW* 550). One must note the condition of Hill's judgement here, if Hill perhaps cannot quite: he reads Eliot's reading of Bradley in a certain way, perhaps to underwrite his own readings of the British Idealist. In *Knowledge and Experience* (the 1964 Faber edition of his doctoral dissertation on Bradley) Eliot writes that "[t]here are two (or more) worlds each continuous with a self, and yet running in the other direction – *somehow* – into an identity".[23] Eliot clearly shows an interest in precisely this element of Bradley's style here. One might perhaps argue that Eliot's parenthesised "*somehow*" shades into parody, as if for a moment he is doing the voice; or one might argue that Eliot is emphasising the very aspect of Bradley's style which Hill accuses him of ignoring. On balance, I think Eliot may here be demonstrating a mannerism in this parenthetical "*somehow*", a necessary evil where there should be a functional necessity – but whatever the precise nuance of the Possum's tone here, it does not look like he is ignoring this aspect of Bradley's style, as such. However, what might possibly have been an undesirable aspect of Bradley's thought for the young Eliot is enabling and vital for Hill, I think precisely for the reasons that Eliot, as academic philosopher and sometime student of Bertrand Russell, but also as increasingly committed to orthodoxy of faith, rejected.

Though Eliot abandons the "eros and alienation" which Hill discerns in Bradley's style, not to mention his philosophy, I would suggest that this abandonment is foreshadowed, at least, before the "threnos" of the last chapter of *The Use of Poetry and the Use of Criticism*, which is where Hill points to, in Eliot's turn from tradition to orthodoxy in 'The Function of Criticism'. However, Hill's emphasis is increasingly on selfhood; not simply the "passive[ly] attending upon"[24] the self of Confessional poetry (as part of the cult of personality), but the achievement of selfhood which is crucial to Bradley's ethics and Gerard Manley Hopkins's existential theology, the "instressing of his own inscape" (*CCW* 563) (Hopkins being an important exemplar for Hill's later work as well). When Hill writes in 'Citations I' in *A Treatise of Civil Power* "of Alanbrooke's war diary", of "*possession of himself,* | *as a means of survival and, in that sense,* | *a mode of moral life*" (*CCW* 560) he is occupying the Bradley of *Ethical Studies*: "the question in morals is to find the true whole, realizing which will practically realize the true self".[25] And yet, says Bradley, the self's moral progress is dependent upon this whole never being fully realised: "I must progress, because I have an other which is to be, and yet never quite is, myself; and so, as I am, am in a state of contradiction."[26] This "state of contradiction" is the organising principle and the radioactive generator of Hill's later poetry, an aporia which is very close to Hill's definition of 'eros', which is the spirit of Hill's later poetry, being its "theory of energy":

> Bradley's eros, if we want a theory of energy that will make a topos out of a technic and that will be answerable across a wide range of expectation, is a much safer bargain. Bradley writes, "We have the idea of perfection – there is no doubt as to that – and the question is whether perfection also actually exists". (*CCW* 571)

Eros is the state of apprehension between belief and unbelief, the ideal and the actual, the achieved and the unachievable. This is the 'topos' and the 'technic' of Hill's later poetry, and why the final poem in *The Daybooks* ends without a full stop – a typographical gesture towards the unrealisable whole at the very moment of its realisation. Bradley's statement recalls Sidney's in *An Apology for Poetry*, a sentence which is very important to Hill's thinking: "Sith, our erected wit maketh us know what perfection is, but our infected will keepeth us from reaching unto it."[27]

The way of apprehension

T.H. Green was an idealist like Bradley who, as Hill claims, had a "respect for concreteness" (*CCW* 109); that is, he enquired beyond the data while acknowledging always his being radically within the data. Bradley and Green, then, are exemplars of the "sensuous interest" which Hill espouses throughout the later criticism, which Eliot allegedly abandons (*CCW* 376). Hill's assessment of Green's ethical thrust is given early on in 'Perplexed Persistence', an account which becomes increasingly illuminative of the later mode: "The nature of the world is such as we are constrained to recognise, the ineluctable fact, but to be content with the rich discrepancies which this offers is nonetheless dangerous and is sometimes treacherous" (*CCW* 110). In other words, the embracing of facticity which drives Hill's later work does not, should not, entail an abandoning of metaphysical desire. This is a central ethical and political focus of Hill's later work, characterising his embattled position. The postmodern culture of "rich discrepancies", its relativism, its "plutocratic anarchy", Hill is constrained to recognise, though he recognises at once that it is "dangerous and … sometimes treacherous".

"[T]he way of apprehension, the syntax of becoming" (*CCW* 534), discerned in F.H. Bradley's writings, Hill identifies as the authentic technical approach for his later work, just as it is authentic existentially. It implies a semantically and structurally 'feeling forward' towards an unknown and ultimately unrealisable completion. In the essay on Green of 1975, Hill writes of "Green's 'real bridge', Mill's 'in reality' and Marshall's 'in the place of'" which "seem attempts at an illicit bridging of 'the chasm between which the Kantian analysis of judgement left between subject and object'". Significantly, in these forms of "illicit persuasiveness" there is "a hint of the despotic" (*CCW* 111). Bradley's theory of judgement, however, leaves no such chasm, and therefore no such "illicit persuasiveness" is required; his 'somehow-ness' is therefore an ethical generosity – on the part of the reader also, one might remark drily. But no; Hill explains it as "the *somehow* of realization", not "the *somehow* of abdication" (*CCW* 534); it is analogous to the seemingly ineffable process of writing poetry – presumably when it is written well, and without recourse to an online thesaurus – when "[s]omehow is whatever protracted or split second activity of the mind makes real the presence of the right word" (*CCW* 533–534).

The concept of apprehension – and its radiance – occurs in Hill's later criticism in various telling places, often in relation to the re-readings of Eliot which energise his later poetry and prose:

> [Eliot's] finest work – and here I include critical theory and practice together with the poetry – reveals the closest and keenest affinity with the Bradleian moment of intelligible apprehension: I mean by this the sense that his best writing gives of being the appreciative spectator of its own enlightenment.[28]

One might say further to this that Hill's later work is driven by its affirmative, Bradleian, sense of being 'somewhere between', as with Eliot at his best moments, a state of contradiction, of inherent difficulty, through which the mind emerges occasionally, unexpectedly, into the arena of its own enlightenment: "the reality of a poem such as *Marina* exists somehow and somewhere between the intelligible apprehension, understood as the rudiments of grace, and the briefly unintelligible affrighted apprehension with which Hercules, in the poem's epigraph, comes belatedly to his senses" (*CCW* 540).

Hill's later sense of direction is powered by the conviction that Eliot belatedly took leave of his senses, and that he himself will not make the same concessions and compromises. Apprehension for Hill means a providential grasping of 'things' in their already-oneness, something akin to what Hill calls "the act of mercy or grace" (*CCW* 404): not so much atonement as attunement – a translated term from Martin Heidegger (an important figure for Hill's later work) describing a state in which "[t]he pure 'that it is' shows itself".[29] It is like Keats's negative capability. A Heideggerian sense of attunement bears a similar relation to atonement as apprehension bears to comprehension in *A Midsummer Night's Dream*:

> Such shaping fantasies, that apprehend
> More than cool reason ever comprehends.[30]

The "way of apprehension" (*CCW* 534) which Hill pursues in his later work is this feeling of "shaping fantasies", a commitment to spontaneity and the feeling forward through language and structure that he calls the "syntax of becoming". And this is what Hill meant when he enjoined his audience, in an Oxford Professor of Poetry lecture in 2012, to imagine him writing from within "a small intense radiance of apprehension, a miniature vortex of intuition".[31]

Notes

1. Geoffrey Hill, 'Poetry and "The Democracy of the Dead"', Oxford Professor of Poetry lecture, 3 December 2012.
2. Peter Popham, 'Geoffrey Hill Is Our Greatest Living Poet', *New Statesman*, 6 December 2012, for example.
3. Though the publication of Hill's posthumous book of poetry *The Book of Baruch by the Gnostic Justin* was published in April 2019, after this book was written.
4. Geoffrey Hill, 'A Deep Dynastic Wound', Oxford Professor of Poetry lecture, 30 April 2013.
5. Or as Ezra Pound declares, "*KRINO, to pick out for oneself, to choose.*" Pound, *ABC of Reading* (Faber: London, 1951) p. 30.
6. Peter Robinson, 'Contemporary Poetry and Value', *The Oxford Handbook of Contemporary British and Irish Poetry*, Peter Robinson ed. (Oxford University Press: Oxford, 2013) p. 731.
7. This is discussed in chapter 2.
8. F.H. Bradley, *Ethical Studies* (Henry S. King & Co: London, 1876) p. 78.
9. Geoffrey Hill, 'How Ill White Hairs Become a Fool and Jester', Oxford Professor of Poetry lecture, 30 November 2010.
10. T.S. Eliot, *The Use of Poetry and the Use of Criticism: Studies in the Relation of Criticism to Poetry in England* (Faber: London, 1964) pp. 31–32.
11. Bradley, *Ethical Studies*, p. 88. "There are times indeed, when we feel the increase of progress means increase of pleasure, and that it is hard to consider them apart. I do not mean those moments (if there are such) when the music-hall theory of life seems real to us."
12. William Morris, *Political Writings of William Morris*, A.L. Morton ed. and intro. (Lawrence & Wishart: London, 1973) p. 85. Hill uses this phrase in various Oxford Professor of Poetry lectures, and in his acceptance speech for the Truman Capote Award in 2009. These usages will be discussed elsewhere in the book.
13. Geoffrey Hill, interview with Carl Phillips, 'The Art of Poetry: 80', *The Paris Review*, Spring 2000.

14 T.S. Eliot, *Selected Prose of T.S. Eliot*, Frank Kermode ed. and intro. (Faber: London, 1975) p. 69.
15 F.H. Bradley, *The Principles of Logic* (Kegan and Paul: London, 1883) p. 10.
16 For example: "Whether the object contains, or does not contain, a self and not-self in connexion, on either view there is a real felt subject." F.H. Bradley, *Essays on Truth and Reality* (Clarendon: Oxford, 1914) p. 195.
17 Emmanuel Levinas, *Totality and Infinity: An Essay on Exteriority*, Alphonso Lingis trans. (Kluwer: Dordrecht, Boston, and London, 1991) p. 33. Levinas's phrase here recalls Hill's phrases "metaphysical fantasy" ('Our Word Is Our Bond', *CCW* 157) (quoting J.L. Austin) and "metaphysical fancy" ('The Tartar's Bow and the Bow of Ulysses', *CCW* 200). I feel this is a more precise term in some contexts than 'eros'.
18 Kant introduces this concept in his *Prolegomena to Any Future Metaphysics*. "When we regard the objects of sense, as is correct, as mere appearances, we thereby at the same time confess that a thing in itself lies at their foundation." *Kant's Prolegomena and Metaphysical Foundations of Natural Science*, Ernest Belfort Bax, trans., biography, intro. (George Bell and Son: London, 1883) p. 62.
19 Bradley, *The Principles of Logic*, p. 146.
20 Ibid., p. 145.
21 Christy Rush, interview with Geoffrey Hill, 26 May 2011, *The Oxford Student*. http://oxfordstudent.com/2011/05/26/interview-geoffrey-hill-oxford-professor-of-poetry
22 John Haffenden, *Viewpoints: Poets in Conversation with John Haffenden* (Faber: London, 1981) p. 98.
23 T.S. Eliot, *Knowledge and Experience in the Philosophy of F.H. Bradley* (Faber: London, 1964) p. 143.
24 T.S. Eliot, 'Tradition and the Individual Talent', *The Sacred Wood: Essays on Poetry and Criticism* (Methuen: London, 1934) p. 58.
25 Bradley, *Ethical Studies*, p. 69.
26 Ibid., p. 78.
27 Quoted by Hill in 'How Ill White Hairs Become a Fool and Jester'.
28 Geoffrey Hill, 'T.S. Eliot Memorial Lecture', MS BC Hill/4/35, p. 25, Brotherton Library, University of Leeds.
29 "The pure 'that it is' shows itself, but the 'whence' and the 'whither' remain in darkness." Martin Heidegger, *Being and Time*, John Mcquarrie and Edward Robinson trans. (Blackwell: Oxford, 1967) p. 173. Atonement here is a reference to Hill's early essay 'Poetry

and "Menace" and "Atonement'" (*CCW* 3–20). Hill says, among other things, on the topic of 'atonement': "When the poem 'comes right with a click like a closing box', what is there effected is the atonement of aesthetics with rectitude of judgement" (*CCW* 12).
30 William Shakespeare, *A Midsummer Night's Dream*, Harold F. Brooks ed. (Methuen: London, 1979) p. 103. Act V, Scene 1.
31 Geoffrey Hill, '"Legal Fiction" and Legal Fiction', Oxford Professor of Poetry lecture, 5 March 2013.

Chapter 2

A postscript on modernist poetics?

In 'Modernism / Post-modernism', an as-yet-unpublished piece, Geoffrey Hill gives a glimpse into his first encounters with modernist writing, and the galvanising effect they had upon him:

> when as a fifteen year old schoolboy in Britain I discerned Tate's ["Ode to the Confederate Dead"] in an anthology it showed me, more than any other poem that I have since read (more even than Yeats's "Byzantium" poems or Wallace Stevens's "Sunday Morning") how I could see my way to becoming a modern/modernist poet.[1]

This autobiographical vignette affords an insight into the power that modernist poetry has exerted on Hill, but also into his alternative perspectives on modernism, having reached out to the work of Allen Tate rather than, say, W.B. Yeats or T.S. Eliot, or even Ezra Pound, of whom in the same piece Hill remarks that he "found his structures uninstructive", and that he only "learned … from his methods at a later date".[2] The influence of Pound is more evident in a book such as *Speech! Speech!*, for instance, but Hill's relationship with modernism in his later work can be characterised by his engagement with the more unexpected elements in modernism – certainly from the perspective of a British poet-critic – represented by Allen Tate and the American New Criticism, and more broadly by a questioning and revoking of more 'mainstream' modernist poetics represented by such figures as W.B. Yeats, T.S. Eliot, and Ezra Pound. Hill's abiding and urgent sense of his being a high modernist influences his readings of the poetry of the past, too: "I am a committed high modernist, even in my reading of the Tudor poets, or of Pope."[3] Both of these attestations belong to Hill's later career; to gain a clear sense of where Hill sees himself as coming from in this period, therefore, one must seek to gain a perspective on his relationship with modernism.

Hill is both deeply influenced and deeply troubled by modernist literature. If in his earlier work Hill sought "the fullest possible objectification of the subjective", as a "misreading of 'Tradition and the Individual Talent'"[4] (T.S. Eliot's seminal work of literary criticism, dated 1919), in his later work an alternative model for the relation of subject and object is explored. This relation is at the heart of modernist aesthetics and politics – especially Eliot, Yeats, and Pound – and Hill's later work is a critique, sometimes explicitly, of it. This new relation between subjective and objective is found in part through a reading of F.H. Bradley which is also a revocation of T.S. Eliot, as the previous chapter argued, but this alternative model finds expression and vindication in readings of other figures, too; indeed, it is characteristic of Hill that his rereading of modernist poetics finds its justifications in a number of periods of English literature. In the later work, there is a questioning of certain of the central tenets and poets of literary modernism: of T.S. Eliot's impersonality and later pragmatism, as the previous chapter argued; and of the cultural politics of figures such as Ezra Pound and W.B. Yeats:

> Yeats with his clangour of despotic beauty,
> Pound's destructive matrix, creative hatred. (*BH* 871)

But there is much taken from the examples of Pound and Yeats too, certain key features of their thought which Hill finds enabling for his sense of Bradleian eros: Pound's logopoeia, for instance, as "the dance of the intelligence among words", or Yeats's antinomies: "Between extremities | Man runs his course".[5] There is also an engagement with writers peripheral to or influential on literary modernism in Hill's later work, and on modernism in broader historical and intellectual senses: figures such as Ludwig Wittgenstein, F.H. Bradley, Walt Whitman, Gerard Manley Hopkins, Isaac Rosenberg, and even Martin Heidegger. Hill's later work in criticism and poetry constitutes in no small part a strenuously ethical re-reading of the modernist tradition. Whereas 2002's *Style and Faith* focused largely on English writers of the seventeenth century, *Inventions of Value* and *Alienated Majesty* have much more of a nineteenth- and twentieth-century focus. The focus on nineteenth-century writers in particular is indicative of a shift in Hill's later work which it is the purpose of this chapter to trace, in part, and of later chapters to pursue more fully.

The influence of modernism on Hill's reading of English poetry is evident in *The Orchards of Syon* II:

> Shakespeare
> clearly heard many voices. No secret:
> voicing means hearing, at a price a gift,
> affliction chiefly, whereas despair
> clamps and is speechless. Donne in his time
> also heard voices he preserved on wax
> cylinders. Some of these I possess
> and am possessed by.   (*BH* 352)

This passage describes the absorption and reconstitution of Eliot's early poetics – the poetics of eros and alienation – and in a more general sense in modernist writing. As such, this is a chorus-style commentary on Hill's approach in the poem and in his later phase at large, which while writing *The Orchards of Syon* had been coming thick and fast for some time. "[V]oicing means hearing" recalls Hill's own remark that "What we call the writer's 'distinctive voice' is a registering of different voices" (*CCW* 241), itself recalling Eliot's seminal pronouncements in 'Tradition and the Individual Talent': "Someone said: 'The dead writers are remote from us because we *know* so much more than they did.' Precisely, and they are that which we know."[6]

While Hill is influenced by modernist poetics in a deep if general sense, he is crucially influenced by Eliot's view of influence itself, and of the importance of tradition and history in the formation of the self: a view not restricted to Eliot and a royalist, classicist, Anglican sensibility, but indicative of that historicist instinct, or commitment, echoed by Karl Marx in *The Eighteenth Brumaire of Louis Bonaparte*: "The history of the dead generations weighs down like an Alp on the brains of the living."[7] Despite Hill's revocations of 'Tradition and the Individual Talent', Eliot's essay survives at a deep level in Hill's later work, along with its various afterlives in modernist poetry and criticism.

'Sensuous intelligence' and its contexts

Perhaps the most crucial concept associated with modernism for Hill is that of the sensuous intelligence, a concept gleaned from modernism, particularly, once again, from Eliot. In 'The Metaphysical Poets', his 1921 review of Herbert Grierson's anthology, Eliot describes a "dissociation of sensibility"[8] which set in after the English Civil War, the separation of thought and feeling which helps explain where eighteenth-century English poetry went wrong, producing the discursive sterility of the Augustans on the one hand and the emotional excess and imprecision of the Romantics on the other: "[i]n the seventeenth century a dissociation of sensibility set in, from which we have never recovered; and this dissociation, as is natural, was aggravated by the influence of the two most powerful poets of the century, Milton and Dryden".[9] So influential was Eliot's theory that it went a long way in creating John Milton as the modernist *bête noire*, with even Robert Graves sending him up in the mid-century 'historical' novel *Wife to Mr Milton*; though this anti-Miltonism occurred roughly contemporaneously outside this modernist milieu as well, Ivor Gurney writing, in a letter from the trenches of France in 1916, that Milton "wrote the most detestable half-English, sounding more like a Bohn translation than anything else".[10] The common element here is that Gurney, like Eliot and Pound, is interested in the relationship between poetry and music, a relation which Milton is perceived to have broken; but for the modernists, especially Eliot, Milton represents the breaking of an even more fundamental relation, that of thought and feeling.

However, Hill does not go along with the common view of the modernists that Milton was a sort of hyper-Cartesian, proto-Augustan poetaster, equating him instead in a vital respect with the Romantic poet, critic, and philosopher Samuel Taylor Coleridge: "I would say confidently of Milton, slightly less confidently of Coleridge, that they recreate the sensuous intellect."[11] This is one of Hill's most valuable seals of approval, in direct contradiction of Eliot's assessment. And elsewhere:

> The major difference, as I understand it, between the semantics of Bacon, Hobbes, and Locke, on the one hand, and those of

Milton and Coleridge on the other, is that the former regard the deliberated and undeliberated ambiguities of language as elementary obstacles to the improvement of communication whereas the latter understand them to be complex indices of innate, inveterate human nature.[12]

So, Hill sees in Milton precisely that which modernist orthodoxy of the first half of the twentieth century asserted is *not* there, namely the "sensuous intellect", a sense of language as being implicated with thought and feeling, as being a resistant and active medium, of ambiguity as being endemic to its vitality. The modernists made a literary zombie of Milton, an absent centre of English literature and letters, with either a pernicious influence or a negligible one: "Milton is the worst sort of poison",[13] wrote Pound, while Eliot observed "the deterioration ... to which he subjected the language",[14] as begetter of the sterile eighteenth century, the (alleged) great dead end of English poetry. Hill has sought to rehabilitate Milton on the terms of the "simple, sensuous, and passionate"[15] poet that he sees himself as, in Milton's phrase, and which Coleridge saw Milton as; and Milton is an exemplary presence in Hill's later poetry, subject of *Scenes from Comus* and various poems in *A Treatise of Civil Power*, as politically engaged, sensuously intelligent poet, critic, and polemicist. (One might object, of course, that how Hill's work answers to the "simple" aspect of the Miltonic formula is less than clear.)

It is perhaps quite telling that Hill associates Milton with Coleridge with respect to sensuous intelligence. Hill avers that he "received instruction from Coleridge many years before"[16] he encountered certain other works crucial to him; Hill's very early poem 'Genesis', originally subtitled 'A Ballad of Christopher Smart', shows evidence of encounters with Coleridge, not least *The Rime of the Ancient Mariner*. And in *Shakespeare, Ben Jonson, Beaumont and Fletcher*, Coleridge identifies the same moment in Milton's writings as a crucial moment: "Speaking of poetry, [Milton] says, as in a parenthesis, 'which is simple, sensuous, passionate'",[17] which Coleridge goes on to attempt define and refine, though in a way which suggests that he may have been influenced in his view of Milton by Joseph Addison's many articles on the poet in *The Spectator*: work which, Hill argues in the 2008 lecture 'Milton as Muse', served both to popularise and to "emasculate"[18] Milton's work:

> Simplicity ... supposes a smooth and finished road, on which the reader is to walk onward easily, with streams murmuring by his side, and trees and flowers and human dwellings to make his journey as delightful as the object of it is desirable, instead of having to toil with the pioneers and painfully make the road on which others are to travel.[19]

It is safe to say that Hill differs from Coleridge on the definition of Miltonic simplicity, and it is not finally clear that Hill ever really finds himself in a settled relationship with it. "The learned readers of J. Milton" of *Scenes from Comus* may include Coleridge, though Coleridge's own description of Milton's "simple, sensuous, passionate" formula strangely ignores or elides the "Weight of the world, weight of the word" (*BH* 430) which Hill's poem describes, and is in large part a meditation upon. If one were to attempt to sum up Hill's sense of sensuous intelligence in language, it might be that it entails a simultaneous perception of the weight of the world and of the word: that is, that language is not a varnish on the surface of experience, or a passive medium to convey the author's sentiments, but that language, history, and the self are coexistent.

In Coleridge's defence, this is difficult matter to define; it is perhaps impossible to encapsulate finally. What Hill calls the "sensuous intelligence" Eliot described as "thinking through the senses, or ... the senses thinking", though Eliot's sense of this is, by his own admission, vague, though couched in the scientific language typical of Eliot's early criticism: "the exact formula remains to be defined".[20] However, elsewhere Hill has defined it in the most disarmingly straightforward terms, as "the coexistence of the conceptual aspect of thought and the emotional aspect of thought as ideally wedded";[21] though the word 'ideally' here, archly placed, puts the sensuous intelligence into a Bradleian realm of somehow-ness, a realm in which the proposition "rests in its own intelligibility".[22] The presence or otherwise of sensuous intelligence is itself a matter for the sensuous intelligence of the reader, as Hill demonstrates by reference to Hilaire Belloc, quoting four lines quoted, in turn, by Ivor Gurney in another letter home from the trenches: "Of Courtesy, it is not less | Than Courage of Heart or Holiness, | Yet in my Walks it seems to me | That the Grace of God is in Courtesy." Of these lines by Belloc, Hill remarks: "The verse is very lively but it is not alive with sensuous intelligence" (*CCW* 439). The absence or presence of sensuous intelligence is here the difference between the lively and the alive; that is, between surface intelligibility and living density. Making it a little more concrete, Hill also defines the term by a phrase of Yeats, as "the ability to choose the intellectually surprising word which is also the correct word" (*CCW* 409). So, to attempt another definition of the term, perhaps the sensuous intelligence entails the coexistence of discursive, ordering reason and the energies of the surprising and irruptive, with the two containing and conditioning each other.

One might say that, like intrinsic value, sensuous intelligence is necessarily a thing "of which the exact formula remains to be defined", that it is by definition indefinable, and that much of Hill's later criticism is a working-out of just such ultimately indefinable formulae, this 'brute fact' of poetics having been recognised as vital, if mysterious,[23] the "brute mass and detail" of *The Triumph of Love* LXX – "there, by some, to be pondered" (*BH* 259). Some, but not all, will be sympathetic to Hill's mission. Like T.H. Green, it is the quality of the 'perplexed persistence' of Hill's criticism which distinguishes it, a quality which Hill confers also on his ideal reader, describing the "perplexed persistence of readers of good will".[24] That is not to say, however, that the reader's persistence will meet only with perplexity: the two late volumes of essays, on value and alienation respectively, bristle with dense clarity and bursts of intelligent perception. Crucially, however, whereas sensuous intelligence implies a reversal of Eliot's dissociation of sensibility, Hill's use is not inflected by such absolutist, high modernist notions of a final coherence within the self and within civil society, or indeed in the work, the final atonement of subjective and objective. He has referred in the early essay on Green to the "illicit bridging of 'the chasm between which the Kantian analysis of judgement left between subject and object'", an "illicit persuasiveness" carrying "a hint of the despotic" (*CCW* 111), perhaps like Yeats's "despotic beauty". This "hint of the despotic" is made manifest in modernist poetics by the aestheticised politics of Eliot, Yeats, and Pound: "In high Modernist aesthetics are politicized and politics aestheticized", Hill writes in 'Modernism / Post-modernism', an apprehension crucial to Hill's critique of modernism.[25]

I would suggest that there is a moral-political ambivalence to Eliot's Bradleian convictions as early on as the essays in *The Sacred Wood*; despite his avocations of associated sensibility, Eliot remains mistrustful of emotion. Aristotle is the vehicle of this mistrust in 'The Perfect Critic':

> For everything that Aristotle says illuminates the literature which is the occasion for saying it; and Coleridge only now and then. It is one more instance of the pernicious effect of emotion.
>
> Aristotle had what is called the scientific mind – a mind which, as it is rarely found among scientists except in fragments, might better be called the intelligent mind. For there is no other intelligence than this, and so far as artists and men of letters are intelligent ... their intelligence is of this kind.[26]

Eliot's readings of Coleridge and Milton differ fundamentally from Hill's on this point; and Hill's notion of intelligence contradicts Eliot's here too, according to his explanation of the matter in the interview with the *Paris Review* in 2000:

> The idea that the intellect is somehow alien to sensuousness, or vice versa, is one that I have never been able to connect with ... The intelligence is, I think, much more true [than "intellect"], a true relation, a true accounting of what this elusive quality is. I think intelligence has a kind of range of sense and allows us to contemplate the coexistence of the conceptual aspect of thought and the emotional aspect of thought as ideally wedded, troth-plight, and the circumstances in which this troth-plight can be effected are to be found in the medium of language itself.[27]

Furthermore, Eliot's remarks here countermand his espousal of the sensibility of Donne in 'The Metaphysical Poets', which, admittedly, came shortly after the essays of *The Sacred Wood*. Eliot's view of intelligence is from the outset conditioned by this Aristotelian ideal, and this in both the artist and the 'man of letters', this latter persona being the one which, in Hill's view, comes to predominate in Eliot. The epigraph to the short final section of 'Tradition and the Individual Talent' is from Aristotle, too, translating as "Doubtless the mind is more divine and less subject to the passions".[28] In this respect, Eliot's 'decline', as Hill sees it, may have been (at least in retrospect) predictable from these early essays in *The Sacred Wood*, at least in terms of the sensuous intelligence, and is not quite so much of a betrayal of youthful commitment. What Eliot praises in the context of the metaphysical poets is what he deplores elsewhere, a typically Possum-like ambivalence.[29]

The recognition and espousal of this quality, or method, does not originate with Hill, then, and is a central concern of modernist poetics. Yeats, Eliot, Pound, and others sought a co-inherence of the discursive intellect and the intuition and energy of sensuousness, explicitly or implicitly as an index of complete being or of final political coherence. Hill is an outspoken adapter of this modernist ethos – and it *is* an ethos – but not a subscriber to its political implications in those poets. There is, in fact, a distinctly anti-Cartesian cast to modernist poetics,[30] most explicitly in the ideas of the sensuous intelligence (in its various forms) and of the dissociation of sensibility, which is the name for the socio-cultural decline brought about by the dereliction of the sensuous intelligence. (In this respect, Milton's revolutionary politics are a more than negligible factor in the 'literary' judgement of Eliot and Pound.) As becomes apparent in *Knowledge and Experience*, Eliot prefers Leibniz, author of *Monadology*, to Descartes. In Eliot's assessment of Leibniz's general reaction to Descartes, one can discern the reasons for Hill's following Eliot on this point: Leibniz develops "an idealistic metaphysic, largely based on Descartes, based upon self-consciousness".[31] It is a Leibnizian self-consciousness which animates Hill's later work. And in *Scenes from Comus*, we encounter the Leibnizian penumbra in the quotation from Thomas Vaughan, alchemist and prose stylist extraordinaire: "*The Monad begetteth the Monad and doth | reflect upon itself its own fervour*" (*BH* 424). That balance – which is also Bradleian – between otherness and self-reflection is the general topos of Hill's later work – rather than their radical separation which is the Cartesian emphasis.

In 'A Précis or Memorandum of Civil Power', the Cartesian *cogito* is gone beyond, with a little help from the French philosopher Gabriel Marcel:

> *Cogito a bare*
> *threshold*, as G. Marcel sagely declares,
> of what's valid.
> Come round to the idea, even so
> belated, and knock. Echo the answer
> in spare strophes that yield almost nothing
> to the knowledge
> outside them raw with late wisdom.   (*BH* 581)

In this passage, Hill equates his "late wisdom" to Gabriel Marcel's Heideggerian overturning of Cartesian dualism, while attesting to the quality of alienation also, in "spare strophes that yield almost nothing | to the knowledge | outside them". The alienated literary artefact – the Hill-poem – goes beyond the discursive intelligence, even in a poem as discursive and philosophical as this one. And yet, it seems Hill's "late wisdom" has something to do with his coming to see the cogito of Descartes as a *"bare threshold"*, and the errors of judgement in Pound, Eliot, and Yeats to be in some measure due to their assumptions of a Cartesian duality of subjective and objective, and the consequent desire to atone them.

Hill takes the high-modernist obsession between subjective and objective and develops it into something enabling for his later phase, this later phase issuing in large part, as I have argued, in a critique of modernist poetics and politics. There is at times a Heideggerian cast to Hill's thought, just as F.H. Bradley's work recalls certain ideas in *Being and Time*; and there are explicit references to Heideggerian ontology in Hill's poetry and critical prose. Hill's interest in Heidegger may originate in the German philosopher's overlap with F.H. Bradley's conception of "immediate feeling". Just such a Heideggerian moment in F.H. Bradley is quoted in 'Dividing Legacies': "We ... have experience in which there is no distinction between my awareness and that of which it is aware ... There is an immediate feeling, a knowing and being in one" (*CCW* 374). Bradley's immediate feeling is thus very close to Heidegger's sense of 'mood', translated by Macquarrie and Robinson as "attunement".[32] Hill's later poetry aspires to the condition of attunement, rather than atonement, one might venture, this Heideggerian sense of attunement recalling Hill's self-description as working within "a small intense radiance of apprehension, a miniature vortex of intuition".[33]

Hill's sense of alienation as "thrown-ness" has a Heideggerian dimension, too (*CCW* 530). This, in the Heideggerian sense of *geworfenheit*, entails a sense of arbitrariness, of worldly recalcitrance, echoed in Hill's claim that "Like eros, also, language has its arbitrariness" (*CCW* 571); and in *Scenes from Comus*, that "Weight of the world, weight of the word, is" (*BH* 430). In *Speech! Speech!*, "*Gelassenheit* is a becoming | right order, heart's ease, a gift in faith" (*BH* 294): Heidegger's *Gelassenheit* entails an availability to quiddity, an acceptance, even an embracing, of the arbitrariness and facticity of the world: "the careful | fabric of our lives ripped through | by the steel claws of contingency" (*The Triumph of Love* [henceforth *ToL*] LXXV; *BH* 260). It is indeed a "becoming", that existentialist word-of-power recalling Bradley's sense of the "endless becoming and incompletion of the world".[34] 'Facticity' describes that which is brute fact and that which cannot be assimilated by interpretation, an approximation of writing to being which is crucial to Hill's later work and which is referred to frequently there: to say that a statement of Bradley "rests in its own intelligibility",[35] for instance, or to refer to the "strangeness of truth"[36] is to evoke a Heideggerian sense of facticity. *Gelassenheit* is one emblem for Hill's later period, then.[37]

Bradleian eros has a Heideggerian element, too, that of being-towards-death. Eros as Hill defines it is "the power that can be felt in language when a word or half-finished phrase awaits its consummation" (*CCW* 548). If we take death to be the ultimate consummation, and death to be the horizon of being, as Heidegger asserts, then it is a horizon never reached and always present in its absence, once again "the endless becoming and the incompletion of the world". We are given here a diagnosis of "becoming | right order", in which right order is becoming – that is, beautiful and apt – but also in which becoming, in the existentialist sense of Heidegger and Bradley, is right order. Hill's notion of a "syntax of becoming" is therefore of a piece with his "late wisdom". This Bradleian idea plays to a greater spontaneity and sense of 'self-discovery', line by line and clause by clause, so crucial to his later poetry. This commitment to spontaneity is attested to by the large amount of amendments through the various appearances of his later work: 'Pindarics' and *Clavics* undergoing amendment and revision between initial publication and appearance in *Broken Hierarchies*, for instance, and *A Treatise of Civil Power* being significantly reorganised and revised from initial pamphlet form (with Clutag Press in 2005) to book form (with Penguin in 2007).

Modernist legacies

There is a post-Eliot emphasis in a broader sense in Hill's work. Since the 1950s, Hill has been influenced greatly by the American New Critics, as they are known, that post-Eliot generation running from around 1925 to 1965[38] and including such luminaries as R.P. Blackmur, Lionel Trilling, Robert Penn Warren, Allen Tate, and John Crowe Ransom, a generation of critics who set a precedent for Hill's development of Eliot beyond Eliot's own conclusions. This New Critical discourse seeks to establish and defend the reality of the poem, not as the product of a mind, or of history, nor as an amalgam of language-features, but as a separate, 'alien' reality. Hill cites Graves's and Riding's *A Survey of Modernist Poetry* and Empson's *Seven Types of Ambiguity* as seminal early works in this early post-Eliotic vein (*CCW* 553). The influence of New Criticism is evident in Hill's early work, and he continued to quote such proponents as R.P. Blackmur in his Oxford Professor of Poetry lectures.[39] He has grown within and away from this modernist tradition, and has developed the modernist practice of ambiguity into an ethical outlook. But, of course, this ethos was implicit in modernist ambiguity; Hill has, rather, lit upon it and expanded it into a way of re-reading, or recreating, modernist practice within his own ethics of writing. This is to say, modernist writing has influenced his ethos, and his ethos has influenced the way Hill reads the modernist tradition. William Empson, for instance, is a frequent reference point in the late lectures and essays, as is Robert Graves. It is (perhaps) a way of seeing Hill's recreative relationship with modernism to see Empson and Graves as exemplary British figures in Hill's later work, with Eliot, Pound, and Yeats as much more troublesome influences. To his "belated surprise", Graves exemplifies Hill's later method, representing the "crux of techne with mental and emotional crisis", Hill adding that "when you have techne without crisis, the result is poetry similar to that written by the Movement poets of the 1950s"[40]: lively, perhaps, but not alive.

Such topics were so common in mid-twentieth-century American criticism that the critic James Benziger remarked in 'Organic Unity: Leibniz to Coleridge' in 1951:

> Perhaps only one who has been long interested in the phrase *organic unity* is wholly aware of how commonplace it has become in twentieth-century criticism ... The organic form, said Coleridge – translating Schlegel almost word for word – "is innate; it shapes itself as it develops itself from within, and the fullness of its development is one and the same with the perfection of its outward form." Or, as we should be more likely to say today, the organic poet thinks immediately in terms of his medium, and his thoughts are inseparable from their expression.[41]

The idea of the poet's "thoughts being inseparable from their expression" is indeed very close to Hill's notion of "expressiveness",[42] described in terms of the choreographer Mark Morris and Gerard Manley Hopkins in 'What You Look Hard at Seems to Look Hard at You', an Oxford Professor of Poetry lecture, a notion which shares a boundary with sensuous intelligence and Heideggerian attunement. Of Coventry Patmore's incredulity to Hopkins's claim that the sonnet 'Hurrahing in Harvest' was "the product of half an hour's extreme enthusiasm", Hill remarks:

> Patmore's own phrasing in that protest may give some indication as to why Hopkins felt it necessary to write as he did. Patmore's phrase "the spontaneous expression of your poetical feeling" does seem to suggest that Patmore presupposes a sort of time-lag between a sensory reaction to which you can legitimately apply such a restrictive term as "poetical feeling" and the conversion of it into appropriate poetical utterance ... Patmore seems to speak for the great body of opinion against which Hopkins was writing: that there is something magically hived off from feeling, and it is called "poetical feeling".[43]

In the essay 'Poetry and Value', in a discussion of Coleridge and Leibniz, mining the same seam as Benziger, Hill offers another definition of this position: "Language ... does not issue from reflection but is an inherent element within the activity of reflection itself; it is an integral part of the body of reflection" (*CCW* 488). Hill's idiom here, comprising the 'inherent' and the 'integral', is attuned to the idiom of New Criticism, and, as I suggest, arises largely from it, though it is qualified and given historical depth by reference to such poets and theorists of poetics as Milton, Coleridge, and Hopkins.

Benziger, with Schlegel and Coleridge, is essentially describing Hill's sense of when "impulse and effect are at one" (*CCW* 23). This state of being "at one" is probably something akin to Bradley's 'perfection': Christopher Ricks has remarked on Hill's conception of 'atonement' in 'Poetry as "Menace" and "Atonement"': "To speak of atonement *between* x and y (instead of atonement of x and y) is to concede that it is not truly an at-one-ment, since it would have to be an at-one-ment (a setting at one) of x and y, not between them."[44] Ricks is right to point this out, and this is just the sort of semantic tremor which is Hill's critical stock-in-trade, and endemic to his sense of 'crisis'. In this small qualification is writ large Hill's attitude towards perfectibility, and ultimately towards atonement. Hill's later essays and poetry explore this sense of between-ness, of striving for an impossible at-one-ness, which lies at the heart of his Bradleian sense of eros. Coleridge's Schlegelian invocation of "perfection" in the passage quoted by Benziger is the red flag here: in 'A Postscript on Modernist Poetics' Hill quotes Bradley's "We have the idea of perfection – there is no doubt as to that", glossing this with the remark that "This is flatter than a flat assertion, and yet a brief flicker lights up the flatness: the momentary uncertainty as to whether 'no doubt' goes with 'perfection' or with 'idea'" (*CCW* 571). This "momentary uncertainty" between there being no doubt about perfection or no doubt as to the idea of perfection encapsulates Hill's sense of the erotic. "If asked for Bradley's basic affirmation of eros this is what I would point to", writes Hill. "Disappointing, in a sense; and, if disappointed, we can turn to the concluding pages of *Essays on Truth and Reality* where the erotic element as we understand it is more explicitly considered" (*CCW* 571), wherein Bradley refers to "the becoming and the endless incompletion of the world" (a crucial definition of eros nowhere cited by Hill).[45] And Bradley goes on:

> To deny that this side of things is fact would in my view be absurd. But on the other hand to accept this side of things as real in itself and unconditionally, and to proclaim it as being in its own character the last word about the Universe, to me seems no less ridiculous ... In this volume I have urged that what matters and what is ultimately good is the Whole, and that there is no aspect of life which, abstracted and set utterly by itself, can retain goodness. And on the other side I have insisted ... upon the absolute, the unassailable right of every aspect of life to its own place, function, and liberty. Even the separation of play and earnest, I have pointed out, has but relative worth. And the attempt to lower science and art to the rank of mere instruments springs, I urge, once more from this propensity to mistake some perverted distinction for a separate Power, and to sentence whatever it excluded from this to unreality or mere subservience.[46]

The 'Concluding Remarks' of *Essays on Truth and Reality* are the mirror-image of the 'Conclusion' of Eliot's *The Use of Poetry and the Use of Criticism*, which reads "in the style of a threnos" as Hill asserts (*CCW* 563), its "And... And..." enacting that striving towards an unknown conclusion, the "syntax of becoming". But this passage reads also as a 'perfect' fusion of ethos and practice in a way which is readily transferrable to poetry. What is the poet doing in the process of writing a poem, or trying to, but balancing "place, function, and liberty" against an imagined "Whole", and enacting the coexistence of "play and earnest" as the sensuous intelligence? Or rather, that is what Hill's 'ideal' poet would be doing, and what his championed poets *have* done, in his eyes. It is this fusion of precision and abstraction which marks Bradley's style, and which distinguishes this passage as an example of it.

One might point to the literary criticism emerging from the modernist milieu as a source for Hill's commitment to "immediate context" (*CCW* 557) also; William Empson's *Seven Types of Ambiguity* or *The Structure of Complex Words* are the classic studies of what Hills calls "immediate context" in the modernist and New Critical era. In *Seven Types of Ambiguity* a passage occurs which exemplifies Hill's conception of word value:

> Racine always seems to me to write with the whole weight of the French language, to remind one always of the latent assumptions

of French, in a way that I am not competent to analyse in any case, but that very possibly could not be explained in intelligible terms. Dryden is a corresponding English figure in this matter; Miss Gertrude Stein, too, at this point, implores the passing tribute of a sigh.[47]

According to Empson, this cannot be "explained in intelligible terms". Hill agrees with this fundamentally, but maintains that this quality *can* be perceived, *somehow*, even if it cannot be made ultimately intelligible:

> I am, in my approach to literature and literary criticism, an "intrinsic value" person. I try to imagine it as a palpable quality; if a poem or a prose passage succeeds, I tell myself, then one ought to be able to weigh it in a pair of craftsman's scales.[48]

The entire poise of this passage, its position, is contained in that small parenthesis "I tell myself", a "brief flicker" which asserts the right to metaphysical desire here and elsewhere in Hill's later work: it is both an affirmation and a disavowal – very Hillian. It is repeated in a passage in *The Triumph of Love* which contemplates similar metaphysical desire:

> Even now, I tell myself, there is a language
> to which I might speak and which
> would rightly hear me;
> responding with eloquence; in its turn,
> negotiating sense without insult
> given or injury taken.
> Familiar to those who already know it
> elsewhere as justice,
> it is met also in the form of silence.   (*ToL* XXXV; *BH* 249)

In the essay 'On the Ontological Mystery', Gabriel Marcel equates the intrinsic, a parallel term for 'being' in the essay, with, if not quite unintelligibility, then certainly a resistance to intelligibility: "being is what withstands – or would withstand – an exhaustive analysis bearing on the data of experience and aiming to reduce them step by step to elements increasingly devoid of intrinsic or significant value".[49] In a private letter, Hill's editor Kenneth Haynes summed up Hill's (and perhaps his own) grasp of the political position of intrinsic value: "The value of the work is its ability to say 'no' to its interpretation."[50] Intrinsic value is that which cannot be assimilated or translated into terms other than its own. Hill's sense of intrinsic value is of a kind with Cleanth Brooks's famous injunction against the so-called "heresy of paraphrase",[51] Brooks being one of the most important American mid-century New Critics; just as it is of a kind with Heidegger's *Gelassenheit*.

However, Marcel's definition of intrinsic value is not in terms of an absolute: the data in question become "increasingly devoid" of intrinsic value. The idea of intrinsic value as somehow mediated and yet of necessity an absolute has a bearing on Hill's approach to the problem, too:

> A crucial issue remains. In so framing the matter, do I confuse intrinsic with mediated value? Here again [Joseph] Butler has shown that, in some if not all circumstances, intrinsic and mediated value cannot, may not, be separated. It is my "obligation to obey this law [in] its being the law of [my] nature"; that is, in and of itself, the intrinsic being that I mediate. (*CCW* 477)

Again, "cannot, may not be separated" is an instance of what Hill identifies as the Bradleian 'somehow': it is a semantic flicker whose terms are mutually qualifying: it may not be because it cannot be, or it cannot be because it may not be? To say something cannot be done is a very different thing from saying that something may not be done: one belongs to fact, and the other to value. To some, this may well look like equivocation. But the underlying feeling of this is that, in matters of intrinsic value, fact and value are *somehow* one and the same: a mutual identification given some justification by the 'Concluding Remarks' of Bradley's *Essays on Truth and Reality*. Again, this might be dismissed, arguably, as little more than wishful thinking given a certain authority by appeal to F.H. Bradley.

Graves and Riding also use Gertrude Stein, less archly than Empson, as an example of "mechanical" writing without word value:

> These words have had no history, and the design that Miss Stein has made of them is literally "abstract" and mathematical because they are commonplace words without any hidden etymology; they are mechanical and not eccentric.⁵²

Eccentricity is a vital element in Hill's sense of word value and the political place of poetics. Hill remarked in an early essay that "[t]hat which is eccentric is not concentric; it does not share a common centre" (*CCW* 130). The belletrism of Eliot, as Hill sees it, assumes just such a 'common centre', an audience of initiates or devotees; perhaps concentricity often entails the ability, the self-assumed authority, "to make opinion appear to be genuine ratiocination" (*CCW* 469), as Hill remarks of Hobbes, and in the reader "the tendency to mistake power for authority" (*CCW* 489). This latter diagnosis forms part of the nub of Hill's critique of high modernist poetics, and the gist of Hill's critics' objections to his own later criticism. To follow the terms of Graves and Riding, the eccentric is not mechanical: it is language with three dimensions.

Hill has quoted Donald Carne-Ross's description of the "massive, truculent English" of Dryden,⁵³ and its massiveness and truculence are not simply matters of vowel-music and rhythmic patterning, if we take Empson's remark to be axiomatic for Hill. To attend to the value of words is to attend to the "whole weight" of the language, of its "latent assumptions". This is surely not simply a matter of education, but a matter of intuition also – perhaps it is *primarily* a matter of intuition, a feeling in and through words. This kind of value, which seems to be coming close to a sense of 'intrinsic value', "could not be explained in intelligible terms", and here Empson seems to borrow some of F.H. Bradley's sceptical mysticism, or at least to trade on the "latent assumptions" of the intellectual milieu of 1930, or what was acceptable to the contemporary intelligentsia (and it was still possible to speak of an intelligentsia); in *A Survey of Modernist Poetry* Graves and Riding identify "the eternal difficulties which make poems immortal",⁵⁴ which is perhaps more intelligible than the Bradleian gesturing of Empson, but which partakes still of the idioms of intrinsic value. This sort of idiom is not completely alien to Hill either, but his adjustments are telling. Serious writing, he remarks in one Oxford lecture, is "between politics and eternity".⁵⁵ This, as the previous chapter discussed, is characteristic of Hill's reading of F.H. Bradley's 'eros', against the perceived belletrism of the likes of Eliot, and perhaps even Empson on occasion; eros is that acute sense of being between the absolute and the particular, and of being, *somehow*, of both and of neither.

Graves's and Riding's *A Survey of Modernist Poetry* (1927), and Robert Graves in a more general sense, seem to exemplify Hill's later reaction to modernism, implicitly in his later essays, and often explicitly in his Oxford Professor of Poetry lectures. In *A Survey of Modernist Poetry*, for instance, Graves and Riding insist that "Language in poetry should not be treated as if it were a paint-box, or the poem as if it were something to be hung on the wall, so to speak"; this recalls Hill's criticism of contemporary poems being like "selfies",[56] that is, sacrificing word value for self-portraiture. Indeed, Graves and Riding reiterate a core tenet of post-Eliot modernist poetics, which recalls Hill's notion of 'alienated majesty' even as it evokes Eliot's impersonality:

> the important part of poetry is now not the personality of the poet as embodied in a poem, which is its style, but the personality of the poem itself, that is, its quality of independence from both the reader and the poet, once the poet has separated itself from his personality by making it complete – a new and self-explanatory creature.[57]

Graves's and Riding's "new and self-explanatory creature" is angelized by Hill into an "alien being" (*CCW* 566). This tenet recurs and resonates throughout Hill's criticism, forming the subject of *Alienated Majesty*, a volume of essays which explores the origins of this quality in Emerson, Whitman, and Hopkins, before turning to Eliot and F.H. Bradley, and, in the final essay, Yeats.

And W.B. Yeats crops up throughout *Liber Illustrium Virorum*: in one poem, Hill writes "Yeats – and yet again I fail to avoid | Him as my seamark – plotted some Roman | Fascisti-Shakescene but lost that bid" (*Liber Illustrium Virorum* [henceforth *LIV*] XL; *BH* 724) – "sea-mark" being a word that appears in *Coriolanus* to which these lines allude (as well as *Othello*, incidentally). Yeats is one of the three bad examples of modernist politics, the others being Pound and Eliot;

in fact, high modernist poetics are distinguished in Hill's criticism (in prose and poetry) for their political shortcomings. And yet, Hill clearly takes much from Yeats as a poet also, not least the idea of the "monad of linguistic energy" (*CCW* 578) which is the "unit comprising antithetical, even mutually repellent forces" (*CCW* 577). Indeed, Hill's allusions to Yeats are often approbatory, even though they must be ironically so: "I buy terrific gyre" in poem XXXIII; and, more ironically still, "Reintroduce us to good mother-wit" in poem VIII, "mother-wit" seemingly taken from an essay by Yeats on eugenics.[58] Yeats is often associated with pose and posture, as in poem 19 of *Ludo*: "what an air, | eh, Yeats, great double-breasted winter coat | collared with fur!" (*BH* 610. And in the essay 'Language, Suffering and Silence', Hill describes Yeats (within the specific context of the argument) as "like a D'Annunzio in Irish tweeds" (*CCW* 403). The association of Yeats with posture Hill shares with C.H. Sisson, a poet-critic on whom Hill lectured at the University of Bristol in 1984, and who crops up a couple of times in Hill's later criticism; Sisson writes, for example, that "Yeats was a great egotist, and frivolous enough to think it worth while cutting a figure even after his death";[59] and of 'Politics', that "It is understandable, but it is too pre-conceived to impress us as poetry."[60] The import of this in the context of Hill's later work is that the "understandable" and the "pre-conceived" imply each other.

In *Liber Illustrium Virorum*, Yeats is conflated with Coriolanus, too, that Shakespearean character of patrician hauteur, invoked as "broken"[61] in Eliot's *The Waste Land*. *Liber Illustrium Virorum* contains many references to Yeats, and Eliot hovers behind the sequence too:

> Aufidius meanwhile
> Volscian style
> Exultantly at ease,
> No baggage and no *crise*,
> Secure in self-keeping ...   (*BH* 688)

Aufidius is here offered as an alternative figure within the Coriolanus tradition, perhaps the symbol of an alternative approach to high modernist poetics, given the context; and particularly since Hill writes that "*Coriolan* remains one of the major 'lost' sequences in English poetry of the twentieth century and *Four Quartets* is the poorer for Eliot's having 'lost' it" (*CCW* 543). Coriolanus, and Eliot's *Coriolan*, then, represent Hill's relationship of revocation with modernism, particularly with regard to Eliot. Here the figure is symbolic of "self-keeping", rather than the "continuous self-sacrifice" of Eliot's formulation in 'Tradition and the Individual Talent'. Aufidius, the Volscian, stands at the receiving end of Coriolanus's taunt, excerpted by Eliot as the epigraph to the subsequently suppressed 'Ode on Independence Day, 1918': "To you especially, and to all the Volscians, great hurt and mischief" – an epigraph that suggests a contempt for the 'gentle reader', if ever there was one.

Coriolanus might be described as an 'alienated' figure: alienated, anyway, from the *vox populi*. 'Alienation' and its cognates is a word with a dense history, and with the connotation nowadays of being dissatisfied with the normal way of doing things: if someone feels left out of something, such as society, say, they feel 'alienated'. The word is also associated with Marx, and the worker's alienation from his or her productions. Hill's usage is affected by these various connotations, but there is a rationale given for what seems like Hill's diverging uses of the word. In 'Alienated Majesty: Ralph W. Emerson', Hill quotes a journal entry in which Emerson cites 'Alienation' and 'Otherism', and goes on to remark:

> Clearly, Emerson's 'Otherism' is not 'altruism' but what in German is known by two words, *Entfremdung* and *Verfremdung*. The first means *estrangement*, the second is *artistic (especially theatrical) distancing*. It is arguably a prime function of the imagination to grasp both senses at once ... (*CCW* 494)

Arguably: and it is certainly Hill's argument that this is so, and this goes a long way to explain why "the young Eliot was about ... eros and alienation" (*CCW* 556): artistic distancing (Eliot called it impersonality) is the concomitant of social estrangement. However, the failure to recognise *Verfremdung* at work, its effects and affects, results in another kind of alienation: "Royce and James are finally estranged from their own deepest intelligence by a failure to recognise the existence of such an *aporia*" (*CCW* 496). I would suggest, though, that this estrangement is not an absolute condition in Hill's view but is caused by deficiencies in our present political culture, as I argue in chapters 5 and 6; and at this point it should be specified that *Entfremdung* is a word from Marx, evoking thereby the classic Marxist sense of the individual divorced from his or her creative nature by capitalist modes of production.[62] The alienated and alienating verbal artefacts of Shakespeare and his generation, for example, were not socially estranged. *Hamlet* was a hit. The conditions of political modernity, in their emphasis on the individual, erode the distinction between self and personality, according to Hill (*CCW* 496); they are conditions in which "the creative self cannot maintain its independence from the cultural personality". Lamentably, for Hill, the self is now insufficiently alienated from personality in literary work, and in art and life generally (*CCW* 497).

A further note on eros

Eros is all about the desire for consummation, which is not quite an ideal state, but exists *somehow*, neither as actuality nor idea, reminiscent of Emmanuel Levinas's "metaphysical desire", as I have said. Metaphysical desire is not one type of desire, as such, but the energy and structure of desire itself: that is, the always-thwarted impulse towards possession, which is at once an impulse for consummation and annihilation. Hill quotes Bradley: "We may be told that the End, because it is that which thought aims at, is therefore itself (mere) thought. This assumes that thought cannot desire a consummation in which it is lost. But does not the river run into the sea, and the self lose itself in love?" (*CCW* 548) There seems to be a bit of a contradiction in the description of eros in 'Eros in F.H. Bradley and T.S. Eliot': "Eros is the power that can be felt in language when a word or half-finished phrase awaits its consummation"; and yet "Pope is one of the most immediately erotic of poets" (*CCW* 548). Perhaps this is saved by "immediately"; also by "Eros is so palpably present in rhyming verse that it seems like a parody of itself". It is the expectation of fulfilment which is repeatedly offered in rhymed poetry – offered but never finally satisfied.

To understand Hill's sense of eros fully, one must appreciate how he sees it working in Bradley, and how it is explained in *Ethical Studies*. The essential character of eros is insatiable faith:

one associates it with dramatized agnostic yearning: Tennyson's "Oh yet we trust that somehow good | Will be the final goal of ill" is a sublime instance.⁶³

It is an affirmative version of the "heretic's dream of salvation expressed in images of the orthodoxy from which he is excommunicate".⁶⁴ Eros is summed up in a sentence from *Ethical Studies* which Hill does not provide in his criticism: "I must progress, because I have an other which is to be, and yet never quite is, myself; and so, as I am, am in a state of contradiction."⁶⁵ Eros is a continuous self-attention which is simultaneously an acute sense of otherness, without the possibility of these two qualities being united (as the soul might be united with God, say). It is a never-ending drive towards the horizon. In 'A Postscript on Modernist Poetics', Karl Rahner is called in to give evidence to Hill's case: "Being expresses itself, because it must realize itself through a plurality in unity" (*CCW* 567). It is this sense of plurality in unity which is at the heart of Hill's ethical outlook, which can be traced to Rahner, to Bradley, to Kierkegaard, and to Yeats, too, who is a vital point of conflict and contact for Hill's later work.

What is Rahner's "plurality in unity" if not ambiguity? This is one of the legacies of modernism to which Hill is indebted, and there is perhaps more of Robert Graves, Laura Riding, and William Empson in the later work than there is of Eliot and Pound; or, at least, more of a sense of affiliation with *A Survey of Modernist Poetry*, *The Structure of Complex Words*, or *Seven Types of Ambiguity* (*CCW* 553). Ambiguity is a necessary element of what Hill calls word value, since "questions of value are inseparable from questions of translation" (*CCW* 384). Connotative ambiguity, the precise semantic and etymological quality of a given word in its context, is the hardest thing to translate. The attention to the multiplicity of meanings conferred on a given word by its history, usage, and reception, is what Hill means by "immediate context", and also by "word value". Ambiguity implies the control of multiple meanings by the author, but also an energy within the word – which may be the closest thing we can get to its 'intrinsic value' – which bespeaks the arbitrariness, the recalcitrance, and the radiance of language. In Graves's and Riding's *A Survey of Modernist Poetry*, and in William Empson's *Seven Types of Ambiguity*, there is a salutary attention to matters of immediate context; it is not quite true to say that the focus on technique and language elides ethos, however, as the one implies the other, as Graves, Riding, and Empson are aware, and as all writers and critics worth their salt are aware.

Hill does not see this modern – read modern*ist* – tendency in Bradley, who does not on the whole "tolerate ambiguity"; but in this, Bradley is "writing against the pull of what, around the time of his death, in 1924, would become the strongest inclination in modern British literary criticism" (*CCW* 553). The extent to which Bradley was aware of contemporary trends in literary criticism is debatable, despite his brother having been Oxford Professor of Poetry at the turn of the century and a noted literary critic. I would suggest, however, that if ambiguity is largely absent from Bradley's style, a style which answers (if obliquely) to the demands of expositional rigour, it is surely at the heart of what Hill calls eros: it is ambiguity in the negative sense, that is, a being between absolute states, in a state of disequilibrium always desiring equilibrium. It is present in Bradley's conception of self-consciousness, in which self-attention cannot make the self into an object, as an object of knowledge, because this would then render the knower incapable of knowing, as would the case in reverse: "The self … may become an object, and yet the self must also be felt immediately, or it is nothing … I am fully aware that this statement is in one sense not intelligible."[66] Bradley's self-confessed unintelligibility on this point would have been anathema to Bertrand Russell, but is for Hill, perhaps, an instance of "the power of intelligible mystery",[67] or of "the strangeness of truth"[68] that, finally, "rests in its own intelligibility".

Notes

1 Geoffrey Hill, 'Modernism / Post-modernism', BC MS 20c, Hill/4/23, p. 22, Brotherton Library, University of Leeds.
2 Ibid.
3 Hill, '"Legal Fiction" and Legal Fiction'.
4 Hill, 'The Art of Poetry: 80'.
5 W.B. Yeats, *The Major Works, including Poems, Plays, and Critical Prose*, Ed Larrissy ed., intro., notes. (Oxford University Press: Oxford, 1997) p. 132.

6   Eliot, *Selected Prose of T.S. Eliot*, p. 40.
7   Karl Marx, *Der Achtzehnte Brumaire des Louis Bonaparte* (Berlag: Stuttgart, 1914) p. 7. "Die Tradition aller toten Geschlechter lastet wie ein Alp auf dem Gehirn der Lebenden."
8   T.S. Eliot, *Selected Essays* (Faber: London, 1932) p. 288.
9   Ibid., p. 288.
10 Ivor Gurney, letter to Ethel Voynich, *War Letters* (Midnag/Carcanet: Manchester, 1983) p. 49. Anti-Miltonism has a long history, though, far pre-dating the modernist era: see Christopher Ricks, *Milton's Grand Style* (Oxford University Press: Oxford, 1963) chapter 1.
11 Hill, 'The Art of Poetry: 80'.
12 Geoffrey Hill, 'Noetics and Poetics', BC MS 20c, Hill/4/17/2, p. 11, Brotherton Library, University of Leeds.
13 Ezra Pound, *Literary Essays of Ezra Pound*, T.S. Eliot ed. and intro. (Faber: London, 1954) p. 216.
14 T.S. Eliot, 'Milton (I)', *Selected Prose of T.S. Eliot*, p. 258.
15 John Milton, *Areopagitica* and *Of Education*, Michael Davis ed., intro., and notes (Macmillan: London, 1963) p. 105.
16 Hill, 'Noetics and Poetics', p. 8. "I received instruction from Coleridge many years before I came to the teaching of Augustine or was introduced to Wittgenstein's radically Augustinian commentary, the *Philosophical Investigations*."
17 Samuel Taylor Coleridge, *Shakespeare, Ben Jonson, Beaumont and Fletcher: Notes and Lectures* (Edward Howell: Liverpool, 1874) p. 3.
18 Geoffrey Hill, 'Milton as Muse', lecture delivered at Christ's College, Cambridge, 29 October 2008.
19 Coleridge, *Shakespeare, Ben Jonson, Beaumont and Fletcher*, p. 3.
20 Eliot, 'Swinburne as Critic', *The Sacred Wood*, p. 23.
21 Hill, 'The Art of Poetry: 80'.
22 Hill, 'T.S. Eliot Memorial Lecture', p. 7.
23 The ontological implications of this are to the purpose in this context.
24 Geoffrey Hill, 'Civil Polity and the Confessing State', *The Warwick Review*, 2:2, June 2008, p. 10.
25 Hill, 'Modernism / Post-modernism'.
26 Eliot, 'The Perfect Critic', *The Sacred Wood*, p. 13.
27 Hill, 'The Art of Poetry: 80'.
28 Eliot, *Selected Prose of T.S. Eliot*, p. 43.
29 Hill's avowed enthusiasm for Dante's *De Monarchia* is interesting in this context, Dante's treatise providing a justification of authority in

the terms of this Aristotelian intellect (via Thomism) – precisely the model that Hill is seeking to overturn in his later work, having overcome earlier in life an attraction to the idea of the absolute intellect of Averroes. (See Haffenden, *Viewpoints*, p. 98. "Averroism was the doctrine of monopsychism, that is, that there's only one single Intellect, or 'intellective' soul for the whole of humanity, and it seemed to me at first sight a most comforting doctrine … but afterwards I felt it was not a doctrine to be embraced at all; it seemed to be the archetype of the totalitarian state.") Geoffrey Hill, 'Between Politics and Eternity', BC MS 20c Hill/4, Brotherton Library, University of Leeds. I discuss Hill's interest in this text more fully in chapter 6.

30 The anti-Cartesian, or pre-Cartesian, element to Eliot's Bradleian sense of "sensuous interest" is pointed out by Hill in 'Dividing Legacies' (*CCW* 376). "It further appears … that Eliot values the pre-Cartesian elements in Donne's poetics that are at the same time Cartesianism turned on itself: 'the sensuous interest of Donne in his own thoughts as objects.'" "Cartesianism turned on itself" serves as a very broad but not inaccurate precis of the philosophy of Gottfried Leibniz.
31 Eliot, *Knowledge and Experience in the Philosophy of F.H. Bradley*, p. 186.
32 Heidegger, *Being and Time*, p. 173. "The pure 'that it is' shows itself, but the 'whence' and the 'whither' remain in darkness."
33 Hill, '"Legal Fiction" and Legal Fiction'.
34 Bradley, *Essays on Truth and Reality*, p. 471.
35 Hill, 'T.S. Eliot Memorial Lecture', p. 7.
36 Geoffrey Hill, 'Thoughts of a Conservative Modernist', BC MS 20c, Hill/4/22, p. 12, Brotherton Library, University of Leeds.
37 Of 'this' in F.H. Bradley, again demonstrating a proto-Heideggerian element of Bradley, and also in Charles Sanders Peirce: "the 'this', I take it, comes upon us with something of Peirce's 'Brute Actuality'" (*CCW* 570).
38 Hill, 'How Ill White Hairs Become a Fool and Jester'.
39 Ibid.
40 Hill, 'A Deep Dynastic Wound'.
41 James Benziger, 'Organic Unity: Leibniz to Coleridge', *PMLA*, 66:2, p. 24.
42 Geoffrey Hill, 'What You Look Hard at Seems to Look Hard at You', Oxford Professor of Poetry lecture, 6 May 2014.
43 Ibid.

44 Christopher Ricks, '*Tenebrae* and At-One-Ment', *Geoffrey Hill: Essays on His Work*, Peter Robinson ed. (Open University Press: Milton Keynes, 1987) p. 67.
45 Bradley, *Essays on Truth and Reality*, p. 471.
46 Ibid., pp. 471–472.
47 William Empson, *Seven Types of Ambiguity* (Penguin: London, 1995) p. 25.
48 Geoffrey Hill, 'Address of Thanks to the Sponsors and Jury of the Truman Capote Award for Literary Criticism in Memory of Newton Arvin', *Iowa Review*, 40:1, 2010, p. 186.
49 Gabriel Marcel, 'On the Ontological Mystery', *The Philosophy of Existentialism* (Citadel: New York, 1956) p. 14.
50 Kenneth Haynes, letter on Hill's *Thoughts of a Conservative Modernist*, BC MS 20c, Hill/4/22, Brotherton Library, University of Leeds.
51 Cleanth Brooks, *The Well Wrought Urn: Studies in the Structure of Poetry* (Dennis Dobson: London, 1949) pp. 176–196.
52 Robert Graves and Laura Riding, *A Survey of Modernist Poetry* (Heinemann: London, 1927) p. 281.
53 Hill, 'Poetry and the "Democracy of the Dead"'.
54 Graves and Riding, *A Survey of Modernist Poetry*, p. 75.
55 Geoffrey Hill, 'Poetry, Policing, and Public Order (1)', Oxford Professor of Poetry lecture, 29 November 2011.
56 Hill, '"Legal Fiction" and Legal Fiction'.
57 Graves and Riding, *A Survey of Modernist Poetry*, p. 124.
58 W.B. Yeats, 'On the Boiler', *The Major Works*, p. 391. "Take a pair of twins and educate one in wealth, the other in poverty, test from time to time; their mother-wit will be the same."
59 C.H. Sisson, 'W.B. Yeats', *The Avoidance of Literature* (Carcanet: Manchester, 1979), p. 257, p. 258 *passim*.
60 Ibid., p. 258.
61 T.S. Eliot, *Collected Poems 1909–1935* (Faber: London, 1936) p. 77.
62 This Marxist sense of alienation which informs Hill's later work is discussed in greater depth in chapter 6.
63 Hill, 'T.S. Eliot Memorial Lecture', p. 3 of draft notes.
64 Haffenden, *Viewpoints*, p. 98.
65 Bradley, *Ethical Studies*, p. 78.
66 Bradley, 'What Is the Real Julius Caesar?', *Essays on Truth and Reality*, p. 418.
67 Hill, 'Thoughts of a Conservative Modernist', p. 7.
68 Ibid., p. 12.

Chapter 3

'Turbulently at rest': order and anarchy in the later work

In his poetry, as in his criticism, Geoffrey Hill contemplates and argues through vexed questions; but his style in both forms is, at the same time, itself a vexing of its various informing questions. Hill's style is, in fact, itself a major contribution to that literature of 'perplexed persistence' which he ascribes to T.H. Green in his essay of 1975: "his value as an ethical writer is due to the same cause which makes his speculation perplexed and self-contradictory", writes Green of Joseph Butler (*CCW* 109): though self-contradiction becomes translated, in Hill's poetry, into the trope of paradox, a device which is more than simply a rhetorical flourish (though it is that, too), encapsulating much of Hill's modus operandi in political and theological terms. Paradox is a way of working through, or beyond, aporia – a word which appears in Hill's later work, and which is crucial to it – and there is a distinctly paradoxical flavour to much of F.H. Bradley's ethics and metaphysics. Two lines from poem 51 of *Oraclau | Oracles* serve as an apt epigraph to this element of Hill's later style:

> Disorder cannot be brought to the point
> Which is the point of disorder.   (*BH* 757)

Disorder cannot, by its nature, be brought to the ideal consummation of a settled order, but that is its very 'point': its end is its endlessness. These lines exist in a state of irreducible equity, though they speak of disorder: again, a critical aspect of Hill's late style, which, like his own observations on the style of John Donne, "confesses [its] own inordinacy while remaining in all things ordinate" (*CCW* 263). Through paradox, semantic play, and a simultaneous cohesion and coming-apart which is also a self-reflexive remark on the poet's own style, these lines characterise much of Hill's approach in his later work, and particularly *The Daybooks*.

The ambiguity of the word 'point' here, implying an 'end' both in terms of purpose and of duration, is itself to the point. In Hill's later approach there is a necessary co-inherence of poise and collapse, which is similar to Hill's view of language and its semantic ambiguity, described in 'A Postscript on Modernist Poetics' as "a theory of energy" (*CCW* 571). A passage on Yeats in one of Hill's later essays could stand, also, as a statement on his own late work:

> What he is looking for in his late writings is a unit comprising antithetical, even mutually repellent, forces, in which the calculated is at one with the spontaneous: integration that is simultaneously diremption; a kind of monad of linguistic energy. ('A Postscript on Modernist Poetics', *CCW* 578)

Yeats is often a point of reference in this later work, particularly in *Liber Illustrium Virorum*, both in approbatory and condemnatory senses, as I argued in the previous chapter. For Hill, it is language's ambiguities and connotative dissonances which constitute its "linguistic energy", and his view of language is that of the *felix culpa*, the fortunate Fall, of St Augustine: "[l]ike eros, also, language has its arbitrariness" (*CCW* 571). It is the capacity and fate of poetry to concentrate to the *n*th degree the postlapsarian nature of language, and Hill's Bradleian sense of a perfection which exists *somehow* is in fact a version of 'Romantic agony': that is, "This grime, this always working to perfect | That which by nature must remain imperfect" (*Al Tempo de' Tremuoti* [henceforth *ATdT*] 86; *BH* 930). As such, Hill's theology of language and sense of politics intertwine; but whereas the centre of Hill's theological concern is the relationship between perfection and imperfection, this chapter will deal with the political version of this relation in Hill's work, namely order and anarchy.

In poem XXIX of *The Triumph of Love*, the co-inherence of anarchy and order is offered as an image of polity, "England's | iron-bound storm-tree turbulently at rest" (*BH* 248). In the *Oxford English Dictionary*, 'turbulent' has just the kind of double connotation favoured by Hill in the context of order and anarchy: in definition 2, it is both 'stormy, tempestuous', and 'Of a state of mind or thought,

Order and anarchy in the later work   49

social or political affairs, etc.'. Clearly this notion of being "turbulently at rest" is at the cusp of private experience and public action for Hill. His later work explores the relationship between the ideal and the real, the metaphorical and the literal, just as it explores the relationship between writing and justice, if there is one; and his later style can be read as an embracing of the anarchic forces within the self and the world, even as these forces are scrutinised as dangerous elements within the self and its effects.

Will and law

Clavics carries, as epigraph, an epitaph to the seventeenth-century English composer and musician William Lawes:

Concord is conquer'd: In this Urne there lies
The Master of great Musick's mysteries,
And in it is a riddle like the *cause*:
Will. Lawes was slain by such whose *wills* were *laws*. (*BH* 789)

Killed in the siege of Chester in 1645, Lawes fought on the side of the Royalists. English, and indeed European, history in the seventeenth century was painful and turbulent, abundant in visions of order and anarchy by political theorists and artists, literary and visual, alike; the most famous image in this mould being *The World Turned Upside Down*, a popular trope in the broadsides of the day. The seventeenth century is defined, not just in England, by civil war, scholarly controversy, intellectual and social upheaval.

As the epitaph makes show of, the name Will Lawes contains 'will' and 'law', given a nice contrast by the epitaph's writer, too, in its final line, "*Will. Lawes* was slain by such whose *wills* were *laws*". If the name Will Lawes suggests a harmony of will and law – and the line's capitulation suggests an ironic contrast between the martyr and his killers – then the manner of his death suggests a fatal disharmony; fatal, perhaps, for a version of England, also. However, Lawes's epitaph itself delights in the controlled anarchy of English, as here, where 'concord' and 'conquered' are almost, but not quite, full rhymes, a relationship which emphasises their fatal disharmony by positing their harmony. This is exactly the kind of collocation in which Hill himself delights in *Clavics*, invoking us, and himself, in poem 3 of the sequence to "Grant fidelity to heterophones" (*BH* 793) – heterophones being words which are spelt the same but pronounced differently – which is an injunction to recognise order and anarchy simultaneously, as in the name of Will Lawes. It is the paradoxical atonement of "concord" and "conquer'd" which Hill is interested in: it is their heterophony, rather than their homophony, which brings them together in a Yeatsian "monad of linguistic energy"; that is, a monad which is *not really* a monad.

Similarly, music in *Clavics* represents the conflation of harmony and dissonance: it is what "Crashaw names *love*", but it is also "a maker | Up of discord | And a demon to play" (*BH* 827). Lawes's music is known for its dissonance and disorientating contrasts, a mode which Hill works in his later poetry to great effect. In fact, in one poem in *Clavics* we find "Will Lawes auditioning for Ronnie Scott" (*BH* 805), and elsewhere, we are told that "Lawes is a mod" (*BH* 821). In fact, the very stanza-form of the sequence produces a "dissonance | Unresolved beneath resolution" (*BH* 793):

> The grace of music is its dissonance
> Unresolved beneath resolution
>   Of flow and stance:
>   Our epic work –
>   Cadenced nation –
>   Figuration
>   Running staidly amok,
>   Discord made dance. (*BH* 793)

"Discord made dance", indeed. The concatenation of order and anarchy, and the theological and political connotations of that sense of poetic (dis)order, is at the heart of Hill's later work, and of *The Daybooks* in particular. Hill posed this problem in an Oxford Professor of Poetry lecture, quoting Christopher Ricks: "Does poetic order correspond in any detailed way to social order? What sort of regime is maintained in a particular verse structure?"[1] Flow and stance here correspond to the "syntax of becoming" and the poem's form, or frame. No matter how much the poem is 'finished' – in the metaphor of *Clavics*, like a key in a lock – as a concentration of language it always embodies some degree of anarchy, some element of demonic play.

The two recurrent themes of *Clavics* are music and polity: that word 'discord', like 'disharmony', has a double connotation of 'contention' (as in civil strife) and 'dissonance' (*OED*). And, in poem 40 of the sequence, "Mourning rare Lawes, grief-enscrolled business, | Bravely refines | Music's harsh concord with the laws of state" (*BH* 830). Like mourning, or celebration, poetry is a part of the *res publica* though it is not at its executive centre: poetry is an act, or an artefact, which refines and reimagines the polity, or else itself connives with official sentiment – a position which is often mocked in the later poetry, particularly *Speech! Speech!*: "the Brits | are heroes living as they have to" (*BH* 335).

Hill is profoundly implicated as poet and critic in the relationship between writing and justice. His work is deeply involved with the notion of a poetic order which exists in parallel to social order, but which does not pretend to mirror or predict it; or, most perniciously and dangerously of all, purport to bring it about. In an interview with John Haffenden in 1981, Hill made a remark which stands over his imaginings of order and anarchy even in his most recent work:

Haffenden:
Do you have strong feelings about the function of art and poetry, or do you feel that when we look to art for consolation, sublimation or transcendence we should remain sceptical about its value?

Hill:
What is wrong with accepting both parts of that proposition? To succeed totally in finding consolation in art would be to enter a prelapsarian kingdom. Father Christopher Devlin has a very fine phrase to define the themes of Hopkins's sermons – "the lost kingdom of innocence and original justice", which is a lovely resonant phrase; and without in any way aligning myself hubristically with Hopkins, I would want to avail myself of Devlin's phrase, because I think there's a real sense in which every fine and moving poem bears witness to this lost kingdom of innocence and original justice. In handling the English language the poet makes an act

of recognition that etymology is history. The history of the creation and the debasement of words is a paradigm of the loss of the kingdom of innocence and original justice.²

Typically of Hill, transcendence and scepticism go hand in hand. Language remains a "paradigm" of "innocence" and "justice", and not its place of residence. A paradigm, etymologically speaking, is something which is exhibited beside something else as a comparison; it is analogous. Certainly, in this later work, Hill is, quite openly, revelling in the anarchic energies of language, as in *Ludo*, a sequence whose very name suggests just these energies, which are also reminiscent of the games of childhood: "Emerod-ridden rear end well-riddled by rod. And?" (*BH* 606). And nothing; and everything: the point is the play, as in the play of childhood, which imitates and parodies the arbitrariness and intrigue of the adult world. The self-referentiality of Hill's later work is indicative of the self-referentiality of language. In *Ludo* we have "Nonsense verses set down versus conscience" (*BH* 620), in which conscience corresponds, perhaps, to law (and there is the paraphernalia of Freudianism to support this reading, explored further on in the present chapter). This is will as wilfulness, the poet as wilful child. The *OED*'s two connotations of 'wilful' establish the word in Hill's context as compounding elements which are crucial to his latter modus operandi: "obstinately self-willed or perverse", and "crafty or wily". Certainly in *Ludo*, as throughout *The Daybooks* and the later poetry more generally, the notion of wilfulness, of being "obstinately self-willed or perverse", is taken up and used more and less seriously.

In poems which adhere to rigid formal structures in *The Daybooks*, the relationship between will and law is inevitably very apparent to the poet. As Hill writes in poem 18 of *Al Tempo de' Tremuoti*:

> Syntax as coitus. Call Original Sin
> *Freedom being what it is* (not Wittgenstein
> Though something like him). Under and above,
>
> *Scattering bright* (Donne). Angels and nematodes.
> Even if in sex only, one can say
> *I will and yet my will does not obey.* (*BH* 895)

So, if syntax is like sex, then in syntax one experiences the infidelity of the will – Sidney's "infected will" – as joyful and generative. If sensuality is a result of the Fall, then it is constitutive also of free will, "*Freedom being what it is*". In poem 19 of *Ludo*, too, Hill goes back to the will: "What's here anarchic and libidinous | Shakespeare names *Will*" (*BH* 610). In the very next poem, "Grief is everywhere", which "will not grow | with watching; arbitrarily though law | bends natural justice to accommodate will" (*BH* 610). Here the tension between will and law is made explicit; and it is in the nature of Hill's view of the anarchic laws of language that the pun on 'will' is the most generative of meaning.

So, the law, which we take to be immutable and objective, is actually a compromise, a compounding of natural justice with will, according to these lines from *Ludo*. In other words, natural justice and will are different in kind, not simply in degree. Natural justice, or natural law, is a legal term which denotes an ideal standard against which lawmaking and arbitration is measured. Lloyd L. Weinreb defines it as "the idea of justice", and also as "radically separate fact and value, descriptive and normative discourse, 'is' and 'ought'".[3] It is like Yeats's triumphantly defeated attempt "to hold in a single thought reality and justice".[4] In other words, natural law is to the human will what the ideal is to the real, the value to the fact; its existence, though ideal, is a painful reminder of our duality, of our being "apart from nature and a part of it",[5] and of the essentially metaphorical nature of absolute justice. As such, "arbitrarily", in Hill's poem, is itself given a double bias here, as the adverbial form here means 'capricious', or something which is done 'at will', even as the word suggests, also, "the idea of justice", or arbitration. The will, by nature infected, bends and warps whatever it encounters; neutrality, arbitration which is not 'arbitrary', is, all things (not) being equal, beyond the capacity of wilful humans. As early as 'The True Conduct of Human Judgement', an essay on *Cymbeline* from the early 1960s, Hill asserts that "Shakespeare is perhaps ready to accept a vision of actual power at cross-purposes with the vision of power-in-grace; the 'real world', in fact, 'in which the life of the spirit is at all points compromised'" (*CCW* 69). Indeed, Hill, in typically half-self-mocking fashion remarks, in a poem added to the *Broken Hierarchies* version after the initial publication in 2012 of *Clavics*, "Quasi-Shakespearean this play on *Will*" (*BH* 830). Hill sees this theme of will versus natural justice as crucially Shakespearean, but, just as crucially, this Shakespearean context as itself a part of the wider context of an acute sense of polity in Elizabethan and Jacobean literature. The English sixteenth and seventeenth centuries, with their histories of state violence and struggle, and their proliferation of literary and political writings, provide Hill with a rich context for the relationship between writing and polity.

In his essay on Robert Southwell, Hill cites a critical judgement that the Elizabethan poet's work, such as 'The Burning Babe', is the product of a "well-ordered will", suggesting that Southwell is, for Hill, an exemplary instance of will and law being united, creating a work in which "impulse and effect are one" (*CCW* 23). And in this essay of 1979, which is in large part a meditation on the connotations and implications of 'equity', Hill writes of "the *naturalis aequitas* of Roman jurists", which constituted a "recourse to general principles of justice … to correct or supplement the provisions of the law" (*CCW* 27). Here, too, "impulse and effect are one": the biasing effect of individual will does not intervene in the actions of these – somewhat fantastical – "Roman jurists". Southwell, who represents equity and a probably idealised purity of will, dies a martyr; he is a victim of the judiciary, not its arbiter. (Hill tends to write about martyrs: that is, idealists or fantasists of power-in-grace who fall victim to actual power.) This ideal state, this *naturalis aequitas*, corresponds also to Martin Luther's "natural law", of which Luther wrote in a letter of 1544: "every man, confronted by the natural law, must ask, Would you that others should do to you what you do to them?"[6] This vision of natural law is of a moral life in which "impulse and effect are one": it is an imitation of Christ, a counsel of perfection. Ultimately for Hill, however, this is necessarily, though no doubt lamentably, a symptom of metaphysical desire, as much a "semantic relic" as intrinsic value, as 'Translating Value' has it, no less valuable, though certainly more dangerous, for this. Indeed, another of Hill's latterly avowed religious influences, Karl Barth, writes in *The Epistle to the Romans*, "I see that the law which proceeds from Spirit, compelling, necessary, and inevitable though it be, is excluded from my existence as a man".[7] This natural justice, natural law, or *naturalis aequitas*, is to the human will, then, what silence is to language (and this is a direct critique of Eliot's symbolist mysticism in *Four Quartets*):

> Even now, I tell myself, there is a language
> to which I might speak and which

would rightly hear me;
responding with eloquence; in its turn,
negotiating sense without insult
given or injury taken.
Familiar to those who already know it
elsewhere as justice,
it is met also in the form of silence.   (*ToL* XXXV; *BH* 249)

This section of *The Triumph of Love* poem is couched, though "turbulently", in its disrupted line-breaks, in idioms of equity and reciprocity: "to which I might speak and which | would rightly hear me"; "in its turn"; "given ... taken". The poem can describe equity, but its very medium is itself wilful and disordered.

In an interview with *Paris Review* of 2000,[8] Hill equates silence with incoherence:

> Even now when the things are coming fairly quickly, I do feel that everything that I write is a kind of battle won – or lost – against silence and incoherence. And I think there is something naturally incoherent in me, just as I think there is probably something, at some level, anarchic, because the kind of obsessive concern I have with order in the early work is one that somebody has who feels all the time how endangered order is, and what a potential threat to order *he* is.[9]

Hill is pitched against the seduction of metaphysical wraiths and judicial sentences, while acknowledging that they haunt human values, and haunt his own politics, aesthetics, and religious sense; and this is the import of his critique of intrinsic value, which, in effect, amounts to silence or a kind of God's-eye view: the intrinsic implies "not ... that the value is conferred by the admiration, but that society will in the end be brought to recognize the value that has always been there" (*CCW* 388). And yet, Hill is deeply involved with the history of the idea of intrinsic value, "intrinsic natures", and the "inhaerent" in his later essays and lectures. The debate around intrinsic value is that of materialism versus idealism; Hill is deeply involved with language as material, though occupying the shadow of the ideal. For Hill, an appeal to justice, as an appeal to silence, may equate to that "stylish aesthetic of despair, that desire for the ultimate integrity of silence" (*CCW* 11), against which he writes, sometimes explicitly, always implicitly, in his later poetry.

Scenes from Comus, in particular, explores idioms of equity and "equipollence" (*Scenes from Comus* [henceforth *SC*] 2:1, *BH* 431), which, in tractate-ish tone, posits that

> Weight of the world, weight of the word, is.
> Not wholly irreconcilable. Almost.   (*SC* 1:20; *BH* 430)

The semantic drift of this is that the weights of word and world are 'almost not wholly irreconcilable'. The semantic torsion here registers the fact that it is an argument, a self-argument, an embodiment in the material of language of the difficulty of the issue, and not simply a *credo*. The complication of sense registers the complicated relationship between word and world. The emphatic "is" presents the facticity of that mysterious relationship, a relationship "that very possibly could not be explained in intelligible terms", in Empson's words.[10] The two lines actually contradict each other, a self-contradiction echoed in the following lines: "Almost we cannot pull free; almost we escape | the leadenness of things." This is an instance of what Hill calls in *Oraclau* "Torquing upon hwyl, wrestling grammar" (*BH* 748) ('hwyl' being a word in Welsh meaning something like inspiration), in which 'to talk' is 'to torque', and in which inspiration and grammar, or perhaps transcendence and "leadenness", are subject to each other's workings.

The word 'will' and variants has nineteen entries in the index to *Collected Critical Writings*; 'self-will' – a compound word compounding Nietzschean self-overcoming with gameful childishness – has five. Hill is apt to quote others on the subject of will, but in 'Poetry and Value' he writes, in a passage which considers Coleridge's *Aids to Reflection* and the significance of the word 'reflection' itself, that

> "Reflection" is not here identifiable as a "passive attending upon the event" or even as a "wise passiveness" but in metaphors of, and associations with, energy conceived of as a "co-instantaneous yet reciprocal action" of the individual will and an empowering law. (*CCW* 488)

This passage recalls the Yeatsian "monad of linguistic energy". Hill reflects, here, on the co-inherence, in Coleridge's philosophy of language, of will and law, or of Act and Being. As Coleridge writes in *Biographia Literaria*, chapter 13, "The primary IMAGINATION I hold to be the living Power and prime Agent of all human Perception, and as a repetition in the finite mind of the eternal act of creation in the infinite I AM. The secondary Imagination I consider as an echo of the former, co-existing with the conscious will, yet still as identical with the primary in the kind of its agency, and differing only in degree, and in the mode of operation."[11] The primary imagination, then, exists in an otherworldly state, in which Act and Being are united in the primal word, 'I AM'. However, Hill writes in the early essay 'Redeeming the Time' of Coleridge's linguistic idealism (in both the philosophical and political senses of 'idealism'), that the primary imagination, that "living Power and prime Agent",

> represents an ideal democratic birthright, a light that ought to light every person coming into the world. In the event, the majority is deprived of this birthright in exchange for a mess of euphoric trivia and, if half-aware of its loss, is instructed to look for freedom in an isolated and competitive search for possessions and opportunity. Therefore the secondary imagination, the formal creative faculty, must awaken the minds of men to their lost heritage, not of possession but of perception. (*CCW* 101)

As with Lloyd L. Weinreb's definition of natural law, the emphasis here is on the chasm between *is* and *ought*. The primary imagination is, for Hill, akin to the "lost kingdom of innocence and original justice": Coleridge is, here, as he was in earlier life (with Robert Southey) a utopian. Hill brings out the political or quotidian baggage, ignored by Coleridge, in that word 'ideal', here invested with the connotation of something fervently wished for – 'what I would *ideally* like …'. Coleridge's idealism is recast by Hill, here and throughout his poetic writing, as wishful thinking; and Hill's poetic trajectory is towards ever greater contemplations of the "infected will" in human moral life as in poetry. Coleridge writes also that the secondary imagination "dissolves, diffuses, dissipates, in order to recreate; or where this process is rendered impossible, yet still at all events it struggles to idealise and unify".[12] I will not attempt here a lengthy discussion of Hill's relationship with Coleridge's philosophy of language; it suffices to say here that the struggle "to idealise and unify" is often explicitly the focus of Hill's poetry, and this struggle, *as* struggle rather than as achievable end, is in the background of much of his writing in criticism and poetry throughout his career, and is often explicit in the later poetry: this is the Bradleian erotic impulse in action. Where Coleridge relegates "conscious will" to the secondary order of imagination, Hill, while not rejecting this diagnosis as such, sees this ideal order of imagination as being forever metaphorical.

It should be said, here, that 'human moral life' and poetry are, for Hill, inseparable; as he puts it in 'Our Word Is Our Bond', "'rhetoric' is part of the ontology of moral action" (*CCW* 168). And this is the point: the struggle "to idealise and unify" in language is a paradigm, indeed, for the ceaseless implications and complications of the moral life. Hill – as with his revocation of Coleridge in 'Redeeming the Time' – is insistent on the sphere of the primary imagination as being metaphorical, as with Christopher Devlin's remark on Hopkins. However, in the poetry, the desire for the primary imagination, the "lost kingdom", to be real, is a source of energy, as is the relationship between poetic order and social order, which may (or may not) be another kind of wraith.

A passage in *Clavics* 28 echoes an image from Pound's *Cantos*, in which the poet imagines himself "as a lone ant from a broken anthill, | the wreckage of Europe, EGO SCRIPTOR".[13] In Pound, Coleridge's primary imagination, the I AM, is writ large – literally – in the black capitals of the newspaper headline or political slogan. 'I am a writer', screams Pound, 'the only durable thing among this wreckage'. This "EGO" is underwritten in Hill's poetry, particularly his insistently self-reflexive later work: and the passage from *Clavics* runs:

> As to the ant when chance disturbs the State,
> Divisions huge, minute, crude, delicate,
>   Like egg-and-spoon
>   White grub – rice grain –
>   She works her reach
>   With pitch and stretch
> Staithed in that giant crèche.

>   No metaphor.
>   The butterflies, high flyers on high winds;
>   Invisible to us they plane and soar
>   Beyond our minds'
>   Troubled conventioning and do not err. (*BH* 818)

As in the critique of Coleridge's primary imagination, the transcendent is given a worldly twist: the butterflies are "high flyers" who have taken wing "when chance disturbs the State", as likely a description – no metaphor – of the 2008 economic collapse as any other in *The Daybooks* ("Anarchical Plutocracy" [*Clavics* [henceforth *C*] 23; *BH* 813 *inter alia*] being the ultimate game of chance). Not to err is not to be implicated in grammar, which is the result of the Fall. Hill has described the opening sentence of *Paradise Lost*, for instance, as a seminal paradigm of "deviant ethics".[14] The opening poem of *Odi Barbare*, too, establishes a relationship between the difficulty of the poetry and the ethical difficulty of the world as we find it, "Not moronic but a fell world of equals, | Things to fall for, deep in our study sessions, | Ready metered set to a mark perfection / Staggers away from | Anarch's paradiso the infrastructure" (*BH* 835). The modulation between 'fell' and 'fall' here is characteristic; and it is apt, too, that this sequence, which is an engagement with the legacy of Philip Sidney, should make play, in fallen language, with the Fall: "Measure loss re-cadencing Sidney's sapphics | Not as words fall but as they rise to meaning" (*BH* 835). The concentration of poetic language allows words to "rise to meaning", perhaps: a statement of optimism for the capacity of poetry to transfigure the coercive and compromised nature of language, though this transfiguration may be hard-won by both poet and reader alike, "deep in our study sessions", and ultimately that rising to meaning is to refocus the fallen nature of selves and words. Again, the relationship between language and order is Hill's subject matter – though crucially, despite finding itself in an "Anarch's paradiso", the poem imagines "Luck permitting love and its grave verdictives" (*BH* 835).

There is previous form from Hill on the subject of verdictives, a word coined by J.L. Austin in *How to Do Things with Words*: "verdictives … are typified by the giving of a verdict, as the name implies, by a jury, arbitrator, or umpire. But they need not be final; they may be for example, an estimate, reckoning, or appraisal. It is essentially giving a finding as to something – fact, or value – which is for different reasons hard to be certain about".[15] As with the statement by Lloyd Weinreb on natural justice, the relationship between fact and value hovers behind Austin's considerations. Verdictives make claims *about* the world, but make no claims *on* the world. "But they need not be final": here we see an ethical hinterland to the prolificity of Hill's later output, which openly refuses to have had the final word in a Poundian, legislative sense (something which Pound himself failed to do in *The Cantos*) – and which ends, in the last line of the last stanza of the last poem of the last sequence of *Broken Hierarchies*, without a period:

The stars asunder, gibbering, on the verge   (*ATdT* 95; *BH* 936)

Hill's later poetry is ever "on the verge", denying itself the specious glamour of any notion of consummation, even in the formal poems of *The Daybooks*: "Talk of closure keeps open the matter", as poem 28 of *Clavics* puts it (*BH* 818), itself a neat statement of Bradleian eros. In fact, this "theory of energy" is at the heart of Hill's later approach: "[e]ros is the power that can be felt in language when a word or half-finished phrase awaits its consummation", writes Hill in 'Eros in F.H. Bradley and T.S. Eliot' (*CCW* 548). The ending of *Al Tempo de' Tremuoti* defers erotic consummation forever, in an image of the cosmos which is simultaneously an image of infinite energy and infinite emptiness. In other words, the specific energy or power of poetic language lies in its unfinishedness, its being "turbulently at rest", "this always working to perfect | That which by nature must remain imperfect".

Modernism and justice

This sense of being on the verge, being "a babbler | in the crowd's face" (*BH* 601) is bound up, then, with Hill's divergence from the political and theological ethics of high modernism, specifically Ezra Pound and T.S. Eliot. However, while the divergences from Pound are quite stark (and laid out as early as 'Our Word Is Our Bond' of 1984), Hill's differences with Eliot are rather more complicated. For instance, in *Al*

Tempo de' Tremuoti, "There is no true feeling without structure. | This may have been disputed" (*BH* 927). The sequence deals with Italy, and particularly in that context this statement strongly recalls Eliot's in his essay 'Dante' (1929), in which he remarks that "political and ecclesiastical organization are only required because of the imperfections of the human will"[16] (a classically conservative statement); and, of *The Divine Comedy*, that "[e]very degree of the feeling of humanity, from lowest to highest, has … an intimate relation to the next above and below".[17] Whereas Eliot writes here of hierarchies of feeling in an image of ideal order – and ideal order is Eliot's focus from 'Tradition and the Individual Talent' to *Four Quartets* – Hill has elected to call his collected poems *Broken Hierarchies*; and Hill's arguments against such notions of idealism and ideal order have been set out above. I would argue that Hill's very choice of title for his life's work bespeaks this fundamental divergence from the politics and ethics of T.S. Eliot. "[P]olitical and ecclesiastical organization", as Hill is ever aware (elegist of the nineteenth-century working class as he is), is as apt to police and coerce the human will as it is to correct its "imperfections"; and the difference between hierarchy and hegemony is alluded to at various points in Hill's later poetry: what Eliot calls hierarchy, Hill calls (in Gramsci-like fashion) hegemony.[18]

There is a persistent sense in Hill's later work that the politics of modernism go along with a misunderstanding of the role and nature of metaphor. For example, poem 10 of *Al Tempo de' Tremuoti* presents a mock-apocalypse, predicated upon a wrong-headed concatenation of word and thing:

> Augustine, Khlebnikov, parting the Red Sea.
> New time upleaping to a double wand.
> Gehenna shown to be the Promised Land.
> Salvation re-rehearsed futurity.
>
> Nihilation of all negatives; hierarchies
> Of abandon; polarities annulled;
> Syntax delivered and a world re-spelled;
> Anarchy riding it with firecrackers. (*BH* 892)

The proximity of 'word' and 'world', here, and "hierarchies | Of abandon; polarities annulled", are as illusory and delusory as "Gehenna shown to be the Promised Land". One might allow oneself the suspicion, here, that Hill is revelling rather too much in the rhetorical effect of juxtaposition; that he is having his cake and eating it, signing his own disclaimer with the image of "Anarchy riding it with firecrackers". But essentially Hill is questioning here the notion of linguistic idealism: that is, a precise relationship between word and thing – or signifier and signified, in the language of structuralism. *The King of Time*, which Hill refers to later in this poem, is a study of the Russian Futurist poet Velimir Khlebnikov which dwells often upon his association of word and world: for instance, Charlotte Douglas, the volume's editor, writes of Khlebnikov that "For him, the shift in sound that produces a shift in meaning was a shift in the structure of the universe".[19] In other words, the poet is a miracle-worker. With Augustine, Khlebnikov sees a direct correspondence between nature and the word: hence the absurd image of them "parting the Red Sea", like Moses, who had divine sanction from the word of God, inscribed on the tablets of the law. Perhaps, then, Hill's use of "futurity" carries a suggestion of the absurd presumptions of futurism. As a futurist, Khlebnikov partook of the violent, world-shattering ethos-aesthetic of modernism, with all its political and moral errors, so glaring to the present official political culture. Khlebnikov, Douglas continues, wished to "reclaim a power for poetry by reaching back beyond ... intellect ... to the roots of language".[20] This "reaching back beyond ... intellect" recalls Eliot's definition of the 'auditory imagination' as much as it recalls Coleridge's primary imagination, or Devlin's lost kingdom, and echoes the cultural rhetoric of modernism; but there is a suggestion of euphemism on the part of the editor, that to reach beyond intellect may in fact entail its abandonment. The utopianism, the nostalgia of this desire to reclaim "a power for poetry" is characteristic of early-twentieth-century cultural politics; and it is these very cultural politics with which Hill is explicitly at odds in his later work, as when he describes Yeats as a "D'Annunzio in Irish tweeds" (D'Annunzio being an Italian futurist who became a fascist politician) ('Language, Suffering and Silence', *CCW* 403). It is safe to say that Hill is more historicist than futurist, and that this "reaching back beyond ... intellect", that is, 'beyond' the historical significances and pressures of language, would be considered by him a dereliction. Hill sets out his position explicitly in 'A Postscript on Modernist Poetics':

A poem re-enters history in a multitude of circumstances, and it may indeed do so as an effective agent, or hostage. Nonetheless, whatever historical effects it may produce, or be made to produce, are as collusive with good and ill or as absurd as those of any other historical entity. Yet the poem – the true poem … is not exhausted by the uses to which it is put; it is alienated from its existence as a historical event. This intolerable condition, rejected, may lead a poet to a political aesthetics; embraced, to an apolitical one; these twin betrayals – Yeats's "Three Songs to the One Burden" on the one hand and his "On being asked for a War Poem" and "Politics" on the other – haunt modernist poetics. (*CCW* 579/580)

So, true poetry – that is, poetry of real value – neither attempts to dictate history nor is indifferent or meaningless to it; the "true poem … is not exhausted by the uses to which it is put" because, as Kenneth Haynes remarked in a letter to Hill, "[t]he value of the work is its ability to say 'no' to its interpretation".[21] Again, Hill's position here is one of negotiation, an invigilating between extremes: between a political and an apolitical aesthetics, between politics and eternity. The symbolist nostalgia of Khlebnikov – another early-twentieth-century modernist – is an abdication of this vigilance: it is "Gehenna shown to be the Promised Land", a sentence which resonates strongly in the mind of the post-world-wars reader, and indeed may well be reference to contemporary Israel, a frequent cipher for the presence of the infected will within the utopian (Gehenna, meaning broadly 'hell', being originally a place where children were burnt as sacrifices to Baal or Moloch in *Jeremiah* 19:5).[22] Indeed, Khlebnikov's poetry is another example of that incantatory primitivism also explored by T.S. Eliot – though for different purposes and in a different language – in *Sweeney Agonistes*, for example. The recurrent blunder of modernist poetics is that, in Hill's view, they reach either for 'turbulence' or for 'rest', and, as such, *over*-reach politically and ethically (and often aesthetically). Hill's position, as I have argued already, entails constant vigilance (the word Hill uses is 'attention'), being "turbulently at rest": an attendance both to historical context and to the "immediate context" of language, from which, Hill argues, Eliot fell away (*CCW* 557), with disastrous effect. This is the anti-sentimental attitude expressed in *Expostulations on the Volcano*, also:

> Since Scottish
> Law is Roman Law, migrate to Scotland
> Where they sentimentalise equities;
> Case-constraints in Equity forgotten,
>
> Re al-Megrahi (not a Scots clan name
> Though some might suppose it is). We have long
> Known sentimentality without claim.
> Translate into Latin | justice its song. (*Expostulations on the Volcano* [henceforth *EoV*] 9; *BH* 637)

The *Encyclopaedia Britannica* disagrees with Hill's statement, here, if one is to take it seriously, claiming instead that "it is a fallacy to suppose that the law of Scotland is founded on the law of Rome: the Scots only turned to Roman, or civil, law when there was a gap in their own common or customary law".[23] On equity, however, there is agreement. "The Scottish conception [of equity] instead consists of a few fairly simple rules aimed at supplementing the law in order to prevent hardship ... The Scottish outlook upon this whole topic places Scots law clearly alongside the continental civil law and not the English system." Hill's position is that the perception of inequity in the world, as in its institutions, is a tragic but *necessary* element of reality among the complexities of society, of the self, and of language. As for that Latin hymn to justice: "Justice is song where song is primitive | As with poetics" (*EoV* 9; *BH* 637). The singing of justice is, for Hill, equated with a politically suspect hankering after pre-modern or perhaps even prelapsarian forms of life, such as the accelerated primitivism of the futurists. It is a twisted version of pastoral. Such longing is natural, of course, as Hill remarks, in the course of a discussion of intrinsic value, in 'Translating Value', disagreeing with Christopher Ricks:

> I do not myself see that a longing for something indispensable is *per se* misguided; though I concede the dangers and would accept that most attempts to embody the "longing" create metaphysical wraiths. (*CCW* 390)

Again, the "poet's job" is not to reconcile the "detail of surface" with the "root in justice" – that "something indispensable" – but to trace the attractions and repulsions of such longing, in the very material of language as in subject matter. His later work is energised and perplexed by recognition of the "'longing' [to] create metaphysical wraiths".

Between active and passive

There are various references in Hill's most recent work to the global financial crash of 2008, all of which fall under Hill's diagnosis of "Plutocratic anarchy" (*Odi Barbare* [henceforth *OB*] 13; *BH* 847 *inter alia*): for instance, "Lords of our time, losers of others' livings, | Negative life equity left our children | With a bone ploughshare" (*OB* 13; *BH* 847). "Negative life equity" is a phrase which again partakes of the idiom of equity and therefore that nebulous notion of "*naturalis aequitas*" or natural law; but "life equity" recalls John Ruskin in *Unto this Last*, in which wealth, with its opposite, 'illth', is recast as a moral quality.[24] Hill's "Negative life equity", while evoking the financial state of negative equity (in which assets put up against a loan are worth less than the loan amount) also evokes Ruskin's concept of illth, about which Hill writes in two of his later critical essays:

> [Wealth, or "intrinsic value"] is whatever we desire shall stand as the moral opposite of illth and collective national bad faith. (*CCW* 388)
>
> ...
>
> Green's objection to Butler's "cross of unreconciled principles" is brusque and inappropriately theatrical though less so than Ruskin's choice of the name "Judas" for the national betrayal of the values of a true commonweal by estimating wealth as commodity values, that is to say, assessing national wealth in terms of what is more truly "illth". (*CCW* 485)

In Hill's dystopian scene in *Odi Barbare*, "our children" are the same children as those in *Scenes from Comus*: "smoke-enriched England I her children ashen" (*BH* 436). It is in the "half-dark of commodity" (*SC* 2:19; *BH* 430), in a nation overshadowed by the smoke of nineteenth-century England, the England of Ruskin and Morris, that wealth is replaced by illth. In *Clavics*, "Anarchical Plutocracy | Proliferates its gyre" (*C* 23; *BH* 813), the "gyre" recalling the "unbroken cycle" of *Odi Barbare*: "Inner cells where rigged Politeia barters | Cash-back rack-victims, || Shall they break us twice in unbroken cycle" (*BH* 847). This "unbroken cycle" is as much the anarchy of late capitalism as it is the Yeatsian gyre of history (the "twice" perhaps referring to the great crashes of 1929 and 2008): each is imagined as a self-perpetuating and objective system which makes passive victims of its members, an 'order' which imposes chaos.

However, it is precisely the moral inhumanity of overlaying objective systematics onto subjective experience which Hill has contemplated throughout his poetry and criticism. Hill's critical idiom has for a long time contemplated the metaphysical attractions of the Coleridge-Eliot school of unifying, as in his inaugural speech as Professor of Poetry at Leeds University subsequently published as 'Poetry as "Menace" and "Atonement"':

> [Of Hill's own phrase "instinctive assent"] [I]f "instinct" is a "natural or spontaneous tendency or inclination", "assent" is "agreement with a statement ... or proposal that does not concern oneself". From the depths of the self we rise to a concurrence with that which is not-self. For so I read those words of Pound: "The poet's job is to *define* and yet again define till the detail of surface is in accord with the root in justice." (*CCW* 4)

It is the "root in justice" which Hill's work in poetry and criticism has pondered obsessively from the very beginning, but justice, particularly, has become a focal point of the later work. However, the notion that the poet's job is to reconcile the "detail of surface" with "the root in justice" is one to which Hill cannot fully give his allegiance, even as he fascinates himself with Pound's dictum, set out in a letter to the Northumbrian poet Basil Bunting in 1936 (whose own poetics are in their own way a prolonged quarrel with this Poundian notion); rather, it is the ethical consequence to this desire to reconcile, or atone, linguistic detail with absolute justice with which Hill is concerned throughout his later poetry and criticism. My argument is that the "active-passive divide" (*CCW* 391) is Hill's ethical concern, particularly in the later work; and that his work constitutes an evolving conception that "the poet's job" is to occupy this divide, which is not an aporia to be bridged or transcended, but is a kind of spark-firing circuit:

> [Of Wordworth's "Michael":] Endurance is one of the great words which lie directly on the active-passive divide, subject to the fluctuations and arbitrariness that Wordsworth cites; and it is here, on the line, that, through language, value is to be realized, provided that the writer can "touch ... his mark with a needle's point", "strike his finger on the place". (*CCW* 391)

There are other references to such a line in various places in Hill's later work, as in his claim that Ruskin's sense of intrinsic value crosses an "indeterminate line"; "democracy", writes Hill elsewhere, "exists along some kind of active-passive divide".[25]

There is a Coleridgean background to this placing of the imagination in the "active-passive divide". In *Biographia Literaria*, Coleridge writes that "[t]here are evidently two powers at work, which relatively to each other are active and passive; and this is not possible without an intermediate faculty, which is at once both active and passive".[26] Coleridge's notion of the mind as a power negotiating between active and passive is a vital influence on Hill, asserting itself in the face of the "vis inertiae". In the letter of Kenneth Haynes to Hill, on Hill's unpublished paper 'Thoughts of a Conservative Modernist', Haynes writes that "[t]he most exciting part of the paper, for me, was to realize that it is the active resistance to the vis inertiae that constitutes value".[27] This is a fair assessment of Hill's position; but I would add that the recognition of the *vis inertiae* (force of inertia) is as vital to the constitution of value as its resistance, even of the *vis inertiae* within one's own resistance.

Hill's refocusing, or reimagining, of "the poet's job" is suggested strongly, if obliquely enough, by some lines in *A Treatise of Civil Power*, in the poem 'A Précis or Memorandum of Civil Power': "I accept, now, we make history; it's not some | abysmal power, | though making it kills us as we die to loss" (*BH* 582). The individual is not simply a passive victim, and neither is he duty-bound to lose himself in objective structures (as Eliot argued in his post-*Waste Land* literary-critical and social-moralistic prose writings); as democratic being, he or she negotiates the "active-passive divide".

As such, literary 'difficulty', that *bête noire* of liberal orthodoxy, is a keeping open, an exploration, of this divide. As Hill writes in *The Orchards of Syon*, "Donne in his time | also heard voices he preserved on wax | cylinder. Some of these I possess | and am possessed by" (*BH* 352). The poet both possesses and is possessed by voices, by language, which may be the voices of the hierarchies or of the *vis inertiae*. "The poet's job" is not the ascetic project to seek to atone herself with the superhuman objective forces of God, or history, or even language – because they are not superhuman or objective, as it turns out. In fact, Hill "would conclude ... not as a general rule, that language is love's correlate" (*CCW* 390): the beloved might be thought of as one whom one possesses (dubiously) and is possessed by (perhaps reluctantly). Hill has been having this debate with himself for some time: in 'Funeral Music', in the 1968 collection *King Log*, he writes "Averroes, you old heathen, | If only you had been right, if Intellect | Itself were absolute law, sufficient grace, | Our lives could be a myth of captivity | Which we might enter" (*BH* 50). This is a crucial moment in Hill's development, and foreshadows, or prepares the way for, the eschewing in his later poetry of the notion of the all-mastering authorial will – comparable with that of History, or God, or as here the Intellect of Averroes. Here, the poem's speaker admits to himself, and to his interlocutor, the twelfth-century Islamic philosopher-theologian Averroes, that "absolute law" is a "myth". Just as the poem re-enters history, as Hill writes in 'A Postscript on Modernist Poetics', history re-enters the poem, and it is the same with the human being: we enter history, and it enters us; we "make history" and "it kills us". So, rather than a fatalistic view of history as an overwhelming force, like a storm – which we find, for instance, as early as 'The Guardians' in Hill's first collection, *For the Unfallen* – his later work evinces this other attitude, which is essentially tragi-comic rather than stoic, so that the poetry becomes the "*sad and angry consolation*" of *The Triumph of Love* (*BH* 286); or, as a poem in *Scenes from Comus* puts it, "The grief of comedy you have to laugh" (*BH* 480).

Comedy, and "[t]he grief of comedy", is a crucial trope in Hill's later work, part of the constant worrying-away at the notions of anarchy and order, and of their symbiosis. It is part, too, of the abstract relations of subjective and objective, active and passive, which undergirds Hill's work. Sigmund Freud writes in the introduction to *Jokes and their Relation to the Unconscious* (a work cited by Hill in the 2005 pamphlet *A Treatise of Civil Power*):

> According to Lipps (1898), a joke is "something comic which is entirely subjective" – that is, something comic "which *we* produce, which is attached to action of ours as such, to which we invariably stand in the relation of subject and never of object" … It will be seen that the characteristic which distinguishes the joke within the class of the comic is attributed by Lipps to action, to the active behaviour of the subject, but by Fischer to its *object*, which he considers is the concealed ugliness of the world of thoughts.[28]

So, Freud's project, like Hill's, is to bring together jarring opposites; his contrast between the definitions of Lipps and Fischer is akin to Hill's 'instinct' and 'assent' in 'Poetry as "Menace" and "Atonement"': that which "comes from us" and that which comes from the "world of thoughts", with all its attendant "ugliness". However much this sounds like a Coleridgean unifying, Freud writes a little further on that jokes are "'a contrast of ideas', 'sense in nonsense', 'bewilderment and illumination'".[29] In his later work, Hill has arrived at an ethos of contrast-in-unity, of "Orders of anarchy" (*ATdT* 6, 891), or the "grief of comedy". Hill has given his readers a nudge in the ribs about this: in the original chapbook version of *A Treatise of Civil Power*, one stanza of the title poem has a "Working bibliography in cell" which includes "Freud – jokes and disquiet".[30] One can expect from Hill that Freud's writings on humour accord, somehow, with his own later philosophy of poetry; in part too, Freud's theories of jokes give Hill a vocabulary for overcoming the influence of the Coleridgean-Eliotic school of objectification, as Hill remarked in interview:

> Forty or fifty years ago, nothing would have induced me to say that there is anything resembling self-therapy or exorcism in the art of poetry or the art of writing. I had been trained, by the Eliot essay "Tradition and the Individual Talent," to deny this. And because I was not quick enough to understand the qualifications that Eliot himself would have entered, I acquired a far too extremist view of what seemed then a total incompatibility of the objective and

the subjective, and I would have said the poem is achieved by the fullest possible objectification of individual subjectivity. Obviously I no longer think so.[31]

And, as he says shortly after this telling comment: "I gradually came to see that the theory of total objectification, attractive as it might appear, was in the end not unlike Averroism"[32] – in other words, that "absolute law" which is rejected in 'Funeral Music'. According to Freud, humour exists through opposites existing concurrently, to evoke that word again: and here we have the Freudian aspect of Hill's abandonment of "absolute law". In his later poetry, Hill explores, not the absolute, then, but the relative – or perhaps, more gleefully yet, "relative absolutes" (itself a phrase from F.H. Bradley) (*SC* 2:18; *BH* 479) – and his use of the tragi-comic mode is a major manifestation of this intellectual structure. Perhaps this latter sympathy towards "self-therapy or exorcism" influences Hill's view of "crisis" as a necessary element of poetic language, as he states in the Oxford lecture in which he mentions Movement poetry: "[w]hen you have techné without crisis, the result is poetry similar to that written by Movement poets of the 1950s."[33]

The poem as a joke in the Freudian sense entails, then, a kind of catharsis which, the *Paris Review* interview would seem to claim, Hill does not feel his earlier poetry offers, with its "far too extremist view of what seemed then a total incompatibility of the objective and the subjective". Jokes, according, to Freud, both express and alleviate disquiet at the same time: "the grief of comedy", if you like. Freud's descriptions of the psychosocial provenance of this function recall not only his own *Civilisation and Its Discontents*, but such writings on the social contract as Hobbes's *Leviathan*, childhood taking the place, in Freud, of a Hobbesian state of nature:

> Though as children we are still endowed with a powerful inherited disposition to hostility, we are later taught by a higher personal civilization that it is an unworthy thing to use abusive language … Since we have been obliged to renounce the expression of hostility by deeds … we have, just as in the case of sexual aggressiveness, developed a new technique of invective.[34]

It is precisely this sense of "personal civilization" which informs and is informed by the objective, historical civilisation to which his works belong, which is present in Hill's "new technique" – though "invective" and "abusive language" is only one part of its texture and meaning. Though an injunction like "You should all fuck less | and pray more" (*Ludo* [henceforth *L*] 46; *BH* 618) certainly comes under the category of invective, not to mention abusive language, the overall effect of Hill's study of "jokes and disquiet" is actually to find another mode in which to negotiate the "active-passive divide", and thereby both to express and to transcend disquiet: to work in a mode of "*a sad and angry consolation*" (*ToL* CXLVII; *BH* 286). As Hill remarked in the interview with John Haffenden in the early 1980s, a poetry of consolation – of *real* consolation – enters that "kingdom of lost innocence and original justice"; poetry of "*sad and angry consolation*" imagines that kingdom and, in imagining it, both conjures it and acknowledges it *as* a conjuration. There is, indeed, something both tragic and ridiculous about this situation. "The glory of poetry is that it is solemn, | Racked with anarchic laughter", says poem 94 of *Al Tempo de' Tremuoti* (*BH* 935); and in poem 2 of *Expostulations on the Volcano*, the poet advertises his "Omens | Uttered by means of antic stand mike" (*BH* 630). And poem 94 of *Al Tempo de' Tremuoti* continues with

>   Genius
> Thriving on various expediences,
> Like Petrarch's shattered and sustaining column,
>
> Transforms bare reflex into rhapsody.   (*ATdT* 94; *BH* 935)

Here Hill is writing of the concurrence of spontaneity and artefact, "reflex" and "rhapsody". "Genius | Thriving on various expediences" is an apt description of the experience of writing formal, rhyming poetry, and of the concurrence of structure and spontaneity more generally, which is the experience of being at once "shattered and sustaining". This is also a celebration of inspiration, a word and concept which has received attention in Hill's criticism. 'Rhapsody', as Hill is no doubt aware, is itself a word which straddles the "active-passive divide": the *OED* gives two definitions which, while not being strictly mutually exclusive, certainly suggest different things in terms of activity and passivity. Definition 1 of 'rhapsody' is "an epic poem, or a part of one, of a suitable length for recitation at one time". Epic poetry suggests the public, the collective, the civilised, even. However, two further definitions suggest differently: "[a] literary work consisting of miscellaneous or disconnected pieces; a written composition having no fixed form or plan" (2a); and "Exaggeratedly enthusiastic or ecstatic expression of feeling" (4). The word 'rhapsody' itself is both "shattered and sustaining": that is, it suggests both disconnection and coherence.

Hill is perhaps alluding, too, to Plato's critique of poets, itself an analysis of the diremption between the active and the passive, as encapsulated in *Ion*, in which Socrates confronts the eponymous rhapsode about the nature of his art. "This gift which you have of speaking excellently about Homer is not an art", says Socrates to Ion, "but, as I was just saying, an inspiration; there is a divinity moving you, like that in the stone which Euripides calls a magnet".[35] Plato banned poets from his ideal republic, of course; justice is achieved within the *polis*, and poets can only travesty or at best imitate justice, their works being copies of reality, which is itself a copy of the Ideal Forms. Ultimately, Eliot had similar compunctions: even in 'Tradition and the Individual Talent',[36] Eliot included as epigraph to the final short section a quotation from Aristotle's *De Anima* ('On the Soul'), "The mind is doubtless more divine and less subject to the passions". Written into the conservative moral tradition of the West is scepticism regarding the relationship between 'poetic justice' and political justice: a scepticism which, partly due to the dreadful example of Ezra Pound, and the subsequent influence of the Movement, has in today's literary climate become orthodoxy. Hill's task, as he sees it, is to buck this prevailing trend, and to concern himself – like Christopher Ricks in the review alluded to in the Oxford lecture – with the issue of the complex relationship between the work of literature and the polity. The poet's role, then, is one of inspired sanity, and this constitutes the unique difficulty to the poet of real value; as Hill writes in *Scenes from Comus*, "All the better if you go mad like Pound" (*BH* 480). On one side lies isolation, on the other conformity.

Hill's use of 'rhapsody' in this context, then, recalls a debate of psychological ethics which runs from Plato's *Ion* through to T.S. Eliot's seminal essay 'Tradition and the Individual Talent', to which Hill refers in his *Paris Review* interview. Hill has moved beyond the notion of the "total incompatibility of the subjective and objective", concentrated in such famous passages of Eliot's as his dictum that "[t]he progress of the artist is a continual self-sacrifice, a continual extinction of personality".[37] Eliot's injunction here is towards an extinction, or perhaps more precisely an objectifying, of subjectivity; an argument which is itself undermined by the essay's definition of tradition as a readjustment of the whole "ideal order"[38] of works in response to the "supervention of novelty", itself revoked in Eliot's later work, for example in 'The Function of Criticism', in which tradition is replaced by orthodoxy – the decisive shift, in Eliot's work, towards ideology and away from "eros and alienation" (*CCW* 556). Hill's later work should be read as a reaction against this abdication, as he sees it, by Eliot. Hill's view of inspiration, as expressed in 'Unhappy Circumstances', attends precisely to this abandonment of the pressure – in the sense of physical pressure, and the 'pressure' of public life – brought by language:

> When "inspiration" ... is taken, as it commonly is, to mean going along with the prevailing windy cant, with whatever currently passes for divine *afflatus*, it becomes indistinguishable from the tamest *bienséance* ... The manna of inspiration is no more than an inspired manner. (*CCW* 189)

So 'inspiration', for Hill, entails, according to this passage in 'Unhappy Circumstances', a coming into one's own, a deep and authentic form of self-challenging and challenging of language; it is not, therefore, as in the Platonic tradition and the criticism of Eliot, an abandonment of moral agency or surrendering to subjectivity (or perhaps the Freudian unconscious).

Eliot's "deepening failure" (*CCW* 556) is perhaps attributable to the fact that he perceived the presence of an aporia, or impasse, between the subjective and objective which had to be surpassed, or perhaps escaped from. Hill's emphasis throughout his criticism, and increasingly, and crucially, in his later poetry, from *The Triumph of Love* onward, is precisely on this "active-passive divide". If we do, indeed, "Look up aphasia and aporia their origins" as the poem 'To the Lord Protector Cromwell' (*A Treatise of Civil Power* [henceforth *TCP*], *BH* 574) invites us to do, we see that aphasia is a pathological inability to speak, and that an aporia, as defined by Hill, is "the no-way, the impasse, the broken middle" (*CCW* 569). I would argue that the aporia, the impasse or divide, whether that be between active and passive or subjective and objective, is equated in Hill's later work with aphasia, the inability to speak, and that this is a sign under which Hill's recent prolificacy is written. Hill's recent critical work on T.S. Eliot and F.H. Bradley, too, explores the relationship between subjectivity and objectivity; in a passage on Gillian Rose, Hill opens this strand of modernist poetics out into a wider ambit:

> The existence or absence of a middle ground is an argument associated in recent years with the late Gillian Rose and with her book *The Broken Middle*. Most definitions of the function of literature in our time assume the existence of a middle ground. I am not convinced that a middle ground is necessary, or that its postulation as a necessity is even required. For as Rose says, "How to represent the aporia … between everyone and every 'one' is the difficulty" … The difficulty which Rose describes arises when the productive or receptive self of every "one" is idly reduced to a word of convenience representing a generic carrier of preformulated opinion. (*CCW* 569)

In his poem 'In Memoriam: Gillian Rose' in *A Treatise of Civil Power*, Hill writes "Poetry's its own agon, that *allows us | to recognize devastation* as the rift | between power and powerlessness" (*BH* 590). This latter phrase recalls Hill's comment in an interview with the *Guardian* newspaper in 2002, that "poetry is both immensely powerful and virtually powerless". If poetry is the opposite of devastation, then, it allows us to comprehend power and powerlessness at the same time, not at either end of some imagined middle ground. And this is the peculiar ability of Hill's later work, or certainly that is Hill's ambition for it: namely, as W.B. Yeats put it, "to hold in a single thought reality and justice".[39] Though what Yeats is describing here is not an atonement but an apprehension.

Notes

1 Geoffrey Hill, 'Monumentality and Bidding', Oxford Professor of Poetry lecture, 11 March 2014.
2 Haffenden, *Viewpoints*, pp. 87–88.

3 Lloyd L. Weinreb, *Natural Law and Justice* (Harvard University Press: Cambridge, MA and London, 1987) preface.
4 Yeats, *The Major Works*, p. 438.
5 Ibid., p. 1.
6 Martin Luther, *Luther: Letters of Spiritual Counsel*, Theodore G. Tappert ed. and trans., The Library of Christian Classics, Vol. 18 (SCM Press: London, 1955) p. 137.
7 Karl Barth, *The Epistle to the Romans*, Edwyn C. Hoskins trans. from 6th edition (Oxford University Press: London, Oxford, and New York, 1968) p. 259.
8 Hill, 'The Art of Poetry: 80'.
9 Ibid., p. 80.
10 Empson, *Seven Types of Ambiguity*, p. 25.
11 S.T. Coleridge, *Biographia Literaria, Volume 1, 1817* (Scholar Press: Menston, 1971) pp. 295–296.
12 Ibid., p. 296.
13 Ezra Pound, *Cantos* (New Directions: New York, 1996) p. 478.
14 Hill, 'Milton as Muse'.
15 J.L. Austin, *How to Do Things With Words* (Oxford: Clarendon, 1975) p. 151.
16 Eliot, *Selected Prose*, p. 226.
17 Ibid., p. 230.
18 "Bless hierarchy, dismiss hegemony" (*BH* 738). This is explored further in chapter 6.
19 Velimir Khlebnikov, *The King of Time*, Charlotte Douglas ed., Paul Schmidt trans. (Harvard University Press: Cambridge, MA and London, 1985) p. 113.
20 Ibid., p. 114.
21 Kenneth Haynes, letter to Geoffrey Hill, BC MS 20c, Hill/4/22, Brotherton Library, University of Leeds.
22 Elsewhere Hill casts metaphysical desire, or utopianism, as "simple projection": "Is it the gulf between simple projection (*Confessing State* – good idea!) and livid (not lived, exactly) establishment? Between the vision (and it was!) of the Israel Symphony Orchestra in Leeds Town Hall, circa 1955, rising to its feet and playing 'Hatikvah', in such a way that I became a weeping Gentile Zionist there and then; and the reality of the Gaza Strip, 2008?" Hill, 'Civil Polity and the Confessing State', p. 19.
23 www.britannica.com/EBchecked/topic/529712/Scottish-law. Accessed 24 February 2015.
24 John Ruskin, 'Ad Valorem', *Unto this Last: Four Essays on the First Principles of Political Economy* (George Allen: London, 1896) p. 126.

25 Hill, 'Civil Polity and the Confessing State', p. 9.
26 Samuel Taylor Coleridge, *Biographia Literaria: Volume 1, 1817* (Scholar Press: Menston, 1971) p. 124.
27 Haynes, letter to Geoffrey Hill.
28 Sigmund Freud, *Jokes and their Relation to the Unconscious*, The Penguin Freud Library, Vol. 6, James Strachey trans., Angela Richards ed. (Penguin: London, 1991) p. 40.
29 Ibid., p. 42.
30 Geoffrey Hill, 'A Treatise of Civil Power' poem 14, *A Treatise of Civil Power* (Thame: Clutag, 2005).
31 Hill, 'The Art of Poetry: 80'.
32 Ibid.
33 Hill, 'A Deep Dynastic Wound'.
34 Freud, *Jokes and Their Relation to the Unconscious*, p. 147.
35 Plato, 'Ion', *The Dialogues of Plato*, Vol. 1, B. Jowett trans. (Clarendon: Oxford, 1871) p. 237.
36 See Tim Dean, 'T.S. Eliot, Famous Clairvoyante', *Gender, Desire and Sexuality in T.S. Eliot*, Cassandra Laity and Nancy K. Gish eds (Cambridge University Press: Cambridge, 2004) pp. 43–65.
37 Eliot, *Selected Prose of T.S. Eliot*, p. 40.
38 Ibid., p. 38.
39 Yeats, *The Major Works*, p. 438.

Chapter 4

'There are no demons': faith and metaphysical desire

Belief and 'suspension of disbelief'

Hill has professed himself a Christian, and yet a Christian who, in 2011, gave the following reply when asked how much his religion defines him as a poet:

> Very little. There was a brief period when the Church of England took me up after I published *Tenebrae* but subsequent books have once more put a distance between us, to our mutual relief I believe. However I adhere to certain old fashioned religious concepts such as the doctrine of original sin and therefore have been much influenced spiritually – not necessarily for the good – by St Paul, St Augustine, Luther and Karl Barth as well as the Hebrew prophets and the teachers of wisdom.[1]

Hill reveals here his investment in the Pauline tradition in Christianity, Augustine, Luther, and Barth being re-interpreters of Paul. However, in religious matters, as in all matters, Hill is also heterodox and eclectic. Indeed, there is a fascination in the later work with esoteric literature, with Christian and Jewish mysticism, namely alchemy and kabbalah respectively – though the fascination with esoterica surfaces in Hill's earlier poetry also: for instance, 'Dr Faustus' in *For the Unfallen*, and 'Men Are a Mockery of Angels' in *King Log*, the latter evoking Tommaso Campanella, a hermetic writer (and poet) of the fifteenth century. Hill's is a sceptical imagination, however – though one might suggest that in his later work, with its frequent allusions to mysticism and esoterica, particularly alchemy, he is less sceptical than *The Sceptical Chymist*: "The Scholastics mean more to me than the New Science", as Hill writes in *The Triumph of Love* (*ToL* CXXV; *BH* 277). However, this interest in alchemy and kabbalah in relation to poetics springs from their very metaphoricity and concern with what Hill (commenting on a passage from Christopher Ricks) calls the "indispensable" ('Translating Value', *CCW* 390). For "indispensable" here, read an objective, timeless standard by and from which to make judgements, such as might exist in an unfallen world: this notion of the indispensable is "effected, as so often, by recourse to the myth of the Fall", as Ricks goes on to argue in the essay in question.[2] In other words, the "indispensable" – intrinsic value – may be inherently bound up with the elegiac, the nostalgic.

This is not to say that Hill believes in the literal, actual existence of the "indispensable", necessarily, only its necessity, and the validity of the desire for it. In the Bradleian sense, it is neither real nor ideal. This particular response to Christopher Ricks presents in microcosm Hill's concern with the relation between faith and what Coleridge called "poetic faith", which is, in the well-known formula, "the willing suspension of disbelief": in other words, the tension between scepticism and what Hill has describes here as the "longing", and elsewhere as "metaphysical fantasy" ('Our Word Is Our Bond', *CCW* 157) (quoting J.L. Austin) and as "metaphysical fancy" ('The Tartar's Bow and the Bow of Ulysses', *CCW* 200). This lifelong concern is writ large in the later work. For all his quasi-Faustian immersion in esoteric and hermetic texts in this later period, Hill's position is equally definable by the very last sentence of *Expostulations on the Volcano*: "There are no demons" (*EoV* 54; *BH* 682). If Hill's position is indeed still that of "a heretic's dream of salvation expressed in the images of the orthodoxy from which he is excommunicate",[3] then this sense of reluctant scepticism has enlarged in the later work to take on ideological and socio-political dimensions.

As Hill avows in the interview with *The Oxford Student*, the doctrine of original sin – elucidated and interpreted throughout the Pauline tradition – is indeed absolutely central to his work as a paradigm for the deviancy of language and its mirroring of the deviant human will. But if there is deviancy and corruption in language and the will, there is a capacity for grace too. In 'Language, Suffering and Silence', Hill makes two telling remarks – one almost in passing, another quite programmatically – laying out his view of a "theology of language". First:

> Language under the kind of extreme pressure which the making of poetry requires, can, on occasion, push the maker beyond the barrier of his or her own limited intelligence. If I were to consider undertaking a theology of language, this would be one of a number of possible points of departure for such an exploration: the abrupt, unlooked-for semantic recognition understood as corresponding to an act of mercy or grace. ('Language, Suffering and Silence', *CCW* 404)

This view works on the assumption that poetry entails "extreme pressure". Hence Yeats's injunction to the aspiring poet Dorothy Wellesley in the 1930s, that "difficulty is our plough", quoted by Hill in 'A Postscript on Modernist Poetics' (*CCW* 567), has a deeper significance for poetic composition, and of reading also: a significance, or perhaps even a seriousness, at which the majority of poets and critics working in the English language today might balk. In the same essay, Hill asserts that "[t]he beauty of Hopkins places us under a very great pressure" (*CCW* 571). Hopkins, a hugely important poet for Hill in the context of language and grace, is also associated with "great pressure", which is the requisite condition of language for those shocks of "semantic recognition" to occur, for writer and reader alike. And a little further on in 'Language, Suffering and Silence', Hill makes his positive statement:

> I would seriously propose a theology of language; and a primary exercise to be undertaken towards its establishment. This would comprise a critical examination of the grounds for claiming (a) that the shock of semantic recognition must also be a shock of ethical recognition; and that this is the action of grace in one of its minor, but far from trivial, types; (b) that the art and literature of the late twentieth century require a memorializing, a memorizing, of the dead as much as, or even more than, expressions of "solidarity with the poor and oppressed". (*CCW* 405)

The inevitability of the link between "ethical recognition" and "the action of grace" is debatable, hence the need, presumably, for a "critical examination", though this is perhaps ultimately down to personal scruple, or, perhaps, the extent to which one subscribes to a Pauline ethics; but, as far as his work is concerned, this critical statement might stand over all of Hill's work in prose and poetry. Just this type of "shock of ethical recognition" is the focus of attention repeatedly in his later critical work. It is the "uncouth anacoluthon" which Hill describes in Hopkins's poem 'That Nature is a Heraclitean Fire and of the Comfort of the Resurrection' – "Enough! The Resurrection" – remarking that "[t]he Resurrection is a kind of eschatological anacoluthon; no amount of standard grammar can anticipate or regularize that moment" (*CCW* 570). Similarly, in the second poem of *Odi Barbare*, in a characteristically self-referential moment – the poem being in fact a kind of a prologue – Hill invokes

> Rumpus, uncouth anacolutha, bullish
> Metamorphs treading out a line. (*BH* 836)

Hill's critical pronouncement about a theology of language is made in "the late twentieth century", so we can safely assume that this second statement quoted here from 'Language, Suffering and Silence' is a self-reflexive critical remark, as well as a judgement on the contemporary panorama as he sees it: poetry *ought to* entail "extreme pressure", or the "very great pressure" of Hopkins's work; and in more decorous terms, it is obliged to a "memorializing, a memorizing, of the dead". Semantic, syntactic pressure, equates to moral and spiritual pressure.

And the image of "[m]etamorphs treading out a line", here, is telling for Hill's later work too: the notion of metamorphosis, of undergoing change at a very great pressure, whether that pressure be spiritual, ethical, or semantic, the three being interrelated, is crucial. (These "Bullish | Metamorphs" also anticipate the imagery of sacrificial bulls in *Odi Barbare*.) And, to be sure, there is a great deal of "rumpus" in the later work too, a linguistic energy and lexical copiousness working within this context of formal and ethical pressure: the 'gravity and grace' of Simone Weil; the simultaneously being "strict and wild" which Hill calls upon contemporary poets to exhibit in one Oxford lecture.[4] Hill perceives grace and mercy as apprehensible, not through some direct influence of God, or in some earthly City of God, but through language in its metaphorical capacity. Language does not constitute reality, ultimately, but symbolises it; as Hill writes in a poem about the theologian Karl Rahner, 'On the Reality of the Symbol', "Metaphysics remain | in common language something of a joke" (*WT*, *BH* 490). Rahner observes that "[b]eing expresses itself, because it must realize itself through a plurality in unity" (*CCW* 567). It is the act of symbolising which is intrinsically human, then, and within which lies our capacity for freedom, which is also our capacity for misprision. Hill quoted with approval, in his first Oxford Professor of Poetry lecture, the well-known statement by R.P. Blackmur, that poetry "adds to the stock of available reality".[5] The full statement, from a 1935 review of a book by Norman McLeod, is:

> The art of poetry is amply distinguished from the manufacture of verse by the animating process in the poem of a fresh idiom; language so twisted and posed in a form that it not only expresses the matter in hand but adds to the stock of available reality.[6]

Blackmur's statement hints at a recognition of the human being as the symbolising agent, the creator-creature, and this is its attraction for Hill, who is similarly fascinated with the borderline between metaphysics and value: this is part of his inheritance from the American New Critics, such as Blackmur himself, and this statement is another of the many in New Critical discourse which feeds Hill's sense of the "brute mass" (*ToL* LXX; *BH* 259) of the poem, that the poem of "fresh idiom" acquires a palpable weight that, one might imagine, might be weighed.[7]

Though Hill is (reluctantly) sceptical of the reality of the metaphysical, he acknowledges the crucial role of metaphysics, of the ideal, in the formation and endurance of human values. In this respect, Hill is firmly within the tradition of Christian existentialism. Kierkegaard writes in *Fear and Trembling* that "inhaling only the unconditional is impossible to man; he perishes like the fish forced to live in the air. But, on the other hand, without relating himself to the unconditional man cannot, in the deepest sense, be said to 'live'".[8] (This statement of Kierkegaard's is repeated by Charles Williams in *The Descent of the Dove*, Williams, who died in 1945, being an important literary and spiritual influence at the Oxford of the early 1950s, mentioned by Hill in his last published piece, 'Mightier and Darker' of March 2016 in the *Times Literary Supplement*.) Bradley's conception of eros is reminiscent of Kierkegaard's statement here. The poem, similarly, is "between politics and eternity". Kierkegaard's "unconditional" is analogous to Christopher Ricks's "indispensable", to which, Hill asserts, one cannot fully address oneself, but which one cannot deny in one's being. In this mode of Christian existentialism, and I would suggest more specifically the Kierkegaardian mode, lies a large part of Hill's late investment in the trope of paradox, a rhetorical trope with moral and spiritual implications – an argument to which I shall return.

The relationship between language and reality, similarly, and the ethical connotations of such a relationship, is a crucial context for Hill's "theology of language". As an exercise of freedom within stricture and constraint, artistic composition adds to the stock of "available reality" by being an achievement of moral as well as aesthetic dimension: it is "*Active virtue*: that which shall contain | its own passion in the public weal" (*ToL* LXX; *BH* 259). Hill does not equate language with ultimate reality, or Kierkegaard's 'unconditional'; his later poetry unites a thoroughgoing scepticism with a fascination with the power of metaphor and belief and the recognition of its necessity, despite one's scepticism. However, Hill has been profoundly implicated throughout his writings by the imaginative possibility of such a relationship between language and reality – a possibility entertained in such New Critical dicta as R.P. Blackmur's. The very first poem of his very first collection, 'Genesis', is all about such possibility:

> Against the burly air I strode
> Crying the miracles of God.
>
> And first I brought the sea to bear
> Upon the dead weight of the land,
> And the waves flourished at my prayer,
> The rivers spawned their sand.   (*BH* 3)

At first sight, this poem seems to emphasise only the notion of *poiesis* as divine inspiration, but actually the poem is decidedly Gnostic in its view of creation: that is, creation is misprision:

> By blood we live, the hot, the cold,
> To ravage and redeem the world;
> There is no bloodless myth will hold.   (*BH* 4)

It is characteristic of Hill's sceptical longing that the speaker here imagines his capacity to "ravage and redeem the world" at once. Rather than equating word and thing, Hill sees grammar and semantics as being indicative, perhaps even constitutive, of what one might fumblingly call 'the human condition', which is the condition of being fallen – or as Hill has put it, that Milton and Coleridge "understand [semantics] to be complex indices of innate, inveterate human nature".[9] Poem 24 of *Oraclau | Oracles*, 'Hermeneutics (1)', for instance, explores the interrelationships of grammar, grace, and the Fall:

> Torquing upon hwyl, wrestling grammar,
> Trusting as Jacob – *torque* to be defined –
> In our disorder here ordained;
> Necessity to unstammer;
> Salvation's first blind flight
> Against the elements, creating sight
> Creation's war of terror and delight:
> Who, formerly malignant as our choice,
> *Fell in one root, recovered by one voice.*   (*BH* 748)

Aside from the recollection of 'Genesis' in these lines, with its "creating sight", Jacob wrestling with the angel is a familiar image to Hill's readers *as* an image, Gauguin's painting 'The Vision after the Sermon' providing the cover image for Hill's Penguin *Collected Poems* of 1985. The human being wrestles with a force which he suspects to be supernatural, or superhuman, by its power: though, whereas the King James Version has an 'angel', the original Hebrew word actually translates as 'man'. The indeterminacy of this translation, or mistranslation, is symbolic of Hill's ambivalence regarding language and its inevitable misprisions, emblematic of the Fall. What we take to be angelic is so often actually a misprision, a metaphysical fantasy – though, for all that, the longing, the imagining, the *wrestling*, is real enough. Jacob's ordeal is simultaneously an epiphany; it is the "terror and delight" of 'Hermeneutics (1)'. Similarly, we are "In our disorder here ordained", order and anarchy co-inhering, the word 'ordain' (Latin *ordinare*) recalling Hill's remark in the preface to *Style and Faith* that Donne "confesses his own inordinacy while remaining in all things ordinate" (Preface to *Style and Faith*, *CCW* 263). The last line of this stanza is taken from Henry Howell's *Last Message and Dying Testimony*, published in 1774 (included in the Welsh-themed *Oraclau* due in no small part, no doubt, to Howell's Welshness) and is in the vein of Hill's continuing meditation on the relationship between the fallenness of language and its grace, as found in poetry of "great pressure". In this stanza, as throughout *Oraclau* and also in *The Orchards of Syon*, glimpses of landscape are glimpsed revelations, in which "The rainbow's | appearance covenants with reality" (*The Orchards of Syon* [henceforth *OS*] XLIX; *BH* 399): which is to say, the 'reality' of grace is a beguiling apparition, an effect of perspective. The covenant is here imagined as a verb, 'to covenant': it is an action, an effort, binding the apparent to the real.

Gerard Manley Hopkins

Hill pays much attention to Gerard Manley Hopkins, in his later poetry (particularly in *The Orchards of Syon*) and criticism, and in his Oxford lectures (the lecture 'What You Look Hard at Seems to Look Hard at You' is an extraordinarily detailed, and counter-traditional, reading of Hopkins's 'The Windhover'). In 'Common Weal, Common Woe', collected originally in *Style and Faith*, Hopkins is examined, primarily as a philologist, and the word 'pitch' is analysed, Hill finding the *Oxford English Dictionary* wanting in its citations of Hopkins's use of the word. However, what is of greater moment to the current argument is Hopkins's own definition of the word, included in Hill's essay: "So also *pitch* is ultimately simple positiveness, that by which being differs from and is more than nothing and not-being" (*CCW* 267). Hopkins's equation of pitch with "simple positiveness" which is "more than nothing and not-being" recalls Hill's statement in 2000 that the writing of a poem entails a battling against "silence and incoherence".[10] Though the figure of Duns Scotus behind Hopkins's notions of 'pitch', 'inscape', and 'instress' casts scant shadow on Hill's usage of 'pitch' (though a sense of *haecceitas* obtains in Hill's sense of the poem "adding to the stock of available reality") one wonders if the Hopkinsian context has permeated Hill's own use of the word, a word which is so central to his notion of the graceful pressure of poetic language, first appearing in 'Dividing Legacies' in *Style and Faith*: "[t]he style of Eliot's address to his audience is a matter of tone; the burden of his analytical criticism is, or ought to be, the question of pitch"; and then, "a discovery of the pitch of Donne's language ... would also be a recognition of sensuous interest" ('Dividing Legacies', *CCW* 375/ 376). Clearly, Hill's sense of pitch is in the attention to "immediate context" which Eliot, according to the essays on Eliot and Bradley in *Alienated Majesty*, falls away from. However, the question remains to what extent this sense of pitch as critical burden is modified by the Hopkinsian connotations of the word picked out in 'Common Weal, Common Woe', related to those considerations of "*self-being*", and "*selve/selving*" which Hill cites as being from the Jesuit poet's "retreat notes of 1880" (*CCW* 267). In these notes, Hopkins writes that

> I find myself both as a man and as myself something most determined and distinctive, at pitch, more distinctive and higher pitched than anything else I see ...
> For human nature, being more highly pitched, selved, and distinctive than anything in the world, can have been developed, evolved, condensed, from the vastness of the world not anyhow ... Nothing else in nature comes near this unspeakable stress of pitch, distinctiveness, and selving, this selfbeing of my own.[11]

There is in Hopkins's sense of pitch in these passages a sense of the contained energy of "human nature", an energy enacted in and symbolised by his "distinctive and higher pitched" feeling for syntax. Certainly, Hopkins's sense of pitch *does* permeate Hill's, as he has shown over the years, and that Hill's acute sense of poetry as "one of the multifarious forms of self-consciousness" (*CCW* 548) is as much influenced by Hopkins's sense of pitch as it is by the Lutheran concept of *homo incurvatus in se* ('humankind turned inward upon itself'), a self-reflexive act which is given an Augustinian provenance in 'Language, Suffering and Silence'.[12] In 'Tacit Pledges', for instance:

Our main concern here is with matters of style: with particulars of syntax, rhythm, and cadence, and with the problems of pitch. Considered in its negative aspect, a writer's style is what he or she is left with after the various contingent forces of attrition have taken their toll. Considered more positively, style marks the success an author may have in forging a personal utterance between the hammer of self-being and the anvil of those impersonal forces that a given time possesses. (*CCW* 407)

Poetry is "personal utterance", then, to the extent that it resists the *vis inertiae* of moral, spiritual, linguistic and aesthetic passivity; and Hill's sense of pitch is a crux of his movement away from the example of Eliot and towards that of Hopkins in this respect. In his emphasis on individual existence, "selving" and "pitch", Hopkins here is firmly within the tradition of Christian existentialism.

The Orchards of Syon is the sequence in Hill's later work which is most apparently indebted to Hopkins. There is the recurrent naming of "Goldengrove", which is taken from Hopkins's 'Spring and Fall': "Margaret, are you grieving | Over Goldengrove unleaving?"[13] which influences the sequence's main theme of autumn and the Fall, "the heavy-bearing trees bowed towards Fall" (*OS* XXII; *BH* 372). The play between fall and Fall is vital, in all that word's senses: the Fall is generative, productive of all "mortal beauty" (*OS* XX; *BH* 370). Here the Garden of Eden is pictured at the time of harvest, as the child Margaret discovers in Hopkins's poem; the trees are "bowed towards Fall", but they are also "heavy-bearing". Parts of the sequence refer to the landscapes of north Lancashire, with "the swaling Hodder" (*OS* XXII; *BH* 382), where "Stonyhursts's ample terraces confer | with the violent, comely | nature of Loyola and English weather" (*OS* XX; *BH* 370). This is Stonyhurst College, where Hopkins spent time in the 1870s. In the journal of 1873, Hopkins, in his luminous, spontaneously measured prose, describes "the path trenched by footsteps in ankledeep snow across the fields leading to Hodder wood through which we went to see the river. The sun was bright, the broken brambles and all boughs and banks limed and cloyed with white, the brook down the clough pulling its way by drops and by bubbles in turn under a shell of ice".[14] The influence of such passages shows in the landscapes of *The Orchards of Syon*:

> Two nights' and three days' rain, with the Hodder
> well up, over its alder roots; tumblings
> of shaly late storm light; the despised
> ragwort, luminous, standing out,
> stereoscopically, across twenty yards,
> on the farther bank.   (*OS* XX; *BH* 370)

The only word which might differentiate this from the self-communing spontaneity of Hopkins's journal entries is the adjective "despised", which situates the ragwort, with the English Society of Jesus, as an unwelcome presence in the English landscape, liable to be uprooted, though standing out luminously – in other words, it adds a moral and historical dimension to the pure apprehension of landscape. And in the same poem, in a sentence which recalls Hopkins's 'Spring and Fall' once more, Hill writes, "Mortal beauty is alienation; or not, | as I see it". This final clause, seemingly pernickety or conversational, is a characteristically Hillian litotes: if 'as' is taken to mean 'because', then this is very close in spirit to the image of the rainbow in *The Orchards of Syon*, which both is and is not the rainbow of Abraham, whose "appearance covenants with reality". The covenant in question is that of metaphor, a crucial locus of human creative freedom: "Reality itself grounded in our metaphors", as Hill puts it in *Al Tempo de' Tremuoti* (*ATdT* 94; *BH* 935). The rainbow appears real, and is invested with symbolic value, though we know it rationally to be an effect of perspective. Again, in the very next poem of *The Orchards of Syon*, "it is smeared | vision that finds Goldengrove some inches | from my face" (*OS* XXI; *BH* 371). Often, in Hill's later work, the act of vision is "smeared", as it were; we see through a glass, darkly, or perhaps the vision is smeared by grief or lachrymosity. And again, in poem XIX:

> > Could
> Goldengrove have been at any time
> *The Wood of the Suicides*?
> It cán be murder, or murderous
> fantasy: wherever you look the leaves
> hanging blood-brown, more real than unreal.   (*BH* 369)

Any contemplation of heaven or hell – Goldengrove and the suicides in Dante's hell – is considered alongside the notion of "murderous | fantasy". Hill's sense of grace is always qualified by his sense of "the leadenness of things" (*SC* 1:20; *BH* 430). His conception of pitch as a simultaneous attention to language and to self-being magnifies his awareness of the unreliability of vision, the slipperiness of language – after all, "We are a fiction even to ourselves" (*CCW* 782) – just as it magnifies his sense of its transient beauty and value. Grace is a "shock of recognition" in Hill's theology of language; it is not a 'state of grace', but an achieved moment, an "uncouth anacoluthon". However, the spontaneity of Hopkins's prose in his journals represents for Hill an example in this direction, even if Hill's personal theology is not as subjectively optimistic or as doctrinaire as that of the Jesuit poet; another aspect of Hopkins's sense of pitch is what he describes in the journal of 1871 as "the pitch of graceful agility",[15] an apprehension of nature which is at once a self-proclaimed principle of style. Where Hill's sense of poetry is that it should be "simple, sensuous, and passionate",[16] as Milton describes in *On Education* (and reaffirmed by Coleridge), his actual poetic style, in tandem with his sense of the fallibility of language and the self, is more aptly summated by that Jacob-like image in *Oraclau*, "Torquing upon *hwyl*, wrestling grammar"; and the same could be said of Hopkins. However we gloss Hopkins's use of the word "graceful" in his journal entry, it is certainly tempting to suppose that Hill's movement towards a more spontaneous style in parts of *The Orchards of Syon* (and beyond) is a kind of spiritual exercise also, appropriate to the setting of Stonyhurst College; tempting, also, to imagine Hill's acute sense of communion with Hopkins, particularly in this setting which he shares across the centuries with the Victorian poet, as being accentuated by Hopkins's note, in his journal of 1873, about having visited "Jeffrey hill".[17]

The fall and the will

While Hill's sense of "murderous | fantasy" acknowledges that what we call reality is usually – or perhaps always – a myth, it simultaneously raises the imagination to the forefront of human agency. I suggest that this is a major locus of Hill's resituating of English

Romanticism within terms of moral agency. Similarly, while Hill is profoundly influenced by the concept of Original Sin, there are strong traces in his work of the Augustinian notion of *felix culpa*, the 'fortunate fall'. St Augustine writes of the notion of *felix culpa* in his *Enchiridion*:

> As for mankind, although born of a corrupted and condemned stock, he still retains the power to form and animate his seed, to direct his members in their temporal order, to enliven his senses in their spatial relations, and to provide bodily nourishment. For God judged it better to bring good out of evil than not to permit any evil to exist.[18]

This is the 'free will argument', as argued in our own day by the likes of Alvin Plantinga: namely, that it was a greater good for God to grant free will than to prohibit evil. It is this freedom which makes grace possible. However, and by the same token, according to Augustinian theology evil is not inherent in nature but in the human will: "The Orchards | of Syon whatever harvest we bring them" (*OS* LXVIII; *BH* 418). This is the difference between Gnosticism and orthodox Pauline Christianity. So, rather than simply gesturing towards some perfect state outside language, Hill's view is that language *itself* embodies the density and grace of the fallen world. It bears repeating that the title of the first essay in his *Collected Critical Writings* is 'Poetry as "Menace" and "Atonement"': in other words, poetry, as the most concentrated form of linguistic composition, embodies to an extreme extent language's, and (dare one say it) humanity's twin capacities for menace and for atonement, the epigraph to the essay taken from the poet and Catholic martyr Robert Southwell, "[t]hus my noblest capacity becomes my deepest perplexity; my noblest opportunity, my uttermost distress; my noblest gift, my darkest menace" (*CCW* 3).

In 'Eros in F.H. Bradley and T.S. Eliot' (*CCW* 563) Hill writes that "[a]s a Christian, [Charles Williams] would have understood the fundamental dilemma of the poetic craft: that it is simultaneously an imitation of the divine fiat and an act of enormous self-will" (*CCW* 563). This "divine fiat" is exactly what Coleridge means when he writes in *Biographia Literaria* of "esemplastic power" being "a repetition in the finite mind of the eternal act of creation in the infinite I AM".[19]

It seems though that Hill is more interested in the statement of Coleridge's which most pertains to "immediate context", "Coleridge's *living powers*" (*OS* XXIV; *BH* 374). Clearly Hill admits this "divine fiat" as an aspect of poetic creation, but crucially poetry is also "an act of enormous self-will"; "the mind of the maker can imitate either God's commandment or Lucifer's 'instressing of his own inscape' as Hopkins splendidly and humbly described it" (*CCW* 563). Hopkins's Lucifer, as much as Milton's Satan, stands here for the "enormous act of self-will" which is forever implicated in what Hill has called the "deviant ethics" of the postlapsarian world.[20] It is the simultaneous perception of deviancy and justice, "divine fiat" and "self-will", which produces the energy – a recurrent word in Hill's later work – of poetry. As Hill writes in poem 6 of *Scenes from Comus*, "in these latter days, language | is the energy of decaying sense" (*BH* 423). Particularly in his later poetry, then, Hill's view of the "inertia of malevolence" (*BH* 423) is counterbalanced by this notion of language's entropy, which in *Scenes from Comus* is manifested in metaphors of nuclear power or volcanic activity. And in poem 8 of *Al Tempo de' Tremuoti*, Hill transforms the Garden of Eden into "Orphic meadows": "Suffice the Fall, *pace* those Orphic meadows. | Each mystic good teased out from forfeit" (*BH* 891). One notes here that peace has become that rhetorical device of polemics, "*pace*".

Matthew Sperling has written of the importance of Augustine's angelic epistemology to Hill, and indeed, as Sperling notes, "*The Triumph of Love* is a book full of angels".[21] However, this observation is counterpointed by Hill's evocation in *Speech! Speech!* of "Augustine's | fellow, who could fart – with most sweet savour – | angels' song" (*BH* 333), a reference to St Augustine's account in *City of God* of people able to fart like angels' song: "A number of people produce at will such musical sounds from their behind (without any stink) that they seem to be singing from that region."[22] Sperling's argument that Hill's allusion here is essentially nostalgic, for "men so graceful they could fart angelic song"[23] is certainly part of the story; but surely Hill is also drawn to the ludic, Lutheran, even Rabelaisian aspect of this bizarre image, aside from its lamentational aspect. Though Hill is influenced by Augustine, he is also influenced by Luther, as he remarked in the interview with *The Oxford Student* of 2011. In *Speech! Speech!* Hill invokes Augustine, but he also invokes Luther.

Poem 117 asks "Why not twist Luther | practised self-parodist?" and, returning to Augustine, invokes the "Unapproachable City of God." (In *The Orchards of Syon*, also, Hill finds the "City of God unlikely" [*OS* XXX; *BH* 380].) In *Speech! Speech!*, "sweet savour" is balanced against scatology, as in poem 99: "AUTHENTIC SELF a stinker; pass it on, | *nasum in ano*, the contagious circles" (*BH* 338), which is a revocation of Augustine's "musical sounds from their behind (without any stink)". While Augustine is certainly an influence on Hill's sense of original sin, I would argue that there is actually as much creative friction with Augustine as there is sense of kinship: in fact, Augustine can represent in Hill's later work certain forms of wrong-headedness, as in *Speech! Speech!*, and also in poem 10 of *Al Tempo de' Tremuoti*, in which we find "Augustine, Khlebnikov, parting the Red Sea" (*BH* 892) – a reference to both men's association of *signum* and *res* (in Augustinian terminology), or signifier and signified, word and thing, which for Hill is a temptation with implications of spiritual pride and also of political enormity.[24] However, there is a rueful nostalgia or longing for such faith: as *The Orchards of Syon* has it, "Enter | sign under *signum*, I should be so lucky" (*OS* XXIII; *BH* 373).

A crucial point of reference for Hill in the matter of original sin is Philip Sidney's *Defence of Poetry*:

> Neither let it be deemed too saucy a comparison to balance the highest point of man's wit with the efficacy of nature; but rather give right honor to the Heavenly Maker of that maker, who, having made man to His own likeness, set him beyond and over all the works of that second nature. Which in nothing he showeth so much as in poetry, when with the force of a divine breath he bringeth things forth far surpassing her doings, with no small argument to the incredulous of that first accursed fall of Adam, – since our erected wit maketh us know what perfection is, and yet our infected will keepeth us from reaching unto it.[25]

This passage is referred to in 'Our Word Is Our Bond', and it provides an idiom which is echoed throughout Hill's criticism, and in the "lovely resonant phrase" of Christopher Devlin's which Hill quoted in an interview with John Haffenden, of "the lost kingdom of innocence and original justice".[26] In a sense, Sidney's argument is quite orthodox and Augustinian: evil is not inherent in nature, but in the human will, and poetic composition is a tension between "divine fiat" and "self-will" – though Hill's conception of poetic composition is perhaps a little more sanguine than Sidney's, as one would expect, given the twin influences of modern Christian existentialism and of Western European secularisation.

This notion of poetry as self-will recurs throughout the later poetry. Hill's later work, being so frequently a self-propagating meditation on the tension between spontaneity and form, is an active reflection also on the tension between self-will and divine fiat, free will and constraint. In poem 6 of *Al Tempo de' Tremuoti*, for instance, "Orders of anarchy: what dead Beckett calls | The *Providential fulcrum*. For a joke" (*BH* 891). This phrase of Beckett's clearly chimes with Hill as much as it sets his alarm bells ringing. "[H]ere is all humanity circling with fatal monotony about the Providential fulcrum", writes Beckett in 'Dante... Bruno... Vico... Joyce';[27] and in similar vein elsewhere he writes that the work of art is "neither created nor chosen, but discovered ... pre-existing within the artist, a law of his nature".[28] In his theorizing about artistic creation, Beckett sounds like he is talking about predestination; and so does Hill, particularly in *Al Tempo de' Tremuoti*, the sequence which opens with a reference to predestination or preordainment, here the birth of Christ:

> A signal pre-election to free choice:
> The mother's face foresuffering, the child
> Big, almost unmanageably held,
> Such attestation in God's passive voice. (*ATdT* 1; *BH* 889)

However, Hill sees predestination as a well-disguised instance of the dialectic of freedom and necessity. In poem 18 of the same sequence, Hill exhorts himself, and his reader, to "Call Original Sin | *Freedom being what it is*" (*BH* 895); and in poem 33, "Freedom to fall is our stability" (*BH* 901). There is a strong Kierkegaardian sensibility in *Al Tempo de' Tremuoti*, in its brooding on freedom and necessity; and, most explicitly of all, in 'A Postscript on Modernist Poetics', "[t]here is something in constraint which frees the mind, and something in freedom which constrains it" (*CCW* 573). There is a distinct consonance with the Danish philosopher's *The Sickness Unto Death*:

Possibility and necessity are equally essential to becoming (and the self has the task of becoming itself in freedom). Possibility and necessity belong to the self just as do infinitude and finitude.[29]

Where Hegel worked to systematise and unify, to synthesise, Kierkegaard, in a lifelong critique of Hegel, insisted on paradox and dialectic, the jarring of opposites, as the authentic structure of the human predicament. Hill sees this structure in Yeats's best writing, too: "What [Yeats] is looking for in his late writings is a unit comprising antithetical, even mutually repellent, forces, in which the calculated is at one with the spontaneous: integration that is simultaneously diremption" (*CCW* 577/578). This is Hill's "Intractability of happenstance" (*ATdT* 19; *BH* 895), providing context for the assertion in *Oraclau | Oracles* that the poet's "Intelligence new made of late" is "By paradox and oxymoron pressed" (*BH* 745). This tension between freedom and necessity recalls F.H. Bradley's injunction, quoted by Hill in 'Eros in F.H. Bradley and T.S Eliot' to "get within the judgement the condition of the judgement": that is, the 'right' or 'true' judgement (or poem) becomes retroactively inevitable by virtue of its rightness and trueness, a dialectic which Hill defines as tautology, though in the process of becoming its 'rightness' is at all times radically in jeopardy.[30] Poem CXXV in *The Triumph of Love* is an extended meditation on this:

> Estrangement itself
> is strange, though less so than the metaphysics
> of tautology, which is at once *vain*
> *repetition* and *the logic of the world*
> (Wittgenstein). Some of its moves – I mean
> tautology's – call to mind chess moves: moves
> that are in being before you – even as
> you – make them. (*BH* 276)

Kierkegaard is a thinker in the Augustinian tradition of *cor corvum in se ipsum* (the heart turned inward on itself): in the Danish philosopher's words, again in *the Sickness Unto Death*, "[t]he self is a relation which relates itself to itself".[31] In Kierkegaard's terms, then, the self can only *become* a self in this act of self-relation. And the dialectic of possibility and necessity finds various symbols, particularly in *Al Tempo de'*

Tremuoti with its evocations of the Fibonacci sequence, as in the very first poem, again:

> Or in alert idleness build a tower
> Of Fibonacci numbers where each term
> Stands in its self-reflection like the sum
> Of those two that precede it: the sunflower
>
> Head is packed with them, and the pine cone,
> Odd symmetries holding the mind at gaze
> Unlike that solipsism of the maze
> Circling the focus of self will alone.   (*BH* 889)

"Odd symmetries", presumably like the unexpected and ordained symmetries of formal verse, are akin to that "other selving" (*SC* 2:41; *BH* 451) which releases the self from the "solipsism of the maze"; "self will alone" is simply egocentrism. What one finds in nature is "Intractability of happenstance"; and this is how the achieved poem symbolises – though, crucially, does not in some medieval scholastic way[32] *constitute* – reality.

Fantasy and belief

This brooding on poetry as somehow standing in relation with reality leads Hill to contemplate various discourses which *do* claim to describe reality directly, or even to *be* reality: here is mathematics, in the Fibonacci sequence; elsewhere Hill invokes quantum physics.[33] As Hill writes in poem 84 of *Al Tempo de' Tremuoti*, "The metaphysical | End of desire is always to be real; | The word and world well-met and going steady" (*BH* 928). This is a taut, effective definition of metaphysical desire, and a description of the political and metaphysical overreaching that often goes with such desire. In a passage which condenses so many of Hill's central themes, again in *Al Tempo de' Tremuoti*:

> Mandelstam and Rimbaud one should try
> To emulate: linguistic alchemy,
> Vicarious redemption by the word:

> Physicists also, such as Schrödinger
> Who'd read the mystics. *Brilliant only child.*
> The particle in its magnetic field,
> Atman to Brahman, void of love or anger… (*ATdT* 37; *BH* 904)

Redemption by poetry is "vicarious"; the power of poetry is metaphorical, in both senses of that phrase. Hill's position towards belief is classically Coleridgean: throughout the later work's meditations on religion and revelation there is "that willing suspension of disbelief for the moment, which constitutes poetic faith".[34] Within "poetic faith" there is an inbuilt scepticism, inevitably, as it is a belief in the power of belief itself. In *The Orchards of Syon*, "Poets | *leap over death* – was that Coleridge? If so, | did anyone see him do it and live?" (*OS* XXXVI; *BH* 386). And in 'Hymns to Our Lady of Chartres', "*Orchard* and *Paradise* (from the Persian) | I would claim for my paradigm the two | most beautiful words we have" (*BH* 168).

Fantasy and fiction, in their relation to belief, are recurrent words, and concepts, in the later work. In *Clavics*, for instance: "Believe it: that there is cunning to twist | Wind's declination of the cypress tops, | You fantasist" (*C* 31; *BH* 821). This is freedom and necessity, spontaneity and form, in the act of contemplation, just as the poet is wishing himself, as fantasist, to believe that there is some "cunning" or purposive will behind the processes of nature, or even control over the poem – even as he has rejected such all-mastering forces. The exhortation, which is really a self-exhortation, to 'believe it', implies the fantasist is at least one step away from the status of believer; whether the believer can at the same time be a fantasist is left open. A fantasy is in musical terms a composition rooted in improvisation, so the word and its derivatives combine for Hill the exigencies of writing and the deeper perplexities of ideology and personal commitment. In *Scenes from Comus*:

> Very little now that I do not
> take to be hers in lieu of deprivation:
> implausible, credible muse whom I
> assuage by night. Unbelievable sex-love,
> to which I gave such credence, she believes
> our slow corruption by the Song of Songs. (*BH* 464)

The stanza is notable for its semantic play on words of belief: "implausible", "credible", "Unbelievable", "credence", "believes". With "credence" and "credible" the word *credo* is recalled, that famous first word of the Apostle's Creed, as if the muse here, in courtly fashion, is both his love and that to which the poet pledges spiritual allegiance. As he writes in *Al Tempo de' Tremuoti*, "The Word begets us crying *Fuck!* and *Ave!*" (*BH* 890), in which it is unclear whether the Word is doing the crying, or whether we, the begotten, are; and so, in the semantic torque of the line, creator and creature are one. The poet's muse here believes that the secular text in the Old Testament is the beginning of the corruption of humanity, and yet *Scenes from Comus* as a whole is erotic, and all about the powers of eros.[35] Again, the poet's noblest gift is his darkest menace, and aesthetics are inextricably linked with the "slow corruption" of humanity – this, in a poem which evokes the poet's Comus-like capacity to corrupt, his recognition of moral corruption in himself and the world, and its emphasis on moments of "equipollence" (*SC* 2:1; *BH* 431) in which the poem's pitch rises to the leadenness of language and the world.

The recurrent references to alchemy and kabbalah in the later work are part of Hill's fascination with the notion that language and reality are linked in some underlying yet mysterious way. Kabbalah holds that physical reality is created out of language (specifically Hebrew) of divine fiat, and so that through study of the Torah's hidden meanings one may find the hidden structures of reality. Alchemy is similarly gnostic, drawing on theories of divine emanations, like kabbalah but in a neo-Platonic tradition, holding that divinity is hidden, locked within the mundane. In poem 87 of *Oraclau*, Hill writes, in anti-alchemical vein, "I can do ashes but not diamonds" (*BH* 769). (This may also have some provenance in Hopkins's in 'Of Nature as a Heraclitean Fire and of the Comfort of the Resurrection'.[36]) Throughout this sequence, set as it is in Wales, with its history of mining as a backdrop, semi-precious stones are used as metaphors for language – comprising, in that sense of Philip Sidney's, both beauty and dross, value and ephemerality – and here coal is used as a metaphor for that "infected will" which "keepeth us from reaching unto perfection" (coal, subject to "great pressure", transforms into diamond). However, the poem continues: "I allow –

I think I do – that to will flaw | For the beauty of amends | Is aestheticism". Again, the metanoia or *dubitatio* of these lines displays that sceptical vacillation discernible in Hill's later work which approaches equivocation: "I allow | – I think I do". In other words, aesthetics are implicated with the Fall, and with imperfection, as Sidney implies in the passage in his *Defence*. The flawed will may be justified by its capacity to "will flaw | For the beauty of amends", which is pure Augustianian *felix culpa*; however, this idea is in turn, according to the same poem, "Spiritual pride, a touch of s.m.". This is "Spiritual pride" such as Hopkins struggled to come to terms with, as evidenced by his burning of all his manuscript poems on his ordination. Obviously Hill is ambivalent about this; but his metaphysical desire cannot be reconciled to his duty to "historical contexture", as he describes in 'Language, Suffering and Silence', in what is crucial statement for situating Hill's theological scepticism:

> If the historical contextures are attended to, our search for an absolute standard of value takes on a complexion of relativity. I find this difficult to admit as a Christian. (*CCW* 401)

Alchemy and kabbalah, then, are once-believed-in fictions, being to modern Western eyes fantastical, archaic narratives claiming to describe the hidden, divine nature of reality. (The very notion of 'ultimate reality' has passed, in our own age, from metaphysics back into physics.) Alchemy is of course a discourse of redemption, of the refining of dross into perfection, the metaphor for which is the turning of base metal into noble metal. It is essentially an extended metaphor for the redemption of the human soul, or the reconciliation of human imperfection with divinity. It is an esoteric, cryptic discourse, a gnosis to which only initiates have the key. As such, there may well be an element of self-parody in Hill's kabbalistic and alchemical references, and perhaps within this self-parody a degree of mocking of the cultural ambience in which these poems take, or are denied, their place. Thomas Vaughan is a point of reference in *Clavics*, whose preface to *Lumen de Lumine* (a work cited in poem 8 of *Clavics*) provides the title of the sequence: "What I have written formerly ... is *Domus signata*, a house shut up: but here I give you the key to the lock."[37] Hill is hostile to the notion of such a 'key' to a settled interpretation: rather, Hill's later sense of things is that the achieved work "rests in its own intelligibility".[38] Alchemical texts employ the semiotic determinism of allegory and parable; if one possesses the 'key', one may unlock the door of meaning. They are gnostic in the purest sense. A *domus signata* is literally a 'house of signs'; Vaughan writes in *Anthroposophia Theomagia* that "[i]t hath been the common error of all times to mistake signum for signatum, the shell for the kernel".[39] Vaughan's critique of "common error" here recalls Hill's of the modernists, and of Khlebnikov's association of word and thing. Vaughan's diagnosis of the lazy, or inattentive, reader also recalls Hill's repeated references to *Qlipoth*, "*the realm of rinds*" (*EoV* 19; *BH* 647), in *Expostulations on the Volcano*. *Qlipoth* is a word in kabbalah meaning the impure forces which surround a 'kernel' or spark of holiness – they are emanations from the Godhead, and as such are imbued with evil as well as goodness. As with alchemy, the nature of *Qlipoth* means that the world is a code to be unlocked by the wise. As such *Qlipoth* recalls Hill's description of reading poetry as postlapsarian language:

> The particular quality of our humanity describable in terms of poetry and value is best revealed in and through the innumerable registrations of syntax and rhythm, registrations that are common to both prose and poetry and to which as writers and readers we attend or fail to attend. ('Poetry and Value', *CCW* 484)

The "innumerable registrations of syntax and rhythm" of Hill's formulation do not occupy the sphere of the metaphysical, as does Thomas Vaughan's *signatum*; but the relationship between what Vaughan calls *signum* and *signatum* (sign and signified, in the idiom of midtwentieth-century structuralist criticism) exercises Hill's fascination. There is direct correspondence between *signum* and *signatum* in music, and the same is claimed for Hebrew; the existence of such a relationship would allow one to enter a "prelapsarian kingdom"[40] of absolute meaning and purpose. It is precisely the goal of alchemical texts to point toward this prelapsarian kingdom; alchemy seeks, or is, "The pitchblende of immortal sign" (*O* 74; *BH* 765) (pitchblende being uraninite, an unrefined form of uranium). However, Hill displays a scepticism, however reluctant, about absolute value, as affirmed by his statement that "our search for an absolute standard of value takes on a complexion of relativity", suggested also by his choice of unrefined uranium for his version of the philosopher's stone. Hill's concern is metaphysical longing, the desire for the "indispensable" (*CCW* 390), the tension between God's grammar and actual grammar, harmony and disharmony:

> *Somewhere* is sacramental belonging.
> Here we find but banking with God's grammar
>   Strung unstringing
> Grace from chance, worked like a novice stammer. (*C* 23; *BH* 813)

So, in his citations of esoteric texts Hill may be having fun – at his own expense as much as anyone else's – at the notion that 'difficulty' can be resolved simply by Googling names and phrases, the simple conversion of *signum* into *signatum* – but there is a serious point being made as well. The 'meaning' is in the very struggle to create meaning, in the torque of language and the poetic line. Metaphysical desire is not only characterised by utopianism and millennialism but also by a Kierkegaardian will to meaning. Meaning for Kierkegaard is an experience of existence, akin to the 'difficulty' of Hill's late work; though the will to meaning, which is the desire for everything to resolve itself into ultimate truth, is the necessary, and necessarily thwarted, condition of this difficulty. "*Somewhere*", writes Hill, "is sacramental belonging", the italicised "*Somewhere*" here recalling the italicised "*somehow*" of F.H. Bradley (*CCW* 532). As in poem 24 of *Oraclau*, "grammar" and "stammer" are rhymed here, exemplifying this position. One notes in this passage from *Clavics* that syntax, in the absence of structuring punctuation, seems to float free of grammatical logic; the "great pressure" of the poetry forces, or allows, the poet to invent semantically, so that the 'achieved' poem is part-grammar, part-stammer: it is "Strung unstringing". (In fact, if the line-breaks are taken to be indicative of the end of a clause, the sense becomes much more logical, and "Strung unstringing" becomes parenthetical, adjectival to the subject, "we".)

In *Oraclau* particularly, alchemy is associated with a certain political nostalgia, the notion undergirding much of Hill's (reluctant) theological scepticism, as when he writes of "*Inert matter* dug from beneath the nation", the inert matter here literally being coal, dug from 'beneath' "the nation" of Wales, which Hill cannot, as he confesses, transform into diamonds. In fact, the utopianism of alchemy is undermined, as it were, at the end of the same poem, to be replaced by "Our acts of love, intelligence and writing: | So with a dormant people roused from sleep. | Milton said that, not something God let slip" (*O* 66; *BH* 762). The law of revelation is cast here as "something God let slip" – against the omniscient creator's better judgement, perhaps. Hill's Christianity is infused then with an attention to "historical contextures" – of language, and of actual human experience – as it is with an inbuilt scepticism regarding metaphysical desire, even the metaphysical per se. Hill has learned more from Milton here than he has from God.

And here I come to the crucial point about nostalgia. Hill is acutely aware of the ethical and political dangers of such utopianism. As Matthew Sperling has observed, Hebrew represents for Hill the closest to music that language can attain – hence in *Speech! Speech!* poem 20 Hill writes that "Poetry aspires | to the condition of Hebrew" (*BH* 298). As Sperling notes, following up the sentence's provenance in Walter Pater, that "[i]n music matter and form can be one, as they aren't in language, with its imperfect correspondence between words and their referents".[41] Sperling describes also in Hebrew "the word thinging itself, the self-enwording thing",[42] though this linguistic utopianism has disquieting resonances in the political arena, as Hill is aware, describing himself as "a weeping Gentile Zionist" who points out "the reality of the Gaza Strip, 2008".[43] 'Tu B'Shevat' in *Without Title* addresses this disquieting reciprocity between linguistic nostalgia and political utopianism (a problem staggered over by Hill's modernist forebears, T.S. Eliot and Ezra Pound). The second poem of the two in 'Tu B'Shevat' evokes the psalmist: "*to the chief musician* – | suffering servant, plenitude that mourns, | singer of griefs unsung, the aleph-tav || of other's fruits and vines." No sooner has the dignity of the First Temple been evoked with the "*chief musician*" (King David), than modern Israel rears its ugly head:

> Moshe Dayan,
> en route to Suez, praised the flourishing
> Palestinian date-harvest,

which was not to the purpose. I salute purpose:
festivals where they strip the vital groves,
attune their joy and wish nobody harm. (*BH* 492)

As such the poem concludes with an appeal for honesty – "I salute purpose" – as opposed to the words of the Israeli military leader Moshe Dayan praising Palestinian industry, which were "not to the purpose". Dayan spoke insincerely, politically. Moshe Dayan's praise for Palestinian fecundity belied his political motives; perhaps 'Tu B'Shevat', particularly in its conclusion, is a salute (a favourite word of Hill's) to truth-telling and settled order, that notion of equity or natural justice which is another form of metaphysical desire in Hill's work. Clearly those last two lines are quite openly an instance of wishful thinking, even whimsical thinking. The very fact that Hill has transposed Zion to 'Syon' in *The Orchards of Syon* bespeaks his wariness of the overlap between theology and politics, and their mutual investment in nostalgia, utopianism, perfectibility.

The Daybooks significantly extend this mode of mistrust of linguistic and political nostalgia, particularly in *Liber Illustrium Virorum* XXXIV–XXXVI. In poem XXXIV, "Of us the Jews, a crucified people, | Have washed their hands; and now as governors | Of Philistia see and speak double; | No more this time Jehovah's sojourners" (*BH* 718). Hill's reaction to the historical and political realities of Gaza (known anciently as Philistia) echoes his attitude to language: he jars together the nostalgia for the transcendent capacity of language to refer to a reality outside itself, to become completely and all-satisfyingly self-sufficient, like music, or Hebrew, and an almost postmodernist sense of linguistic and cultural entropy, finding himself in "This trickster age", as he writes in poem XVII of *Liber Illustrium Virorum* (*BH* 702). In the last line of *Liber Illustrium Virorum* poem XXXVI we find an echo of one of Hill's earliest poems, published in his first collection *For the Unfallen* of 1959, 'Two Formal Elegies', subtitled 'For the Jews in Europe', the last line of which is "The world came spinning from Jehovah's hand" (*BH* 16), an image which, typically for Hill, implies that that which 'makes the world go round' is actually the absence of ultimate purpose or transcendent benevolence. Poem XXXVI of *Liber Illustrium Virorum* discusses the looting of the First Temple by the Flavians, and concludes "Even Domitian | Was a worthy scion,

| From whom we could take much | That's relevant | To have the oiled sphere spinning at our touch". Domitian has the world at his fingertips, while in the early poem the world has spun out of control of the overmastering God (*BH* 720). There is in Hill's view of worldly imperfection a persistent sense that somewhere in the background lurks the spectre of Gnosticism, as in the first poem of *For the Unfallen*, 'Genesis', which has its speaker 'creating' a world from the body of language: "There is no bloodless myth will hold" (*BH* 4).

Metaphysical desire

Hill has been fascinated by esoteric traditions from his earliest work. But why would such esoteric lore be of any interest to a twentieth- and twenty-first-century poet – and a poet quite self-consciously writing in the wake of two world wars? I would argue that (aside from the muscularity and strange luminosity of Thomas Vaughan's prose style, what Hill would call its intrinsic value) there is a hermeneutic indeterminacy in some alchemical texts, in Vaughan particularly, in which the writer is simultaneously empirical and mystical (between politics and eternity, you might say). There is often an indeterminacy in alchemical prose writings between the metaphorical and the literal. For example, a passage in Vaughan's *Lumen de Lumine* describes, as a parable, the personal apocalypse of the truth finally revealed:

> near the daybreak there will be a great calm, and you will see the Day-star arise, the dawn will appear, and you will perceive a great treasure. The most important thing in it and the most perfect is a certain exalted Tincture, with which the world – if it served God and were worthy of such gifts – might be touched and turned into most pure gold.[44]

This is a description of a sunrise, with sunlight as the "certain exalted Tincture", invested with metaphorical value; because the world is impure and unworthy, by its very nature, the precise tenor of the metaphor cannot be revealed; though we are aware that sunlight both is and is not "a certain exalted Tincture". This is *signum* longing to be *signatum*, the ultimate *signatum* being, of course, universal apocalypse, the Day of Judgement, when Truth is revealed. Redemption in alchemical texts must always be, in this sense, "Vicarious redemption by the word". Alchemy is an endlessly deferred 'moment of truth' – like poetry, perhaps – though the intrinsic value of Vaughan's prose, as with any imaginative writing, is a strenuously unfolding – erotic – moment of truth: what Hill calls a "the way of apprehension, a syntax of becoming" (*CCW* 534). As a discourse which centres on the Fall and the nature of worldly impurity, as well as implying metaphysical desire and the slipperiness of signification, alchemy actually fits surprisingly well with Hill's stance on language and the will. Alchemical writing actively contemplates the fantasy of its own absolute value: a "murderous | fantasy", quite literally for Thomas Vaughan, who died inhaling mercury fumes.[45]

Hill's own dramatisation of metaphysical desire is to imagine it as a paradox: "Reality itself grounded in our metaphors" (*ATdT* 94; *BH* 935). Hill has learned the vigilance with regard to such metaphysical desire, in part, I would argue, from the English poet, essayist, and political writer C.H. Sisson, who provides the epigraph to *Mercian Hymns*. In his essay on Sisson published in *PN Review* in 1984 Hill remarks that

> [Michael] Schmidt adds that "when Sisson calls for 'a central authority armed with strong powers for limited purposes' he expresses a tenable and inclusive politics. The phrase 'for limited purposes' is the validating clause, containing the entire tact of his politics, as indeed of his literary criticism". I agree entirely with this. "Strong powers for limited purposes" sums up Sisson's view of poetic, as well as of political, structure.[46]

Again, Hill is interested in the relation between power and purpose, strength and limitation. Art, as Kant claims in the *Critique of Judgement*, is "purposiveness without a purpose",[47] a dominant notion in aesthetics to which Hill returns time and again, from various angles, in his later work, not least in 'A Postscript on Modernist Poetics' in which he evaluates Auden's famous "Poetry makes nothing happen" passage in 'In Memory of W.B. Yeats' (*CCW* 568). Hill readily subscribes to Coleridge's notion of words as "living powers", but maintains scruples about the primary imagination, "the living Power and prime Agent of all human Perception",⁴⁸ the Romantic poet mixing political fantasy and literary theory together as freely as he mixes metaphysics and psychology. Hill pours a large helping of scepticism over such Coleridgean pseudo-politics. In this passage on Sisson, Hill cites his contemporary's "view of poetic, as well as political, structure", a statement which implies their analogousness rather than their identity; however, like Sisson, Hill is aware of the power of metaphysical desire, and aware of the part that invention and fiction play in poetics, and in politics. The idea that "We are a fiction even to ourselves" brings *poiesis* into the realm of psychology and ideology, and can be read as a rejoinder on Coleridge's metaphysics of artistic creation. Where Hill values the fancy above this imagined agency, he is aware, also, of the role of the fanciful in human values, as in his description of "metaphysical fancy" in 'The Tartar's Bow and the Bow of Ulysses'. The poem is a paradigm of this, as Hill points out: "[a] poem … is positioned at some point between the assertion and the dream" (*CCW* 552).

Some of the most fanciful poems in *Oraclau | Oracles* are in the six poems titled 'Hiraeth', a Welsh word with no direct translation meaning something like 'longing' or 'nostalgia'. This is part of Hill's treatment of nostalgia as essentially fantastical: it is a dream of perfection which is manifested in expansive gestures and whimsical rhyme, as in poem 123: "Let us donate this old story | To the geriatric | Programme of the sisters of St Patrick. | If I can cap this it will be a hat-trick" (*BH* 781). There are the expansive exclamatory final lines, too: "I who have swum in love words shore to shore!" (*BH* 780) and "I shall have us – vanishing – strike the air!" (*BH* 782). Hill is not parodying nostalgia, particularly as the whole sequence is a kind of psalm to Wales, elegising also Hill's own working-class Welsh ancestors; and nor is he self-parodying – no one writes bad poems on purpose; but his exaggeratedly venturesome style in the 'Hiraeth' poems is a tonal registration of the fancifulness of nostalgia, of the "metaphysical fancy" lurking within Coleridge's 'fancy'. While nostalgia is an enlivening and perhaps necessary part of political being, it is, like this aspect of poetic writing, subject to discipline; it is an indulgence which is indulged at one's peril. This is highlighted by the poem that immediately follows the 'Hiraeth' section, poem 125, whose opening lines are "True, I do not speak truthfully; how could

I? | We are a fiction even to ourselves" (*BH* 782). In the 'Hiraeth' poems Hill emphasises what he calls elsewhere the "antic" (*EoV* 2; *BH* 630) in order to dramatise the importance of this aspect of self-being, and of poetic writing.

The very fact of the inseparability of politics and religiosity for Hill accounts, at least in part, for his deep interest in the Old Testament in his later work. The departure from his earlier work, beginning with 1996's *Canaan*, is in no small part characterised by this focus on the Old Testament as both textual and ideological source. Hill is a latter-day Christian Hebraist; that is, he occupies the boundary between Christianity and Judaism, as perhaps only a "weeping Gentile Zionist" can. The voice of the Old Testament prophet, of *vox clamans in deserto*, provides Hill with a point of vantage from which to critique contemporary society. Hill sees a hedonistic, morally decadent Britain (and the West) through the lens of religion and often through the guise of the Old Testament prophet – a figure who is always per se belated and cranky: "You should all fuck less | and pray more", as he writes in *Ludo* (*BH* 618). The references to kabbalah and alchemy serve to reinforce this eccentric self-image also. Hill displays that characteristic of the kabbalist which Harold Bloom describes in *Kabbalah and Criticism* as a "*vision of belatedness*"[49] (italics Bloom's) which he ascribes to modernist poetics also, and to John Milton. There is in Bloom's diagnosis a remarkable conflation of some of the most important influences and points of departure in Hill's later work. One can only conjecture if Hill read Bloom's study, or if this is simply a strange serendipity: but Bloom's choice of epigraph for *Kabbalah and Criticism*, ascribed to H. Leivick, is strongly reminiscent of Hill's concern with the co-inherence of order and entropy in poetry, and of techné and crisis:

A song means filling a jug, and even more so breaking the jug. Breaking it apart. In the language of the Kabbalah we perhaps might call it: Broken Vessels.[50]

Or perhaps, rather than 'Broken Vessels', we might call it *Broken Hierarchies*.

Poetry is occasionally presented as an ascetic act, further to the Hopkinsian notion that poetic creation is an act of self-will, as in *Expostulations on the Volcano*, poem 5:

> Spur the nice constraints of rhyme-flagrantive.
> Rhyme is itself re-ordering of will,
> *Directio voluntatis*, a long dive
> Heavenward; held finally to be still.   (*BH* 633)

Directio voluntatis is from Dante's *De Vulgari Eloquentia*, meaning "direction of the will".[51] "Heavenward" is taken from Hopkins, 'On the Portrait of Two Beautiful People': "What worm was here, we cry, | To have havoc-pocked so, the hung-heavenward boughs?"[52] (The word is taken up by Robert Bridges in his dedicatory 'Sonnet to G.M.H.': "Thy plumage of far wonder and heavenward flight!"[53]) Hopkins's ambit is also that of earthly corruption, symbolised in classic fashion by the worm, and grace, that which is "hung-heavenward". The erotic element of poetry which Hill describes in 'Eros in F.H. Bradley and T.S. Eliot' is here mitigated by the ascetic, the re-ordering of will which composition demands of the poet, and which it, perhaps, demands of the attentive reader. As Hill remarked in the *Paris Review* interview, "[t]he instrument of expression and the instrument of self-knowledge and self-correction is the same".[54] Here again is the spiritual and moral dimension of Hopkins's "great pressure", the moralising of the Romantic imagination in which "expression" and "self-correction" are identical.

And it is such pressure which produces a central trope of Hill's later poetry, namely that of oxymoron and paradox, as Hill himself acknowledges in *Oraclau*: "Intelligence new made of late | By paradox and oxymoron pressed" (*BH* 745). There is evidence throughout his work that for Hill the trope of paradox signifies a way, *somehow*, to "ravage and redeem" the deviancy of language. In the early essay 'The Absolute Reasonableness of Robert Southwell', Hill writes that "[t]he existence of the carnal sinners is an oxymoronic treadmill; and their only means of redemption is by way of the divine paradox" (*CCW* 37). Language cannot do justice to the divine paradox, which is presumably inexpressible in language; and Hill remarks also that "ordinate and measurable though it is, [Southwell's style] brings us face to face with violent contradictions". I would suggest that, just as Hill places semantics in the "active-passive divide" (*CCW* 391), so he sees the capacity for grace in language in the tension between oxymoron and paradox. Oxymoron represents the 'violent contradiction' of the world as we find it; paradox is symbolic of the "divine paradox". According to Hill's diagnosis, however, oxymoron is part of the stylistic "treadmill" of mundane speech. It might be more fruitful to suggest that Hill sees the entire project of his later poetry as a reaching towards the power and discipline of paradox, if, to return at last to that great influence on Hill's later work, we take a remark on Hopkins in 'Translating Value' to be descriptive of this later work also:

> [Of Hopkins's description of "unspeakable stress of pitch":] Technically speaking (which, as I follow through the argument, is simultaneously ethically speaking) two matters principally concern me in my own study of Hopkins's writings: (1) how he achieves the "this" (the finished poem) which can properly be said to be the correlative of the "this-ness" of self-being; (2) how he understands and resolves the technical paradox implied by the use of the colloquial "unspeakable"; it is evident that his poems do "speak" the "unspeakable" at a pitch that simultaneously represents intense formality and idiomatic immediacy. ('Translating Value', *CCW* 391)

It is in pitch, that is, in language forged "between the hammer of self-being and the anvil of those impersonal forces that a given time possesses" (*CCW* 407), that the poet essays to speak the unspeakable. It seems that Hill sees poetics as being inherently paradoxical. Paradox works at the very limits of language; it undermines signification and revels in the play of signifiers. As such, within paradox is a gesturing beyond language, to some truth which lies outside of logic and language, and a simultaneous collapsing back within language and signification. It is an attempt "to push the maker beyond the barrier of his or her own limited intelligence". The very last paradox of *Broken Hierarchies* suggests this very fact: "Reality so made: it is like fiction" (*ATdT* 95; *BH* 935). As ever in Hill's later poetry, fiction and reality haunt each other; rhetoric and truth-telling, faith and poetic faith, look remarkably alike. The epigraph to Hill's lately completed

Hymns to Our Lady of Chartres suggests this very ambivalence, cast as "*the Argument*":

> that the doctrine of the Immaculate Conception of the Blessed Virgin in the womb of Anna, unlike the doctrine of the Immaculate Conception of Christ in the womb of Mary, is a sentimental late intrusion that infantilizes faith:
> that, as Henry Adams observed at Chartres, the twin powers of the modern world are inertia and velocity:
> and that, as Péguy said, all begins in *mystique* and ends in *politique*. (*BH* 155)

It is the infantilisation of faith, rather than the truth or falsehood of doctrine, which is at stake in the argument's first paragraph (see also the swipe at Richard Dawkins in *Clavics*); and the third, from Péguy, hovers between scepticism and pessimism. However, it remains to be said that sequences such as *Hymns to Our Lady of Chartres* and *The Triumph of Love* do invoke the numinous, often the Holy Mother in various languages, "Madame" (*Hymns to Our Lady of Chartres* [henceforth *HOLC*] 3; *BH* 158), "Regina Coeli" (*HOLC* 5; *BH* 159), "*Vergine bella*" (*ToL* LV; *BH* 254). However, this evocation of the numen is counterbalanced, perhaps even overbalanced, by Hill's acute sense of "the brute mass and detail of the world" (*ToL* LXX; *BH* 259), and the Péguyan sense, again somewhere between scepticism and pessimism, that *mystique* reaches its end in *politique*, as surely as childhood becomes adulthood: "Relate the *mystique* of Catchems End, | Worcestershire, to the *politique* | of incomprehensible verse sequences" (*ToL* LVI; *BH* 255). The value of the numinous, or the dream, is never in question, particularly as a response to "the brute mass and detail of the world", as in 'To Lucien Richard: On Suffering' in *Without Title*: "The sea | light was visionary, as it sometimes is | to susceptible people. Dead or alive | we sojourn in the world's refuge and abattoir" (*BH* 494). The sea light here may be imagined as the opposite of mass and detail: it is a dazzling blankness. Rather, it is within such "incomprehensible verse sequences" as a paradigm of the world's difficulty that poet and reader may find that "shock of semantic recognition" which, according to Hill, corresponds to "an act of mercy or grace".

Notes

1. Geoffrey Hill, interview with Jessica Campbell, *The Oxford Student*. http://oxfordstudent.com/2011/05/26/interview-geoffrey-hill-oxford-professor-of-poetry/. Accessed 11 March 2015.
2. Christopher Ricks, 'Literary Principles as Against Theory', *Essays in Appreciation* (Clarendon: Oxford, 1996) p. 319.
3. Haffenden, *Viewpoints*, p. 98.
4. Hill, 'Monumentality and Bidding'.
5. Hill, 'How Ill White Hairs Become a Fool and Jester'.
6. Quoted in J.A. Bryant, 'Making Peace with Disorder', *Sewanee Review*, 97:1, 1989, p. 154.
7. Hill, 'Address of Thanks to the Sponsors and Jury of the Truman Capote Award for Literary Criticism in Memory of Newton Arvin', p. 186.
8. Charles Williams, *The Descent of the Dove* (Longmans: London, New York, and Toronto, 1939) p. 218.
9. Hill, 'Noetics and Poetics', p. 11.
10. Hill, 'The Art of Poetry: 80'.
11. Gerard Manley Hopkins, *Selected Prose*, Gerald Roberts ed. (Oxford University Press: Oxford, 1980) pp. 94–95.
12. "By 'crux' is meant the reformer's – indeed the Reformation's – emphasis on *cor corvum in se ipsum*, a trope perhaps derived from Augustine's *detortae in infima voluntatis* [perversity of will twisted away]" (*CCW* 400).
13. Gerard Manley Hopkins, *The Poems of Gerard Manley Hopkins*, W.H. Gardner and N.H. MacKenzie eds, 4th edition (Oxford University Press: Oxford and New York, 1970) p. 87.
14. Gerard Manley Hopkins, *The Journals and Papers of Gerard Manley Hopkins*, Humphry House ed., completed by Graham Storey (Oxford University Press: London, New York, and Toronto, 1959) p. 230.
15. Quoted in Vidyan Ravintharan, 'The Spontaneity of Hopkins's Journal Prose', *Review of English Studies*, 64:267, 2013, p. 839.
16. John Milton, *Milton on Education: The Tractate of Education, with Supplementary Extracts from Other Writings of Milton*, Oliver Morley Ainsworth, ed., intro., notes (Yale University Press: New Haven, 1928) p. 60.
17. Hopkins, *Journals and Papers*, p. 230.
18. St Augustine, *Confessions and Enchiridion*, Albert C. Outler ed. and trans. (SCM: London, 1955) p. 355.
19. Coleridge, *Biographia Literaria, Volume 1, 1817*, pp. 295–296.

20 Hill, 'Milton as Muse'.
21 Matthew Sperling, *Visionary Philology* (Oxford University Press: Oxford, 2014) p. 8.
22 Ibid., p. 9.
23 Ibid., p. 9.
24 As discussed in chapter 3.
25 Philip Sidney, *An Apology for Poetry or the Defence of Poesy*, Geoffrey Shephard ed. (Nelson: London, 1965) p. 101.
26 Haffenden, *Viewpoints*, p. 85.
27 Samuel Beckett, 'Dante... Bruno... Vico... Joyce', *Our Exagmination Round his Factification for Incamination of Work in Progress* (Faber: London, 1972) p. 3.
28 Samuel Beckett, *Proust and Three Dialogues with Georges Duthuit* (John Calder: London, 1965) p. 84.
29 Søren Kierkegaard, *The Sickness Unto Death*, Howard V. Hong and Edna H. Hong, ed., intro, notes (Princeton University Press: New Jersey, 1980) p. 35.
30 In 'Eros in F.H. Bradley and T.S. Eliot', also, Hill sketches a Kierkegaardian view of language through the translator of Kierkegaard, Charles Williams: "Williams was a good theologian and, at his best, a great critic both formally and informally of English poetry because he recognised that language is arbitrary, autonomous, at the same time that it is bound, helpless. In this sense he could recognise in it not only an expression of, but a paradigm for, our human nature" (*CCW* 562).
31 Kierkegaard, *The Sickness Unto Death*, p. 13.
32 See John of Salisbury's *Metalogicon* (1159).
33 An interesting point of comparison here is with Alain Badiou's essay 'Nature: Poem or Matheme?' The confidence of Badiou's claim that mathematics is ontology compared with Hill's brooding on language's *symbolic* rather than *ontological* nature – and the will to meaning as the symbolic longing to become ontological – may suggest, in a broader sense, the cultural marginalisation of literature, and the humanities more generally. Alain Badiou, *Being and Event* (Continuum: London, 2011).
34 Samuel Taylor Coleridge, *Biographia Literaria: Chapters I–IV, XIV–XXII, Wordsworth, Prefaces and Essays on Poetry 1800–1815*, George Sampson ed. (Cambridge University Press: Cambridge, 1920) p. 53.
35 See my own article, 'Eros in Geoffrey Hill's *Scenes from Comus*', *English: The Journal of the English Association*, Autumn 2011, pp. 198–211.

36 Hopkins, *The Poems of Gerard Manley Hopkins*, pp. 105–106. "Flesh fade, and mortal trash | Fall to the residuary worm; | world's wildfire, leave but ash; || In a flash, at a trumpet crash, | I am all at once what Christ is, | since he was what I am, and | This Jack, joke, poor potsherd, | patch, matchwood, immortal diamond, || Is immortal diamond."
37 Thomas Vaughan, *The Works of Thomas Vaughan*, Arthur Edward Waite ed., annotated, intro. (Theosophical Society: London, 1819) p. 242.
38 Hill, 'T.S. Eliot Memorial Lecture', p. 7.
39 Vaughan, *The Works of Thomas Vaughan*, p. 306.
40 Haffenden, *Viewpoints*, pp. 87–88.
41 Sperling, *Visionary Philology*, p. 182.
42 Ibid., p. 187.
43 Hill, 'Civil Polity and the Confessing State', p. 19.
44 Vaughan, *The Works of Thomas Vaughan*, p. 262.
45 Ibid., p. xxi.
46 Geoffrey Hill, 'C.H. Sisson', *PN Review*, 39, July–August 1984.
47 Immanuel Kant, *Critique of Judgement*, James Creed Meredith trans., analytical indexes (Clarendon: Oxford, 1920) p. 61.
48 S.T. Coleridge, *Biographia Literaria: or, Biographical Sketches of My Literary Life and Opinions*, The Collected Works of Samuel Taylor Coleridge Vol. 7, James Engell and W. Jackson Bate eds (Princeton University Press: New Jersey, 1983) p. 304.
49 Harold Bloom, *Kabbalah and Criticism* (Seabury: New York, 1975) p. 17.
50 Ibid., p. 7.
51 Dante Alighieri, *De Vulgari Eloquentia*, Ronald Duncan intro., A.G. Ferrers-Howell trans. (Rebel Press: London, 1973) p. 53.
52 Gerard Manley Hopkins, *Poems and Prose*, selected and edited by W.H. Gardner (Penguin: London, 1963) p. 84.
53 Hopkins, *The Poems of Gerard Manley Hopkins*, p. 44.
54 Hill, 'The Art of Poetry: 80'.

Chapter 5

'Bless hierarchy': the cultural politics of Hill's later work

Hierarchy and hegemony

> Bless hierarchy, dismiss hegemony.
> (*LIV*, *BH* 738)

This single line in *Liber Illustrium Virorum* is a vital moment in the progress of Hill's later work. It occurs at a point of architectonic prominence, being the first line of the final poem of *Liber Illustrium Virorum*; appearing here, it hangs in the memory as the sequence's motto, or emblem. However, one might well ask, on first reading, if the hierarchy here, opposed to hegemony, is the same kind which Hill sees in Yeats and Eliot and their "shared species of hierarchical Toryism" (*CCW* 576); or that of the "hierarchic and stratified commonweal" (*CCW* 468). For many, it might be fairly assumed, the word automatically conjures such overtones, particularly in the contemporary moment in Western society. Indeed, Hill's own usage has progressed from such connotation, from the "'bloudy' hierarchy of Rome and … the tyranny of original sin" (*CCW* 290), for instance. And if Yeats employs the "hierarchical-vernacular monad" (*CCW* 576) in his later work, as Hill asserts that he does, then presumably the hierarchical is opposed to the vernacular. Certainly, when one considers that 'vernacular' originates in the Latin *verna*, meaning a slave born in the master's household, then the opposition of the hierarchical to the vernacular seems to gather some questionable connotations to it – perhaps evoking the master to whom the slave belongs. However, it is the "hierarchical-vernacular" which Hill pursues in his later work, and, in characteristic fashion, his sense of Bradleian eros dictates that his poetry, *somehow*, be of both. In other words, the hierarchical should be striving towards the vernacular, and vice versa. In fact, Hill is at pains in his later criticism and poetry to press home the point that what he means by hierarchy is not the ideal society of the "recalcitrant Tory", a tribe to which F.H. Bradley belonged (*CCW* 556). Hill's sense of hierarchy is pre-political: not quite apolitical, I would venture, but existing prior to any especially delineated sense of economics or of social structure (though the extent to which this is possible is itself an item of debate).

"Intrinsic value is perhaps only a figure of speech; but it is a meaningful figure of speech; and when one speaks today of a total destruction of intrinsic value, people generally know what you mean."[1] Hill's hierarchy is the "largely unknown order of human beings who believe in that impossible thing: intrinsic value."[2] The "unknown order" of intrinsic value is a minute but crucial revocation of Eliot's "ideal order" as evoked in 'Tradition and the Individual Talent'. The priestly overtone of Hill's statement here evokes this necessity of belief even if it is a self-defeating, self-overcoming belief in the Bradleian sense. The poet elects to "Bless hierarchy", when he could have chosen the still-laudatory 'praise', suggesting that this aspect of the concept of hierarchy is to stand out luminously, numinously. He might have written "Bless hierarchy, damn hegemony", to echo Blake's "Damn braces: Bless relaxes",[3] Blake being an exemplar for Hill's later cultural politics, as professed in various places in the poetry, but as it is the line recalls *The Marriage of Heaven and Hell* only distantly – as well as suggesting an invocation to dismiss hegemony in a more concrete sense. As well as the officiations of the priest, and the illocutionary power of the "unacknowledged legislator", 'bless' implies a deeply felt attachment, as if the hierarchy were beloved and perhaps vulnerable. As a 'rule of priests', hierarchy in Hill's sense and in its original sense may evoke "the transcendent kingdom to which only the truly great have access and wherein truth abides" (*CCW* 558), as Hill quotes Simone Weil: a sense of elitism which runs counter to the current accusatory feel of the word, more descriptive of what Hill calls "the democracy of the dead"[4] than the "Commonplace hegemonies" of contemporary polite society. Hill's 'broken hierarchies' stand in contrast to, and as poor phenomenal copy of, Bradley's "unbroken and self-complete Reality" (*CCW* 576) and Weil's "transcendent kingdom"; it is the *Qliphoth*, the 'realm of rinds' of Cabbalistic tradition, that we find in *Expostulations on the Volcano*.

In his review-essay on Charles Williams in the *Times Literary Supplement* (the last work he published in his lifetime) Hill writes:

> In our present condition of oligarchic democracy, "hierarchy" is totally subsumed into hegemony. In reality it stands in opposition to those terms of domination; it relates to matters of right and wrong evaluation, focused on what Ruskin termed "intrinsic value".[5]

So hierarchy as Hill understands it is neither Yeats's aristocratic hauteur; nor is it Pound's pseudo-Nietzschean prejudice; nor is it Eliot's royalist-classicist-Anglicanism. It is a reaction against the conditions of postmodernism, you might say, by recourse to the rhetorics of modernism, which themselves invoke an intellectual culture in which "right and wrong" is possible: that is, in which truth exists, absolute judgement is possible, and by extension artistic merit is more than an ideological shibboleth (subsumed under regimes of power or identity politics). Hill has written in these terms in an as-yet-unpublished piece, 'Thoughts of a Conservative Modernist':

> For the writer, the "self-realization of a being in the other" [Karl Rahner] is, immediately but not finally, self-realization in the otherness of language. This is one of the essential key-perceptions of Modernism, one that enrages the post-modernist self, which resorts to terms of abuse: élitism, arrogance, inaccessibility, incommunicability, self-regarding aloofness, refusal to share psychotic intimacies in verse.[6]

So the hierarchies in question are, in a vital sense, *not* of a piece with the social hierarchies of some Tory wasteland, but rather the hierarchies of the poets, tradition, "the democracy of the dead" – which stands as a reworking or rescuing (via G.K. Chesterton) of Eliot's "monarchy of death", in terms entirely in keeping with Hill's deeply political interrogation of Eliot. Eliot writes:

> As for the first-order minds, when they happen, they will be none the worse off for a "current of ideas"; the solitude with which they will always and everywhere be invested is a very different thing from isolation, or a monarchy of death.[7]

It is "the first-order minds" with which Hill is concerned in his vision of hierarchy; but Eliot's view of the relationship of these minds to the "current of ideas" recalls Hill's criticisms of his developing pragmatism, this "current" being perhaps a little too close to the "prejudicated opinions" at large for Hill's liking. Indeed, this sense of the insidiousness of such currents is crucial to the poet being hierarchical, in Hill's view:

> One of the marks of any good writer, it seems to me, is the extent to which he or she recognises, within the structure of the work at hand, the fact of not being a free agent, of being up against some form of *force majeure* impacted within the assumptions, the prejudicated opinions, of those to whom the work is addressed.[8]

Again, here, the conditions of the judgement should be contained within the judgement. Where Eliot's emphasis is social, Hill's is contextual. Hill's hierarchies are broken because the capacity for "right and wrong evaluation" has been eroded by "oligarchic democracy", the "Commonplace hegemonies": commonplace because they are rife, and because they project themselves as egalitarian. Intrinsic value has been eroded by this post-war culture, but also by the dwindling of any meaningful conception of the metaphysical in common parlance: "Metaphysics remain | in common language something of a joke" (*BH* 490). The push of sense into the next line here enacts the 'erotic' sense Hill has of being between epochs: that is, being of both and neither. "Metaphysics remain" in Hill's later commitment to the likes of F.H. Bradley, T.H. Green, Gabriel Marcel, Martin Heidegger, and Gottfried Leibniz, for example, but then with the next line's onset we are brought crashing back to our own era, where they remain "in common language something of a joke". (The poet's relationship to common language and to jokes cannot be taken as a neutrality, however.) It should be said that Bradley, Green, and Marcel, at least, argue the necessity of the transcendent, or at least the desire for the transcendent, in the full knowledge of its historical erasure; as does Hill.

One might sit back at this point, and object – perfectly within one's rights – that all Hill's pronouncements on hierarchy and intrinsic value are simply truisms. Everybody knows this *really*, but no one wants to talk about this sort of thing any more: there are more pressing political concerns in contemporary aesthetics; and anyway, metaphysics are off the menu. I would counter that, if these assertions are in some vital sense truisms, they are truisms which are indeed avoided in our present cultural dispensation, even slightly taboo in polite society and mainstream media; that, in our current self-conception as a relatively egalitarian society, artistic meritocracy *should* exist more than at any other time in history, but that it does not. Our present society is antagonistic to artists in a unique way: artistic value is considered a metaphysical hangover; the very idea of genius is either hopelessly outmoded or has the rotten taste of elitism about it. "Together, 'genius' and 'intrinsic value' are caught, without hope of success, in the crisis of civil polity to which I have attached Emerson's phrase 'alienated majesty'", avers Hill (*CCW* 525). This idea of elitism is one of our greatest evils: it actually means that those in positions of hegemonic power have to work less hard to stay there, since working-class intellectualism would seem to be, by this topsy-turvy 'cultural logic of late capitalism', elitist. What we may be talking about here is the difference between the artist and the 'professional' – and it is the professionalisation of art, and poetry, which has made it almost into a bureaucratic exercise. It is incumbent on the artist not to talk about these things the more he or she is a 'professional' or has aspirations in that direction. Perhaps to the poet, starting out in his or her reading and attempts to write, this idea of the "democracy of the dead", the ideal meritocracy, is instinctive and intuitive. The American poet-critic Adam Kirsch puts this idea in the terms of an egalitarian democratic proto-politics:

> Every poet begins as a provincial, dreaming of emigration to the city of the honored dead. "I think I shall be among the English poets after I die," wrote Keats ... To live on the fringes of literary society may, then, be an advantage to a poet's literary culture. He sees no reason not to converse directly with the authors he knows

only from books; he does not need his passport stamped by London or New York. This is the freedom that allowed Keats, the cockney poet, to be the direct heir of Shakespeare.[9]

And which allowed Shakespeare to be the heir of Ovid. Keats is a good example here; so is the grammar-school educated Shakespeare, himself the target of the strange snobbery of the conspiracy theorist for a hundred years and more. But by the same token, this conception is not limited to those of humble background; the "city of the honored dead" is open to anyone who merits entry, university-educated or not, regardless of style, school, or period, then: and that is where the problems of definition begin.

What constitutes aesthetic merit is another question entirely. Intrinsic value is, by Hill's own admission, a spectral term; but if it is real in any sense, it must be a quality manifest in a given language, rather than some universal ahistorical abstract quality or property of 'human nature'. It must be the 'genius' of a language. Hill himself sees the potential vagueness of the term as he applies it, though there is a certain necessary vagueness of definition with it: "In my perplexity, 'intrinsic value' is a shorthand tag for acknowledging the writer's inescapable engagement with the density of the medium", says Hill.[10] As Pound puts it, "*Logopoeia* does not translate".[11] As such, to attend to intrinsic value is to attend to the historical genius of a language. If "questions of translation are inseparable from questions of value" (*CCW* 383), then by extension intrinsic value must be the untranslatable element: hence Hill's association of word value with intrinsic value. As Empson remarked, "Racine always seems to me to write with the whole weight of the French language, to remind one always of the latent assumptions of French, in a way that I am not competent to analyse in any case, but that very possibly could not be explained in intelligible terms".[12] Again, in Empson's remark there is the sense that whatever is being apprehended is probably indescribable, though no less a fact for that – a position intolerable to the positivist or empiricist, but indispensable to F.H. Bradley.

Now in socio-political terms this does not necessarily mean that to produce poems of genuine merit you must have read everything in the 'canon' – and it is the 'elitist' notion of the canon that crops up when people are considering these matters – but rather, that all works in that language are evidence, or potential evidence, for the genius of the language, and for its misuse. Such considerations are of course unavoidable in this context. In his essay on Isaac Rosenberg, Hill writes:

> There must surely be more than one canon at any given time: a canon of general acceptance and a canon of intrinsic value. General acceptance presupposes general acceptability. Intrinsic value need not be generally acceptable. I see no reason in theory, however, to prevent a work from taking its rightful place in both canons. (*CCW* 464)

Hill would have placed Larkin in the former, and perhaps himself in the latter category. (Maybe every serious poet does and must.) Shakespeare is the prime example of a poet who is in both categories. *Liber Illustrium Virorum* contemplates such figures as Yeats and Shakespeare in terms of their encounters with "People" (*BH* 738), that is *the* people, as it were, through the lens of the Shakespearean character of Coriolanus – himself defined by his run-ins with the people of Rome. Hill's assertion that the two categories are not mutually exclusive bespeaks the quality of his cultural politics: they are not mutually exclusive in theory, but the degrading nature of the present "plutocratic anarchy" makes them increasingly so in practice. (In this, Hill shows a Miltonic popular radicalism.)

The plight of the poet-critic

In 'The Plight of the Poet-Critic', a review of the aforementioned Adam Kirsch, Carmine Starnino remarks that "Criticism by poets, once the conscience of the art, is now exposed as a theatre of special interests, and acting out of partis pris". In his potted intellectual history of recent times, he also makes the claim that "artistic merit, as a concept, became an ideological fairy-tale".[13] Hill is at pains to make the point, in his later essays and Oxford lectures, that the critic – in his case of course the poet-critic – is *indeed* always coming from somewhere in particular; as was shown in chapter 1, the notion of the judgement containing the condition of its judgement is crucial to Hill's later approach. In 'Translating Value', Hill praises Hume in 'Of the Standard of Taste' in that essay's "self-knowledgeable understanding of how deeply prejudiced we are" (*CCW* 385). The burden of criticism and of poetry is, for Hill, to get the condition of the judgement within the judgement, as has been discussed, not to deny that one is coming from somewhere but to recognise one's own prejudices and assumptions in the warp and weft of one's attempts to overcome those very forces.

What we are left with, according to Starnino, then, is the notion of the poet-critic per se as anachronism, and the notion of artistic merit as "an ideological fairy-tale". As we have seen, Hill engages with this idea, but asserts, or reasserts, the vitality of this very "fairy-tale" as crucial to the poet-critic's eros in the Bradleian sense; fantasy and fantasists abound in *The Daybooks*. "Ruskin's 'intrinsic value' is, in and of itself, such a [metaphysical] wraith; but, according to my argument, it remains a term which points in the right direction, towards semantic realizations that have some substance" (*CCW* 390). That metaphysical hiccup, "some substance", is another example of a Bradleian *somehow* working itself into Hill's semantic textures: if 'substance' is that which really exists, and cannot be broken down into further parts, a Leibnizian monad or Bradleian finite centre, say, then a thing of "some substance" is a thing worthy of analysis, that is, of being broken up to scrutiny (ἀναλύειν, to unloose or undo). 'Realisation' also treads the line between something made real and the apprehensions of memory and the imagination: this is precisely the line which Hill traces in his later criticism and poetry. Poetry "adds to the stock of available reality".[14] Hill believes in belief; to adapt some of Bradley's chapter titles in *Ethical Studies*, it is 'belief for belief's sake'. These ideological fairy-tales are just such naive notions of truth and reality, notions of which artistic merit is the fey cousin. If Michel Foucault's "regime[s] of truth"[15] have supplanted such transcendent categories as truth and artistic merit in postmodern 'theory', then in *The Triumph of Love* we find:

> Power and sycophancy, sycophancy in power:
> power's own cringing to extrapolation
> and false prophecy. Subways of white tile
> smeared with obscene brown banners. Foucault

>   running there for his life. Synaesthesia
>   of appeasement's brain-stench.   (*ToL* CXLIII; *BH* 284)

If one were to try to parse the argument of this strophe, one might say that Hill implies that the concept of power – central to Foucault's relativising of truth – is itself subject to historical contingency. But in terms of immediate context, 'sycophancy', 'cringing', and 'appeasement' suggest a certain impotence in the Foucauldian insistence on power as the ordering agent in human knowledge and practice, or even that moral relativism is a kind of toadying with the oppressor, of a piece with "anarchical plutocracy". A "brain-stench" in this context smacks of distasteful conclusions arrived at by means of abuse of the discursive intellect, devoid of the sensuousness of intuitive ethics, such as, perhaps, the postmodern erosion of transcendent absolutes – such as a moral nature. Moral relativism does not solve the problems of power, says Hill, it merely runs away from them, as an academic might run from intimidating youths in an underpass. Historicist though Hill's imagination is, he does not want to give up the idea of an essential moral nature. Much depends on that debate; the anarchist Noam Chomsky is another 'public intellectual' loath to surrender the idea of an essential moral nature – or, indeed, the idea of the public intellectual.

If the figure of the poet-critic smacks of an anachronistic belletrism, as Starnino claims, then Hill is aware of this and identifies it in Eliot and his milieu: "Analytical finesse and knowing belletrism cohabited in his critical and cultural writings from the first" (*CCW* 544). It is just this belletrism which Hill's attention to "immediate context", in criticism and poetry, works hard to resist – and working hard is the whole point. The belletrism of Eliot, say, emerging from that late-Victorian and Edwardian culture of letters, draws credit on the authority of the figure of the author, the public intellectual: a cultural power which has also been eroded over the past sixty or so years along with conceptions of genius and craft.

Difficulty and the ontological

If one was so inclined, one might symbolise Hill's earlier and later periods with his two translations of Ibsen plays – *Brand* of 1978, and

Peer Gynt of 2016 – and their protagonists. Brand is a Kierkegaardian uncompromising priest; Peer Gynt is a young fool. Both, of course, are outcasts. Even the versification of the two translations might be remarked on in this context of emblematic comparison, that of *Brand* being in taut tetrameters, and that of *Peer Gynt* being a welter of different types of line, including the fourteener, that most ludic of poetic lines. The comparison, albeit broad and impressionistic, is between the stoic and the ludic; and even, in the difference in the poetic line, the taciturn and the prolix. These binary differences are of necessity a mythic simplification, but they serve as emblems of the modes of Hill's two periods.

Indeed, the figure of the Fool, the clown, is essential to Hill's conception of himself in this later period, from *The Triumph of Love* onward, and is something which he consistently emphasises in poetry, interviews, and lectures in this later period. This is certainly to do with some transformation of the private, or inner life, a transformation which he has written about, as in *Speech! Speech!*:

How is it tuned, how can it be untuned,
with lithium, this harp of nerves? Fare well
my daimon, inconstant
measures, mood- and mind-stress, heart's rhythm
suspensive… (*Speech! Speech!* [henceforth *SS*] 3; *BH* 290)

But this is not, cannot be, the whole story. The Fool, as Hill sees it, has a certain social position, ambiguously of the community; the Fool, in Shakespeare, say, is always part comedian, part prophet. There are any number of fools and comedians throughout Hill's later poetry, from Trimalchio in *The Triumph of Love* to the "comedians | Of tragic rigor", say, in *Al Tempo de' Tremuoti* (*BH* 927), the last of the *Daybooks* in *Broken Hierarchies*.

In *Speech! Speech!*, "Scrupulosity | unnerved so, *Gelassenheit* is a becoming | right order, heart's ease, a gift in faith | most difficult among freedoms" (*SS* 11; *BH* 294). Heidegger's *Gelassenheit* means something like an availability to the world's arbitrary quiddity; it is not unlike Keats's state of radical uncertainty, negative capability, a state of openness defined in contradistinction to Wordsworth's "egotistical sublime".[16] This refusal to impose the arbitrary upon the arbitrary Hill describes as "right order", and might be seen as the spirit of his later productivity and facility, which is "a gift in faith" and "most difficult of freedoms". (In this respect the relationship between Hill and Eliot is a little like that between Keats and Wordsworth.) In these two phrases Hill characteristically conflates the spiritual and the political. But rather than alluding to some sudden lifting of the spirit, the "heart's ease" described here is the difficult freedom from his former scrupulosity – though few, I think, would accuse Hill of a lack of scrupulosity at any stage of his writing career. But this is bound up with his sense of himself as public figure, as we find in *The Triumph of Love*, the volume published just previously to *Speech! Speech!*, with its mock-profession of "sick | scrupulosity" (*ToL* LXXV; *BH* 261). Hill may have been "unnerved", then, by the perception among his detractors of his more-or-less pathological scrupulosity. In a *Guardian* profile of Hill, Robert Potts, speaking of the sequence 'Funeral Music' in *King Log* (1968), writes that "the chilling scrupulosity of its phrasing has sometimes misled casual readers".[17] It is this scrupulosity in the face of the casual reader, then, which is the focus of Hill's satire and self-satire. It is not, perhaps, scrupulosity per se, but the ostracisation, indeed the pathologising, of scruple which is the focus of the cultural-political dispute. In *Speech! Speech!*, in which massive irony is a salient trope and a central vehicle of its music-hall satire, "Scrupulosity can kill | like inattention" (*SS* 28; *BH* 302). The scrupulous poet and the apathetic reader are 'on the same page' here, after all.

Scrupulosity might indeed be used as a term with far fewer pejorative connotations than 'difficulty', though the implication in Hill's use of the word is that even it, with its implications of painstaking intellectual labour and moral rectitude, has acquired such connotations in contemporary culture. It is "Symbolic labour spinning straw to gold. | Not the hard labour of procrastination" (*SS* 30; *BH* 303). This evokes the arguments of William Morris in 'Useful Labour versus Useless Toil'.[18] In 'Eros in F.H. Bradley and T.S. Eliot', Hill mentions Graves's and Riding's *A Survey of Modernist Poetry*, and its "study of syntactical ambiguity in a Shakespeare sonnet" (*CCW* 553). It is in the course of this study, and referring to the 'cleaning up' of Shakespeare's punctuation by eighteenth-century editors that Graves and Ridings write:

Shakespeare's punctuation allows the variety of meanings he actually intends ... It is always the most difficult meaning that is the most final ... Shakespeare's emendators, in trying to make him clear for the plain man, only weakened and diluted his poetry. Their attempts to make Shakespeare easy resulted only in depriving him of clarity.[19]

For Hill, as for Graves and Riding, and as for Empson, the value of poetry, of words, is a matter of labour, which for Hill is, or equates to, moral effort: "*Intrinsic value* | I am somewhat less sure of. It seems | implicate with active virtue but I cannot | say how, precisely" (*ToL* LXX; *BH* 259). Graves and Riding overturn the more widely held view of difficulty-as-obscurity, through their own linguistic scrupulosity, to that of difficulty-as-clarity. But it is here that attention to "immediate context" and scrupulosity begin to shade into cultural politics: it is the desire to make Shakespeare "clear for the plain man" which both obscures and reduces his "meaning", which comprises, as Hill would say, his word value and his eros. Graves's and Riding's delineation of the "plain man" is of course politically inadmissible to the contemporary poet, with its 'undemocratic' and 'elitist' overtones (leaving aside its gender specificity). But here it is, also, that contemporary poetry is simply an inversion of precisely this conception of the 'average reader' as the "plain man"; contemporary poets, in their Eliot-like abandonment of word value, *talk down* to the 'plain man', the 'casual reader' – the phenomenon known broadly as 'dumbing down'. In other words, the typical attitude of the contemporary poet is not a revolution in taste and manners, but simply the flip-side of the very 'elitism' which he or she purports to oppose. (It is not unlike that standard figure of contemporary comedy, the upper-middle-class kid who goes to live in Shoreditch or Hackney and suddenly affects a working-class accent.) Indeed, the very notion of the 'democratic voice' and 'elitism' is itself radically confused.[20] What is representative democracy if not elitist? Like most questions, it comes down to the definitions of words. What is triumphing, then, is not cultural-political egalitarianism, but a decline in word value masquerading as egalitarianism, the triumph of velocity over integrity, as Hill might have put it. Or to put it more bluntly yet, it is egalitarianism as a product, the power-relations of the buyer–seller relationship, though partially obscured, or ignored, belying this very ideal. Of course, one sees the problems with the conception of the common reader, the "plain man", and so forth; but according to Graves and Riding, and according to Hill, it is the *condescending* to this "plain man" which is the problem, the underestimation of the democratic citizen: "These I imagine are the humble homes | the egalitarian anti-élitist SUN | condescends to daily" (*SS* 37; *BH* 307). Malone, the editor of Shakespeare's sonnets, enacted the same inverted hegemony as contemporary poets, and as the *Sun* newspaper, when he 'clarified' Shakespeare's sonnets to make them comprehensible to the 'average person' – or so Graves and Riding argue. However, Graves and Riding enter a caveat: "if Malone by his emendations, which have become the accepted Shakespearian text, had not ... presented them fileted to the plain man, the plain man of to-day would undoubtedly be unaware of the existence of the *Sonnets*".[21] Perhaps the "plain man" of Graves and Riding is not so very distant from the 'casual reader' of Robert Potts's *Guardian* article; perhaps the general cultural assumptions of 2002 were not so different from those of the 1920s after all, and perhaps they still are not. Clearly, Graves and Riding handle the phrase gleefully, and repeatedly, but with long-handled tongs.

Hill has said much on difficulty, most directly in an interview of 2000, in a remark worth quoting at length:

> Let's take difficulty first. We are difficult. Human beings are difficult. We're difficult to ourselves, we're difficult to each other. And we are mysteries to ourselves, we are mysteries to each other. One encounters in any ordinary day far more real difficulty than one confronts in the most "intellectual" piece of work. Why is it believed that poetry, prose, painting, music should be less than we are? Why does music, why does poetry have to address us in simplified terms, when if such simplification were applied to a description of our own inner selves we would find it demeaning? I think art has a right – not an obligation – to be difficult if it wishes. And, since people generally go on from this to talk about elitism versus democracy, I would add that genuinely difficult art is truly democratic. And that tyranny requires simplification. And any complexity of language, any ambiguity, any ambivalence implies intelligence. Maybe an intelligence under threat, maybe an intelligence that is

afraid of consequences, but nonetheless an intelligence working in qualifications and revelations ... resisting, therefore, tyrannical simplification.[22]

Hill's statements in interview are always worth the scrutiny; his answers are as carefully constructed and as richly suggestive as anything in his written work (and his interviewers have occasionally testified to his scrupulosity in giving answers). "Tyrannical simplification" most obviously evokes the Newspeak of Orwell's *1984*, and, though a stock point of reference in matters such as this, it is not an irrelevant source for Hill's remark, implying as it does that "complexity of language ... ambiguity ... ambivalence" are properties of a democratic language, itself the birthright of the democratic citizen, the "most difficult among freedoms". It is the notion of freedom as a form of difficulty, and vice versa, which underlies Hill's cultural politics, a 'freedom' based on commodity, a commodious freedom, being no freedom at all. In a later interview, Hill states that "If 'elitist' means belonging to some threatened hierarchy of the intelligence then I think that the poet has an obligation to attune her poetry in that direction".[23] 'Obligation' is a word which occurs in both statements; in the first, art is *not* obliged to be difficult; in the second, the poet *is* obliged to "attune her poetry" to the "threatened hierarchy of the intelligence". Is this inconsistency or subtle difference? The answer is that the most important thing is to whom, or for whom, one writes; one writes for the "hierarchy of the intelligence", what Hill calls in an Oxford Professor of Poetry lecture the "democracy of the dead", and not for that 'democratic' audience which is, in reality, simply people like oneself. That hierarchy of which Hill writes is bound together by "self-realization in the otherness of language", rather than sociocultural affinity (masquerading as egalitarianism).

Despite intrinsic value being recognised as "at best a promissory note", the nature of its promise is investigated by Hill, not least in the essay 'Rhetorics of Value and Intrinsic Value'. Referring to John Locke's *Second Treatise of Civil Government*, he writes:

> As [Locke] argues that intrinsic value is only latent, dormant even, in a piece of land until or unless human labour develops it by work of hand – manures it, that is to say – so [George Eliot] seems able,

in the closing paragraphs of [*Middlemarch*], to suggest that human worth itself may lie deep and dormant and unrealized if it is not thoroughly worked by the "manifold wakings of men to labour and endurance". (*CCW* 472)

Intrinsic value is indeed a phantom until it is "thoroughly worked"; in literary terms, that is, until it is met on willing terms by the reader. The agricultural metaphor crops up elsewhere also. In 'A Postscript on Modernist Poetics', Hill quotes Yeats in a letter to Margot Ruddock: "When your technic is sloppy your matter grows second-hand – there is no difficulty to force you under the surface. Difficulty is our plough" (*CCW* 567). Wellesley returns Yeats's day-labouring idiom back to him, complaining that he has made poetry "a bloody grind" (*CCW* 567). One remembers the origin of 'culture' here, in the Latin *colere*, to tend or cultivate, and of 'verse' in *versus*, the furrow of the plough, more specifically its turn from the end of one furrow to the beginning of another one. In that very definition of 'culture', as cultivation, we are reminded of the cultural politics of Hill's arguments: the self and the work alike are given value by the "manifold wakings of men to labour and endurance", and both are bound to the polity by suchlike imaginative labour. 'Imaginative' is not the same as 'imaginary'.

The term 'ontological reader' crops us in at least four places in Hill's later work. It occurs in 'A Précis or Memorandum of Civil Power', in *A Treatise of Civil Power*: "I trust the arbiter – that's difficult. | My marginal | *ontological reader*, let her recoup | a line or two delivered without pathos" (*BH* 582). This is put in slightly different terms, glossed, even, in *Clavics* as "The enabling reader, the recusant | At my fingertips, for whom I write well | into my scant- | extended age" (*BH* 796). It occurs also in Hill's first lecture as Oxford Professor of Poetry, in which he stated that "The greatest tragedy of the last sixty years has been the extinction of the ontological reader – at least in any public domain".[24] And there is a more protracted consideration of the term in his speech of acceptance for the Truman Capote Prize for Criticism in 2010:

> Until I left the USA in 2006, I owned for a time a book which had been in the library of the classicist and critic Donald Carne-Ross

and which contained his marginalia. To my grief, it was one of a number of books that went astray during my relocation to the United Kingdom. As I recall – and my memory is now faulty – I am indebted to Carne-Ross for his penciled note on the "ontological reader": something about ontological readers not passively reflecting their own pathos. This strikes me as a magnificent perception about a radical kind of relationship between reader and writer and indeed between the writer and her own work: rightly considered it is needful to add. It is my belief that the majority of writers (and readers) does not grasp the nature of the relationship between themselves and their own writing (and reading).[25]

Margot Ruddock seems to be an example of a writer (and reader) who fudges the relationship between herself and her own writing (and reading). The "ontological reader" is capable of approaching the work *actively*, then, alien and alienating though the work is, on its own terms: he or she does not simply project into it his or her own prejudices and emotions, passively.[26] In one of Hill's Oxford Professor of Poetry lectures, a passage from the *Guardian*'s G2 supplement, on an exhibition of Sylvia Plath's drawings, is recited, and described as "at once opinionated and without decisiveness or judgement", which, Hill asserts, is "entirely representative of the oligarchic commodity style in which the creative faculty is sensed as being frenetic yet passive".[27] Similarly, Margot Ruddock is apathetic in the modern sense but not in the classical sense. T.S. Eliot's ideal reader and writer is motivated by *apatheia* (oxymoron intended); and the 'ontological reader' recalls Eliot's description of Aristotle in 'The Perfect Critic': "in whatever sphere of interest", writes Eliot, "he looked solely and steadfastly at the object";[28] he describes also the reader who "we postulate is unable to distinguish the poetry from an emotional state aroused in himself by the poetry, a state which may be merely an indulgence of his emotions. The poetry may be an accidental stimulus".[29] Eliot's 'perfect critic' anticipates Carne-Ross's ontological reader, then; and I would suggest that this is another moment in Hill's later work when his distance from Eliot is not so enormous after all.

The provenance of Carne-Ross's use of 'ontological' in his thumbnail definition must remain a source of speculation, since, as Hill confesses in his acceptance speech, the original book containing the marginalia in question is lost (at least for now); but it is comparable, at least, with George Steiner's category of ontological difficulty. Steiner, in similar manner to Hill, one might remark, works to reorient a traditional Cartesian view of the matter to a Heideggerian one. In 'On Difficulty', Steiner begins by situating the notion of difficulty within that Cartesian schema so endemic to the modern Western tradition. To the question, "What do we mean when we say: 'this poem, or this passage in this poem is *difficult*?'", Steiner offers a breakdown of the traditional view of what difficulty is, namely "an interference-effect between underlying clarity and obstructed formulation". "This", he continues, "roughly is the classical and Cartesian reading of opaqueness, a reading whose inference is necessarily negative".[30] What Steiner is exposing as shibboleth is the 'write what you know' concept of 'creative writing': writing which has "congruence ... with a 'precedent' body of intention, perception, and vocative impulse".[31] Hill has called the injunction to 'write what you know' "that perennial piece of bad advice".[32] (This is the standard response, in GCSE English Lit. class, say, when faced with something difficult: 'what does it *mean*?') The intuition of what you might call the non-ontological reader is that the difficult poem is written in code: it is a scrambled message which can be solved like a mathematical problem (which may or may not also be written in code), like the semiotics of Umberto Eco or Arthur Conan Doyle. Steiner associates his fourth type of difficulty, ontological difficulty, with the "industrialization of language and of the means of dissemination of language [with which came] the semi-literacies characteristic of a technocratic and mass-consumer society".[33] He also associates it with a Heideggerian return to Being, ontological difficulty entailing a "sense of the inauthentic situation of man in an environment of eroded speech". (Steiner actually associates this type of difficulty with "radical modernism", a lineage of which Hill, if not exactly a scion, is not wholly foreign to – the likes of Celan and Mallarmé.) In other words, this type of difficulty is a reaction to the modern world's amnesia about "intrinsic natures" (*CCW* 484/485), you might say; Being, the ontological as such. Steiner's argument is that this type of difficulty is a reaction on the part of "radical modernism" to the unprecedented "erosion of speech" in "technocratic and mass-consumer society". Hill's sense of difficulty is certainly in part animated by such a recognition, as we have seen; and if Carne-Ross's term is in no way directly influenced by Steiner, or by Heidegger (though for all we know it may be), then it certainly shares a locus of concern.

Steiner's diagnosis of the ontological mode in poetry is given further weight in the present context in his subsequent statements, made in the context of remarks about Mallarmé and Heidegger:

> In the riddling fragments of Parmenides, of Heraclitus, of Anaximander, thought and saying are a perfect unity. The *logos* stands in the clearing of being, gathering to itself the "hidden presentness of Being in beings", the quiddity of autonomous existence and meaning towards which Gerard Manley Hopkins had bent his vision.[34]

I would not wish to offer Hill's later poems as "riddling fragments", though one suspects that certain of Hill's less enthusiastic reviewers might support such a description (Nick Laird, for instance, or William Logan); what I am trying to put forward is that thought and saying as "perfect unity" is the source of the difficulty of the pre-Socratics, and, I would suggest to an extent, of Hill's later work – or rather, the *struggle* to unite thought and saying, perfection being the consummation towards which the poet, as Bradley's ethical self, directs itself in the knowledge of its impossibility. In the early essay on Robert Southwell, Hill writes of "impulse and effect [being] one" (*CCW* 23) in Southwell's great poem 'The Burning Babe', and this is at the heart of his notion of alienation. Hill exemplifies this point in his lecture on Hopkins in 2014: "Where Hopkins differs from his contemporaries ... is in his excision of any sense of hiatus between sensation and utterance."[35] And Hopkins is certainly an exemplar in Hill's later "obsessive concern",[36] we might say, with being, with intrinsic value and intrinsic natures.

The acute sense of "the quiddity of autonomous existence and meaning" could itself stand as a paraphrase of Heidegger's *Gelassenheit*, which Hill cites in poem 11 of *Speech! Speech!*: a title which itself evokes "the rapid proliferation of journalistic and popular media of communication – the press, the *feuilleton*, the cheap book"[37] that Steiner designates in 1978, to which we would now add the internet;

but also "the nature of human speech" and "the status of significance".[38] It is this double movement within Steiner's sense of ontological difficulty, of revulsion and reversion, which characterises Hill's later period. Steiner's definition of ontological difficulty seems to be of a different order from his other three types of difficulty (roughly, that which must be looked up; that which challenges expectation; and that which deepens our perceptions and linguistic intelligence). Ontological difficulty is a more self-containing type of difficulty, or a type of difficulty in which the work of art contains itself, withdraws into itself, most completely: a mode of poetic language's being which is travestied in the more orgiastic works of, say, Dylan Thomas and George Barker.

The difference between Steiner's ontological difficulty and his other three types recalls Gabriel Marcel's distinction between problem and mystery: "A mystery is a problem which encroaches on its own data, invading them, as it were, and thereby transcending itself as a simple problem."[39] The "problem which encroaches on its own data" and thereby transcends itself as "simple problem" is very close to Bradley's sense that "you must get within your judgement the condition of your judgement", which is in turn a major tributary of Hill's conception of alienation. "Creation is metamorphic not trans- | cryptic: *doth suffer a sea-change* | take as instance", writes Hill in poem 25 of *Ludo* (*BH* 612). Here there is a subtle difference from Eliot's invocation of Rémy de Gourmont in *The Sacred Wood*, in the chapter on 'The Perfect Critic', which rules that the critic's task is "*ériger en lois ses impressions personelles*" [to erect as law one's personal impressions].[40] There is in de Gourmont's phrase a residuum of power-politics, of the putsch: to erect in law one's personal impressions is to apply, to some extent, an arbitrary will. A major aspect of Hill's later project is to clean up Eliot's poetic theory, to moderate its "hint of the despotic" (*CCW* 111), which arises in part from its assumptions about the gap between subjective and objective states. But returning to Gabriel Marcel: the notion of the poem as a mystery which "transcend[s] itself as a simple problem" would have been attractive to Hill – which is not to say that the achieved poem, as Hill or as anyone else conceives it, does not have 'problems' which can be to some extent solved, as George Steiner's taxonomy of difficulty stipulates also. The idea of language transcending itself, or withdrawing into itself in the Marcel-like vein, is one which recurs in Hill's later work in its various forms, and is perhaps *the* criterion, for Hill, for poetry that is (employing a metaphysical idiom) the real thing.

But despite the Bradleian connotations of some Reality which exists somehow, somewhere (mysteriously within the work itself) Hill's 'hierarchy' evokes Coleridge's 'clerisy' as well. In 'Perplexed Persistence: The Exemplary Failure of T.H. Green', a relatively early essay of 1975, Hill considers, aside from that of Green, the exemplary failure of Coleridge:

> The original subscribers to Coleridge's *The Friend* numbered just under four hundred. He was satisfied, we are told, "to direct his remarks to the 'learned class' he was later to call the 'clerisy'". He required "the attention of my reader to become my fellow-labourer" but from the surviving comments of several self-assured readers … it is evident that some of them considered that he asked too much. (*CCW* 125)

The "learned class", Coleridge's clerisy, certainly smacks of what might be called an 'élite' nowadays, with all that word's pejorative connotations. As Hill writes in 'Pindarics', "The élite | is a smaller crowd. You must accept this | as I must" (*BH* 556). The difference in Hill's desideration of 'élitism' is the tone of stoic resignation: one gets the sense here that Hill is not "satisfied" as Coleridge was to address a "smaller crowd". Hill's manner of address in these lines, in 'Pindarics', and in his later work as a whole, is complicated by the epigraph to this poem, from Cesare Pavese's *Il mestiere di vivere* ('The Business of Living'), which asserts the desire for "slapstick, realistically declaimed to the people" (*BH* 521). It is not that Hill directs his work at a small clique or elite, per se; it is that the "ontological reader" is an increasingly rare species in the post-war world of English writing and public discourse. The sense is, rather, that the ontological reader has been driven underground, and so is increasingly marginalised; there is a persistent feeling that Hill's later work is offered as a form of resistance to the anti-ontological hegemony of the post-war era. "If I am an elitist", states Hill in an Oxford Professor of Poetry lecture, "it is as my tribute to her [Anne Gledhill, Hill's old English teacher] and others of similar ['underprivileged'] background, such as my parents".[41] As poem XI of *Liber Illustrium Virorum* has it:

> Illiterate I would blaze myself the un-
> tutored elect of language: it's that strong –
> Stronger almost than Keats with his mute urn. (*BH* 695)

Keats is one model that springs to mind in this context, as he did for Adam Kirsch; another is Blake, variously: as in the last poem of the sequence: "Hierarchy yet: Blake's lordly plates to *Job* | And he was a sworn Leveller" (*BH* 738). The carefully chosen "lordly" here conspicuously applies to the art, not the artist. And also in *The Triumph of Love*, we find "Blake | in old age reaffirming the hierarchies" (*BH* 279), Blake here providing the exemplar for Hill, in characteristic fashion.

Indeed, Hill has defined this sense elsewhere in terms of both resignation and liberation, "isolation and autonomy":

> I want to root the sense of creative isolation and autonomy in a double seam: first in the commonplace actuality of literary ambition thwarted and fame largely denied; second, and more importantly, in the recognition of verbal power rooted in a kind of rift between self-recognition made public (on the one hand) and public non-acceptance (on the other). (*CCW* 562)

The verbal power in question is a self-recognition which is made in the expectation of the absence of public recognition: and this, I think, is in no small part the source of the trope, so integral to Hill's later work, of comedy, clowning, Pavese's "slapstick". The idea of public "self-recognition" which is largely ignored may strike one as pathetic, but Hill casts it as bathetic, in the "mask of laughter", in order both to satirise and celebrate the necessity of that "public non-acceptance":

> A happy investment, Lord Trimalchio:
> forasmuch as Blake laboured
> in Hercules Buildings, and as "up Dryden's
> alley" is where he was set upon
> to the unstinting plaudits of the trade;
> as "mob" and "fun" came in at the same time:
> forasmuch as the world stands,
> in a small part, exposed for what it is –

tyrant-entertainment, master of the crowds. (*ToL* LXII; *BH* 257)

And herein lies another source of divergence from Eliot. In *The Use of Poetry and the Use of Criticism*, a book which Hill denigrates in the later essays, Eliot writes: "When a poet deliberately restricts his public by his choice of style of writing or of subject-matter, this is a special situation demanding explanation and extenuation, but I doubt that this ever happens. It is one thing to write in a style which is already popular, and another to hope that one's writing may eventually become popular. From one point of view, the poet aspires to the condition of the music-hall comedian."[42] Eliot's vision of the music-hall comedian is rather different from Hill's, and is indeed a vision of the mastery of the crowd. His 'London Letter' of 1922, published in *The Dial*, lamenting the death of Marie Lloyd, is a study of the relationship between popularity and "moral superiority": "Marie Lloyd's audiences were invariably sympathetic, and it was through this sympathy that she controlled them."[43] Hill is precisely opposed to this notion of 'control', as he is suspicious of Eliot's desire for 'power' elsewhere; and his figuration of the comedian is opposed, I think quite consciously, to Eliot's elegy to Marie Lloyd as an elegy for "this capacity for expressing the soul of the people".[44] Hill relocates, or seeks to relocate, the "intrinsic nature" away from such a (subtly) hegemonic idea of the "soul of the people" – a symptom of Eliot's degradation, as Hill would see it – to the intrinsic nature of the linguistic artefact. "Plebs create soul music; he understood | Little of that" writes Hill in *Liber Illustrium Virorum* XXIV, 'he' being Coriolanus – a figure associated, of course, with Eliot, both in *The Waste Land* and in the unfinished *Coriolan* sequence. Coriolanus, in his clumsy relationship with the "lower classes",[45] might stand in for Eliot, here, and for high modernist poetics more generally. The "soul music" which Hill refers to in various moments in his later poetry is both the 'spontaneous' art of the working classes (see Milton's radicalism), and an art which assumes its own 'soul', or 'intrinsic nature', there to be grasped by those who would meet it on its own terms. The association of intrinsic value with what Eliot called "the lower classes" is consistent with how Hill portrays it elsewhere: for instance, the reference to

Anne Gledhill in the Oxford lecture, and in the references to Blake in *Liber Illustrium Virorum*.

This is all a part of Hill's sustained critique of Eliot in his later essays, and his identification of "the progressive deterioration of Eliot's creative gifts in direct contact with the cultural phenomena of enjoyment, taste, distaste" (*CCW* 538), or even, more obliquely, the "current of ideas". Eliot's distant conception of the "lower classes" is of a piece with his increasingly paternalistic attitude, his Lord Reith-like public persona – though one might counter that Eliot's high-handed beneficence is not so different from John Ruskin's in *Fors Clavigera*, a book influential on Hill, especially the later work. There is a general animus towards Eliot's later notion of the 'enjoyment' of poetry, and of enjoyment as passive, apathetic – "tyrant-entertainment" – as I have discussed, in Hill's later work. Such apathy is confronted throughout this later work – indeed, Hill's later phase is characterised in part by this very energy of confrontation – and in *The Triumph of Love*, the long poem which sets out many of the terms of Hill's later approach, it is figured as:

> unselfbeing – each held
> distracted in his doomed body-cockpit
> by a velocity which is also inertia,
> round the clock idle talk-down to impact.   (*ToL* LXXI; *BH* 260)

This is echoed in the epigraph, or "*the Argument*", to *Hymns to Our Lady of Chartres*: "that, as Henry Adams observed at Chartres, the twin powers of the modern world are inertia and velocity" (*BH* 155). In a poem which evokes Wittgenstein from time to time, it is salient to note that 'idle talk' is Wittgenstein's term, roughly, for bullshit: that is, talk with no concern for truth or falsehood, what Hill is wont to call 'cant'. But behind Hill's later work lurks the presence of Heidegger too. It is a term which appears in Heidegger, as well, in the guise of *Gerede*, inauthentic discourse, as opposed to *Rede*. Heidegger's *Gerede* corresponds to Hill's notion of "the linguistic-semantic detritus of our particular phase of oligarchical consumerism":[46] that which is ironically referred to as 'content', in contemporary media-bullshit, being made to provide the steady background hum of conscious life, designed for, even promoting, the passive reader. *Gerede* is the opposite of reading or writing as event, or as Marcellian mystery. The familiarity of the idioms and styles of address veil the 'content' from our conscious perception and do not provoke our active being. This "round the clock idle talk-down to impact" is the ubiquitous presence of news, social media (still in the future at the time this was written), and fake news (ditto). In *Being and Time*, Heidegger writes that "this idle talk is not confined to vocal gossip, but even spreads to what we write, where it takes the form of 'scribbling' [*das Geschreibe*]. In this latter case, the gossip is not based so much upon hearsay. It feeds upon superficial reading."⁴⁷ Heidegger here, whose concern is ontology in the broadest possible sense, is describing the state of absence of the ontological reader: an absence with consequences for the civic realm, and for the being (the *Dasein*) of the individual. It is a state of "unselfbeing", in other words. According to Hill, however, the poet's use of language should be eccentric, as the poet should be eccentric: that is, not *con*centric, not writing with the drift of the language, its clichés, its accepted idioms, its coercive and deadening force, its *Gerede*. Hill, like Heidegger, situates this absence specifically within the modern era: "Oligarchy requires simultaneously debauched and debased response", he declares in the Oxford Professor of Poetry lecture of 2011, 'Poetry, Policing, and Public Order (1)'. "Unselfbeing" is taken from Hopkins' "selfbeing" (*CCW* 391), a state which has similarities with certain ideas in Bradley's ethics, as we have seen.

A few sections later in *The Triumph of Love*, we find Petronius Arbiter, who is enjoined to "Lie back. Enjoy. | Enjoy. Open another vein" (*ToL* LXXIX; *BH* 262). Eliot's 'enjoyment' is here equated with an apathetic decadence, such as that proverbially associated with Petronius, author of the *Satyricon*. It may, or may not, be telling that Petronius provides the epigraph to Eliot's *The Sacred Wood*, in a passage which extols the unmistakable charisma of the poet and 'man of letters'; despite his unlovely clothes, the old man declares "*poeta sum*", "I am a poet". This is little more, really, than an assertion of the authority of the poet-critic, but it evokes the nobility of this figure as well, its charisma. This is of a piece with the culture of letters from which Eliot emerges, and of the culture of image in which we currently find ourselves. Petronius and Trimalchio pop up throughout *The Triumph of Love*, Trimalchio being the clown, the zany figure which is a crucial symbol throughout Hill's later poetry:

> Through such history poets are zanies
> Although their flatteries may be well put
> In the style of something cadgily learned.   (*LIV* XXVI; *BH* 710)

In the shadow of power, the poet is a clown: either to entertain, or to speak uncomfortable truths against the current of opinion – or, perhaps, both. As well as the image of the poet being a 'cadgy learner' (to cadge is to beg, from an old Irish word), the emphasis on comedy throughout the later poetry evokes a few things: spontaneity; a ludic relationship to language; the role of the marginal eccentric; and the artificiality, the poke-in-the-ribs element of poetic writing. As Hill says in one lecture, poetry, like comedy, is all about timing.[48]

To return to an earlier theme, one cannot help but get the impression that the comedian, zany, clown figures in the later poetry have some connection to another recurrent trope, that of the prophet. "Heap | ashes on your head and split your sides" (*BH* 271). There is certainly at least a superficial similarity, in the sense that both figures say things that their listeners, in whatever way, would rather not hear. There is a link between the prophet and the comedian, as suggested in poem 48 of *Ludo*:

> Forgive true poets to seventy times seven
> I
> say
> I say I say   (*BH* 619)

The point is that, following Jesus in Matthew 18:22, you forgive the 'true' poet because she is redeemed by her inventive genius. The "I say" here is a comic or music-hall recasting of what we might call in the context Jesus's 'catchphrase', "verily I say". The phrase "true poet" is itself a kind of joke, appearing in a sequence which revels so much in the inventive play of poetry, and whose title is a Latin word meaning 'I play' (and a board game popular in the twentieth century). Poem 52 takes this up: "Poetry, cheating, and forgiveness, | my three givens, | my thesis" (*BH* 620). And the "true poet" is presented in Hill's work as an *increasingly* embattled figure: "I risk the word 'true' as being perilously appropriate to the increasingly laboured, increasingly exhausted, line of moral succession" (*CCW* 454). 'True' poetry, rather like truth itself, has a semantic value, but is rather difficult to demonstrate – rather because 'true poetry' *is* semantic value in its purest and most strenuous form.

The reference to "false prophecy" in the strophe on Michel Foucault in *The Triumph of Love* is characteristic of Hill's later poetry, in its many citations of and allusions to the biblical prophets. Such allusions might smack of cultural archaism, religious nostalgia, even self-aggrandisement if the poet is taken to identify himself with the figure of the Old Testament prophet – and the epigraph to *The Triumph of Love*, from Nehemiah, does nothing to mitigate this perception. However, I would suggest that there is another way of seeing this trope of prophecy, and indeed of "false prophecy", in the cultural-political terms of the present chapter – namely, of course, in Hill's terms of hierarchy and hegemony. This "hierarchy of the intelligence" is not only the poetic democracy of the dead, the writers of works of "eternal intensity" or intrinsic value; it is also the threatened domain of the public intellectual. Noam Chomsky is one such figure, a writer who has campaigned on behalf of the public intellectual, and whose conception of the figure is akin to Hill's:

> In the Hebrew scriptures there are figures who by contemporary standards are dissident intellectuals, called "prophets" in the English translation ... The prophets were treated harshly, unlike the flatterers at court, who would later be condemned as false prophets.[49]

The difference between Chomsky's position here and Hill's position on this point generally is that for Chomsky this figure is endangered by its very nature, is always necessarily endangered; Hill's emphasis is usually more on the depredations of the current era in this regard. This figure, what Chomsky calls elsewhere the "value-oriented intellectual",[50] is embattled, endangered. In Chomsky's image, this figure is always and per se embattled; in Hill's view, it seems, this figure is particularly embattled in the "plutocratic anarchy" of post-war Europe: it is the ontological reader missing from the public domain, as Hill describes Donald Carne-Ross's term.[51]

Hill is certainly "value-oriented" in his later work, and there is perhaps a shared sense, between Chomsky and Hill, that the orientation towards value will of itself lead the intellectual into the role of dissident in some shape or form. Hill's and Chomsky's use of 'value' implies that this is a quality which is antagonistic to hegemony. To adapt Chomsky's formulation, most contemporary poets today would be, according to Hill, Chomsky's "flatterers at court", that is, reproducers of "the linguistic-semantic detritus of our particular phase of oligarchical consumerism";[52] though for Chomsky himself, an anarchist lacking Hill's innate sense of the elegiac, and of the centrality of nation, this is a timeless state of affairs and within the very nature of power.

It is the role of the *poeta doctus*, the 'learned poet', which is at stake: as a rear-guard action, in the era of "plutocratic anarchy", Hill's priority is to assert the status of public intelligence and of ontological writing. In this sense, then, Hill refigures the idea of the *poeta doctus* into the poet of intelligence, and of sensuous intelligence: in 'Tacit Pledges', "intelligence, such as we find in Rosenberg, is a quality that 'England' has never been overdisposed to acknowledge, for it has never 'delighted and inspired generations of readers'" (*CCW* 423). Rosenberg is a staging-post for the problem of public intelligence: in the essay on Rosenberg, Hill writes, "Poets during the greater part of the nineteenth century were conventionally expected, and repeatedly enjoined, to teach. Wordsworth's original conception of this role was that the poet's privilege and burden is to teach radically new doctrines of relationship: both to the self and to society, and to the self in its relation and disrelation to society. Owen is perhaps the last true representative of this form of Romantic *paideia*, a continuity unbroken from 1798 to 1918" (*CCW* 454). Hill has forgotten, or chosen to ignore, Ezra Pound. In *ABC of Reading*, Ezra Pound quotes one Rodolfo Agricola, that the triple function of literature is "*ut doceat, ut moveat, ut delectet*, to teach, to move, or to delight".[53] It is the association of the *moveat* with the *doceat* which is the bugbear of contemporary poetry and culture more generally: the didactic element of literature is perhaps unconsciously associated with a suspicious politics, or perhaps the didactic element per se is equated with the desire to move, to control the crowd, like T.S. Eliot's vision of Marie Lloyd; and these associations are ingenuous or disingenuous as you prefer. This is part of the "Commonplace hegemonies" (*BH* 719) of which Hill writes: a hegemony which takes the form of the commonplace.

Pound's prescription, taken from this certain Agricola, recalls William Morris in his lecture at University College, Oxford, in 1883,

'Art Under Plutocracy': the "highest intellectual art" of days gone by would "please the eye … excite the emotions and train the intellect", not to mention that it "appealed to all men [sic]".⁵⁴ As Hill asserts, Pound "derived his ethical aesthetics from Ruskin" (*CCW* 466), but it seems that William Morris may lurk somewhere in the shadows too. Or, at least, Pound, Morris, and Agricola are repeating an ancient commonplace. It is a telling revelation of cultural-historical perspective that Hill's position is often taken to be elitist, while William Morris, author also of 'Socialism and Anarchism', clearly did not see himself in such a way. The supervention of Pound between the age of Ruskin and Morris and that of Hill has, at least in terms of literary politics, coloured the issue; more broadly, it was the Second World War and its huge socio-cultural aftermaths which has altered the political landscape so profoundly. Hill himself has realised this:

> *Cursed be he that removeth his neighbour's mark*:
> Mosaic statute, to which Ruskin was steadfast.
> (If Pound had stood so, he would not have faltered.)   (*BH* 284)

"Faltered" seems a generous word to afford Pound in this context, and it suggests a sympathy, an empathy, even. As Pound himself declared, "You cannot call a man an artist until he shows himself capable of reticence and of restraint, until he shows himself in some degree master of the forces which beat upon him" (*CCW* 171); but he did not recognise, or at least he did not meaningfully acknowledge, until it was too late, that such forces exist within as well as outside of the self. Pound arrogated to himself and the figure of the poet too much authority, too much mastery of force. In the term of Coleridge's greatly favoured by Hill, there was not enough of a "drama of reason" in Pound (*CCW* 94). He did not get within his judgements the conditions of his judgements.

Notes

1 Hill, 'How Ill White Hairs Become a Fool and Jester'.
2 Rush, interview with Geoffrey Hill.
3 William Blake, *The Complete Poems*, W.H. Stevenson ed., 3rd edition (Pearson: Edinburgh, 2007) p. 116.
4 Hill, 'Poetry and "the Democracy of the Dead"'.

5   Geoffrey Hill, 'Mightier and Darker', *Times Literary Supplement*, 23 March 2016.
6   Hill, 'Thoughts of a Conservative Modernist'.
7   Eliot, 'Introduction', *The Sacred Wood*, p. xvi.
8   Geoffrey Hill, 'Touching Pitch', BC MS 20c, Hill/4/15, p. 4, Brotherton Library, University of Leeds.
9   Adam Kirsch, *The Modern Element: Essays on Contemporary Poetry* (Norton: New York, 2008) p. 17.
10 Hill, 'Address of Thanks to the Sponsors and Jury of the Truman Capote Award for Literary Criticism in Memory of Newton Arvin', pp. 187–188.
11 Pound, 'How to Read', *Literary Essays of Ezra Pound*, p. 25.
12 Empson, *Seven Types of Ambiguity*, p. 25. As quoted in chapter 2.
13 Carmine Starnino, 'The Plight of the Poet-Critic', *Poetry Magazine*, May 2008.
14 Quoted in Bryant, 'Making Peace with Disorder', p. 154.
15 Michel Foucault, *Power / Knowledge: Selected Interviews and Other Writings*, Colin Gordon ed., Colin Gordon, Leo Marshall, John Mepham, and Kate Soper trans. (Harvester: Sussex, 1980) p. 133.
16 John Keats, *The Letters of John Keats, 1814–1821*, Vol. 1, Hyder Edward Rollins ed. (Harvard University Press: Cambridge, MA, 1958) p. 387.
17 Robert Potts, 'The Praise Singer', *Guardian*, 10 August 2002.
18 Morris, *Political Writings of William Morris*, p. 101. "At present all education is directed towards the end of fitting people to take their places in a hierarchy of commerce." 'Labour' under late capitalist conditions being useless, enforcing the "hierarchy of commerce", it is procrastination merely.
19 Graves and Riding, *A Survey of Modernist Poetry*, pp. 74–75.
20 The recent description of the poet William Letford in a review as a "roofer-poet" is a case in point. The reviewer presumably scores points among the like-minded for making excited noises about Letford's working-class origins; yet one does not see another poet described as, say, a 'professor-poet', or another as a 'broadcaster-poet'.
21 Graves and Riding, *A Survey of Modernist Poetry*, p. 78.
22 Hill, 'The Art of Poetry: 80'.
23 Rush, interview with Geoffrey Hill.
24 Hill, 'How Ill White Hairs Become a Fool and Jester'.
25 Hill, 'Address of Thanks to the Sponsors and Jury of the Truman Capote Award for Literary Criticism in Memory of Newton Arvin (2009)', pp. 188–189.

26 "In the judging of works of art the reader's, spectator's, auditor's 'mood' is at best irrelevant, at worst a gross intrusion. The greatest tribute one can pay to a fine work of art – a tribute that one ought to be able to take for granted – is that its qualities reveal one's own 'mood' to be redundant." Geoffrey Hill, 'Isaac Rosenberg, 1890–1918' (*CCW* 463).
27 Hill, 'Poetry, Policing, and Public Order (1)'.
28 Eliot, *The Sacred Wood*, p. 11.
29 Ibid., p. 14.
30 George Steiner, 'On Difficulty', *On Difficulty and Other Essays* (Oxford University Press: New York and Melbourne, 1978) p. 18.
31 Ibid., p. 18.
32 Hill, 'A Deep Dynastic Wound'.
33 Steiner, 'On Difficulty', p. 42.
34 Ibid., p. 43.
35 Hill, 'What You Look Hard at Seems to Look Hard at You'.
36 Hill, 'The Art of Poetry: 80'.
37 Ibid., p. 42.
38 Ibid., p. 41.
39 Marcel, 'On the Ontological Mystery', *The Philosophy of Existentialism*, p. 19.
40 Eliot, *Selected Prose of T.S. Eliot*, p. 50.
41 Hill, 'Poetry, Policing, and Public Order (1)'.
42 Eliot, *The Use of Poetry and the Use of Criticism*, pp. 31–32.
43 Eliot, 'Marie Lloyd', *Selected Prose of T.S. Eliot*, p. 172.
44 Ibid., p. 172.
45 Ibid., p. 173.
46 Hill, 'Poetry, Policing, and Public Order (1)'.
47 Heidegger, *Being and Time*, p. 212.
48 Hill, 'Poetry, Policing, and Public Order (1)'.
49 Noam Chomsky, *Who Rules the World? Reframings* (Penguin: London, 2016) pp. 20–21.
50 Ibid., p. 20.
51 However, see the arguments in chapter 6 on elegy and the elegiac in Hill.
52 Hill, 'Poetry, Policing, and Public Order (1)'.
53 Pound, *ABC of Reading*, p. 66.
54 William Morris, *The Collected Works of William Morris: With Introductions by His Daughter May Morris*, Vol. 23 (Longmans Green: London, 1915) p. 166.

Chapter 6

'A calling for England': Hill and the political imagination

> The theory and practice of poetry is part of the civil constitution.
> (Hill, 'Poetry, Policing, and Public Order (1)')

> Does poetic order correspond in any detailed way to social order?
> (Christopher Ricks, quoted in '"Legal Fiction" and Legal Fiction')

The body politic and its health

The subtitle of the current chapter is taken from 'To the Lord Protector Cromwell' in *A Treatise of Civil Power*:

> 9
> I had a calling for England: that silver piece
> 10
> I would pierce and hang at my neck, any day.   (*BH* 574)

This chapter will consider how Hill's "calling for England" – a calling which for many millions in the twentieth century entailed, rather, England calling for and upon them – is related to notions of value, memory, and civil power, symbolised here by the silver coin. That "silver piece" is a coin of the realm: 'piece' being an archaic word for a coin, as in 'pieces of eight', but which can also denote an artefact. It is a word which concentrates a crucial tension in the context of civil power and nationhood, an area of concern in which Hill engages strenuously with the writings of John Ruskin.

Coins and precious metals are a recurrent image in Hill's work, beginning in *Mercian Hymns* (1971) – the sequence in which Hill begins to engage explicitly with Ruskin – with the "gold solidus" (*BH* 86), the "Coins handsome as Nero's" (*BH* 93), and the biplane with Ceolred loses, accidentally or on purpose, through the classroom-floorboards, "two inches of heavy snub silver" (*BH* 89). And indeed there is a Ruskinian provenance for this imagery: in *Mercian Hymns* we find the poet "Brooding on the eightieth letter of *Fors Clavigera*" (*BH* 107), and in Poem XI: "Exemplary metal, ripe for commerce. Value from a sparse people, scrapers of salt-pans and byres" (*BH* 93). 'Exemplary' can refer to a type of damages in law, 'exemplary damages', and as such the word, deep within itself, partakes of idioms of exchange and extortion as well as suggesting its intrinsic value, its worked quality. It is this dual nature of the exemplary which exercises Hill's imagination, and the idea of common value: what strikes the attention in this latter extract from *Mercian Hymns* is that value derives *from* the "sparse people", it is not bestowed upon them; their metal is exemplary rather than precious: it is "ripe for commerce".

The tension between these two states, exemplified in Hill more fundamentally in his concern with the tension between active and passive, animates Hill's sense of politics and nationhood, commonwealth and value. Hill's "Exemplary metal" is the first cousin of Ruskin's "national store of continually augmenting wealth" in *Fors Clavigera*.[1] 'Augmenting', in Ruskin's phrase, creates an operative ambiguity between active and passive: the wealth is augmenting by becoming ever larger, and in the sense of inexhaustibly enriching the recipient. The relationship of the individual to the "national store" in Ruskin's phrase is enriching both to that store and to the individual: in this sense, the national and the individual are mutually enriching forces. Ruskin's use of 'augmenting' here as an enactment of the essence of his political vision is indeed exemplary, what Hill calls, in the essay on Hopkins in *Alienated Majesty*, the "uniting of individual genius to the genius of the commonwealth" (*CCW* 531). And elsewhere in Letter 58 of *Fors Clavigera*, Ruskin provides further matter for this context; in his vision of a new society, he asserts that "The metallic currency will be of absolutely pure gold and silver, and of those metals only".[2] Such a vision of society radically re-establishes the relationship between intrinsic and exchange values, and as such the nature of value itself: "*Valor*, from *valere*, to be well or strong (ὑγιαίνω); strong, *in* life (if a man), or valiant; strong, *for* life (if a thing), or valuable. To be 'valuable', therefore, is to 'avail towards life'."[3] Ruskin's sense of value, then, is akin to Hill's of the "energy of intelligence",[4] and to Coleridge's in *On the Constitution of Church and State* of the "*nisis formativus* [shaping power] of the body politic".[5] There is a distinctly nineteenth-century cast to Hill's thought on nationhood, and the places of literature and the public intellectual within it, though such figures as Coleridge and Ruskin are themselves partaking of a much older tradition of political thought, which E.H. Kantorowicz attests in *The King's Two Bodies* (a work cited in Hill's unpublished 'Between Politics and Eternity') as having "pervaded political thought in the later Middle Ages."[6] (Kantorowicz's description of the King's *corpus mysticum* as a "mystic fiction"[7] would have appealed also to Hill's sense of "metaphysical fantasy".)

In the speech to accept the Truman Capote Award in 2009, Hill spoke on the subject of coins of the realm:

> Though not a true numismatist, I take pleasure in coins. One is instructed not to handle them with ungloved fingers, for fear of rubbing off the "luster" or "bloom." Even so, I confess to enjoying them as objects. I would even carry one or two on long-haul flights (when I took these; I am no longer able to) where others might carry a lucky pebble as tactile comforters.[8]

Hill then goes on to describe himself as an "intrinsic value person", entering the caveat that "An objection can be made that writers whom I revere and who proclaim intrinsic value – Ruskin and others – are in fact pursuing a phantom".[9] Hill entertains the notion, however reluctantly, that intrinsic value itself may be little more than such a comforter, intangible rather than tactile, more bluster than lustre, even; and this issues elsewhere in a critique of Ruskin which registers the reluctance of Hill's scepticism:

> Until recently I was essentially an adherent of "intrinsic value" as delineated by Ruskin. I am now much less sure of my position, partly because I am no longer confident that I can discern the point

at which Ruskin himself crosses an indeterminate line between, on the one hand, regarding money as "an expression of right" or entitlement, or as a sign of relations, and, on the other hand, using a monetary trope in which "intrinsic value" is by sleight of will substituted as the vital referent.   ('Poetry and Value', *CCW* 485/486)

It is precisely the "indeterminate line" which determines the energy and strenuosity of Hill's later poetry and criticism, and the ignoring of it, as in his critique of modernism, and here in Ruskin, is the source of certain of Hill's later antagonisms. Elsewhere, Hill writes that T.S. Eliot, in a particular word-usage, is keeping "precisely on a fine line between praiseworthy dexterity and specious contrivance. The art and practice of poetry", he adds, "keeps also to this fine line" (*CCW* 545). The poem's 'fine lines' are tightropes.

Coins and precious metals are often associated with childhood in Hill's work, and therefore with the nostalgia for childhood – and nostalgia itself, that most powerful and potentially pernicious of political emotions. In 'On Reading *Milton and the English Revolution*' in *A Treatise of Civil Power*, an old coin is associated with the ideal society:

God himself is our Zion *where all creatures
are fellow citizens*: the ox with the butterfly,
the butchers in meaty aprons, Aaron's jewels,
a Commonwealth shilling from an oddments box.   (*BH* 562)

In Hill's later work, coins in particular, then, stand for political nostalgia of certain kinds, for thinking which crosses, ignores, or cannot see the "indeterminate line" of ethics. The coin is both an object, beautiful in itself, and "a sign of relations": and as such it is a ready analogy for language, and for the poem.

Hill touches on the "indeterminate line" between these two states of being when he writes in *Liber Illustrium Virorum*, "Corporatist-popul- | ist Gresham's Law degrades People" (*BH* 738). Gresham's Law is a principle of economics that states that 'bad money drives out good': that is, people will keep coins of high intrinsic value and spend ones of a low intrinsic value. In other words, if there is a solid silver coin and a steel coin which have the same face value in an economy, then people will hoard the silver coins and spend the steel ones. Translated into cultural-political terms, Gresham's Law is another symbol of the postmodern cultural malaise of dumbing down, then, as a state of contempt for the intelligence and predispositions of people at large; as Hill puts it in 'Isaac Rosenberg, 1890–1918':

> The true common reader is a natural aristocrat of the spirit, and is far more necessary, far more valuable, to a culture such as ours than are the majority of its writers. (*CCW* 459)

Intrinsic value is anti-postmodern, jarring with any sort of Foucauldian 'regimes of truth' relativism, implying universal and a-historical standards of judgement, or at the very least a-historical standards within a given culture. In the context of literature, intrinsic value is meaningful, but that meaning is difficult to weigh precisely, and requires the most sensitive scales available: those of the Wittgensteinian connoisseur, perhaps. This may indicate the nature of literature itself, according to the pragmatic point of view (of the later Eliot, for instance), and this is a view that Hill himself rehearses, at the close of *The Triumph of Love*, though in true Bradleian fashion encompassing both belief and scepticism:

> So – Croker, MacSikker, O'Shem – I ask you:
> what are poems for? They are to console us
> with their own gift, which is like perfect pitch.
> Let us commit that to our dust. What
> ought a poem to be? Answer, *a sad*
> *and angry consolation*. What is
> the poem? What figures? Say,
> *a sad and angry consolation*. That's
> beautiful. Once more? *A sad and angry*
> *consolation*. (*BH* 286)

The "gift" of poems is their consolation, which is *like* perfect pitch. Perfection is a state outside the world, as indeed intrinsic value may be. The consolation may be sad and angry, then, because the recipient of this gift is aware that it is a consolation prize only, and not the 'real' thing, whatever that would look like. "Publike Dysrasy" is one of Hill's borrowed terms for the plundering of such "gifts" (*BH* 874).

The figure who most insists himself here is W.B. Yeats, who was involved with designing the coinage for the Irish Free State in the 1920s, as alluded to in Poem 35 of *Al Tempo de' Tremuoti*:

> Ireland as Paddy Pearse conceived of it,
> And Yeats projected into that nobler coinage,
> A dream thrust spinning into our own age
> Fanatical and ignorant of profit.   (*BH* 902)

A coinage "ignorant of profit" is the Ruskinian symbol for the perfected society, or Hill's sense of the "gift, which is like perfect pitch", though the epithet "Fanatical and ignorant" does not seem to confer honour on the romantic nationalism of Eamonn De Valera and Patrick Pearse and even Eoin O' Duffy, the fascist, for whom Yeats wrote marching songs. Such romantic nationalism has exercised Hill before, most notably in the long poem *The Mystery of the Charity of Charles Péguy*, first published in 1983. This mode attracted substantial opprobrium a few years before even that, with the sonnet sequence 'An Apology for the Revival of Christian Architecture in England',[10] whose title is taken from a tract by Augustus Charles Pugin, the neo-gothic architect and designer of the Houses of Parliament. Such romanticism, or sentimentalism, you might say, at the heart of nationalism or patriotism is what Hill explores in *The Mystery* and 'An Apology': again, it is the necessity and nature of the fantasy in which he is invested, as well as the exemplary failure. In the later work, Hill explores the fantastical qualities of romantic nationalism perhaps most persistently in *Oraclau | Oracles*, and perhaps most acutely in the series of poems titled 'Hiraeth' within that book, *hiraeth* a Welsh word meaning nostalgia, particularly for Wales. A nostalgia for a foreign nation is analogous to an unattainable love, most poignantly from one's own past, as it is analogous to "the heretic's dream of salvation":

> Great shame
> I cannot speak or sing
> This language of my late awakening
> Nor ask your pardon, Beloved, nor bring

> You, my bride, into the feasting house
> Of first desire, dazed by your wedding dress. (*BH* 780)

Intimations of nostalgia and longing in Hill's later work are characteristically accompanied by knowledge of their impossibility, even by "Great shame". Wales is over the horizon from Hill's kingdom of Mercia, and it is this 'over-the-horizon' quality which is 'erotic' in the Bradleian sense.

In the lecture 'Poetry, Policing and Public Order (1)', Hill declares that "[t]he theory and practice of poetry is part of the civil constitution".[11] Hill values writers who have a strong sense of this civil constitution (and who also take this truth to be self-evident); and it is the idea of polity as constitution, in fact, which recurs in the kinds of quotations Hill picks out to illustrate his sense of this, and which bespeak a certain political tradition which, again, is largely a thing of the past, in official culture at least. To qualify this slightly: many of the writers Hill values evince some sense of civil constitution in terms of the body politic, and the absence of this metaphor from contemporary discourse is a notable absence – though a comprehensible one in an era of mass migrations and globalisation, in which borders and margins are perceived as more permeable and abstract (though Brexit and the rise of right-wing populism suggest a dissatisfaction with suchlike official culture). Hill likes writers who perceive the constitution in the double sense of 'civil polity' and 'body', captured in the image of the 'body politic'. This kind of 'constituted' vision of society has been traditionally expressed as a human body or as a tree; or both, as with Coleridge, who refers in this context to "the circulating sap of life" and "the *nisis formativus* [shaping power] of the body politic".[12] "Life, for instance – the vital *functions* are the result of the organisation; but this organization supposes and presupposes the vital *principle*",[13] observes Coleridge elsewhere in the same text, recalling the description of organic form taken from Schlegel, quoted by James Benziger.[14] In Hill's emphasis on energy – with this imagery of the vortex in '"Legal Fiction" and Legal Fiction', for instance – he may well be influenced by such nineteenth-century conceptions of the role of art and letters in the nation as "vital *principle*".

These nineteenth-century corporatist metaphors form a late addition to a long tradition of the body politic in political thought; the converse to such descriptions and prescriptions of wealth as those from Coleridge are metaphors of 'illth', in Ruskin's terms, or national sickness. In his acceptance speech for the Truman Capote Award in 2008 (a speech which I take to be an autobiographical summation of what is implied throughout his later work) Hill remarked:

> "Publike dyskrasy" is a term I found recently in the writings of Bishop Jeremy Taylor (1613–1667). In terms of civic observation it can be ranked with Ruskin's "illth", the "anarchical plutocracy" of William Morris, and the "Banker's Olympus" of Henry Adams (and later P. Wyndham Lewis).[15]

"Dyscrasy Publike its own gifts to plunder" (*BH* 874), as *Odi Barbare* XL has it. It is the nation's draining of its own vital energies. Put in terms of a general human malaise, perhaps akin to the "infected will" of Philip Sidney, it is also positioned by Hill in more specific historical terms, anachronistically, even, just as the title of Milton's pamphlet *A Treatise of Civil Power in Ecclesiastical Causes* is appropriated for *A Treatise of Civil Power*.

The tree is similarly an image of natural, organic proportion, as in the emblem of the British Conservative Party. However, "Grand baobab commonwealth | Proliferates by open stealth" in Poem XLV of *Liber Illustrium Virorum* (dedicated to Tony Harrison): also known as the upside-down tree, this is an image of 'the world turned upside-down', as the title of a pamphlet of the English Civil War had it, itself taking its title from various places in the Bible.[16] It is a corruption of the natural exemplified also in that it embodies "virtù that from virtus strikes" (*BH* 729), pointing out that the Machiavellian *virtù* originates from the Latin *virtus* (courage, power, worth). In the three poems to Tony Harrison of *Liber Illustrium Virorum*, Hill uses the Nigerian Civil War of 1967 as another example of 'the world turned upside down'. (The war is alluded to also in *Speech! Speech!*, poems 49 and 87, and *Odi Barbare*, poem XXIV.) The natural, organic society is haunted by the spectre of hegemony, the "virtù that from virtus strikes", as in poem XXIX of *The Triumph of Love*, in which the tree which symbolises the State's organic unity, "our politic | transcendent shade", also exhibits the victims of its violence, "hanging amid the branches ... like traitors like martyrs" (*BH* 248). Proportion is ever menaced by disproportion; or perhaps proportion and disproportion, grandeur and enormity, are essentially implicated.

> It's a wild question whether we had or have
> A nation disproportionately imagined
> Like Pakistan today, its founder margined,
> Or Gandhi's India which could never thrive.　(*BH* 902)

A body is in proportion; India and Pakistan are not so much figured here as disfigured, disproportionate. Proportion can signify the organic unity of Leibniz and Coleridge, but it can also signify hierarchy in the more typical sense, as in the Servant's speech in Shakespeare's *Richard II*, Act 3 Scene 4:

> Why should we in the compass of a pale
> Keep law and form and due proportion,
> Showing as in a model our firm estate,
> When our sea-walled garden, the whole land,
> Is full of weeds, her fairest flowers chok'd up,
> Her fruit-trees all unpruned, her hedges ruin'd,
> Her knots disordered, and her wholesome herbs
> Swarming with caterpillars?[17]

Contrary to Coleridgean notions of organic unity, the organic here is symbolic of the state's disunity and disequilibrium – though delivered, one can scarcely fail to observe, in poetic speech which is exemplary of "law and form and due proportion", but animated, driven, by what one might call the "vital principle" of the creative imagination. The state here, politics in general, has failed the artist.

One might see organic conceptions of society as being pertinent in considering this question, as with Coleridge in *On the Constitution of Church and State*:

> A constitution is the attribute of a state, *i.e.* of a body politic, having the principle of its unity within itself, whether by concentration of its forces, as a constitutional pure Monarchy ... or – with which we are alone concerned – by equipoise and interdependency: the *lex equilibria*.[18]

The language Coleridge uses here certainly evokes his organic theories of poetic composition; the "principle of its unity within itself" recalls New Critical conceptions of the poem as objective and self-containing artefact, even Proposition 18 of Leibniz's *Monadology*: "All simple substances or created Monads might be called Entelechies, for they have in them a certain perfection … they have a certain self-sufficiency (*autarkeia*) which makes them the sources of their internal activities and, so to speak, incorporeal automata."[19] (And it is this metaphysics to which Eliot was alluding when he described the poem's "entelechy".[20]) So, to follow Coleridge's logic, a poem is a body politic in microcosm, you might say; and, so, the State is a macrocosmic poem. Perhaps in a general way this is what Hill is onto when he refers to "a poem of State" in *Liber Illustrium Virorum* (*BH* 731), or "Our epic work – | Cadenced nation" (*BH* 793) in *Clavics*, or any number of other examples. In these locutions, however, it is not clear whether the State is like the poem or vice versa, I think deliberately so. An affinity is assumed between the two entities which is either an "intelligible mystery" or is taken to be self-evident. Simone Weil is quoted in 'A Postscript on Modernist Poetics' to this end, too:

> A poet in the arrangement of words and the choice of each word, must simultaneously bear in mind matters on at least five or six different planes of composition … Politics, in their turn, form an art governed by composition on a multiple plane. (*CCW* 573)

However, in *Clavics*, equilibrium is ambivalently desired, as it is by Coleridge for the state: "Music and polity | Agree dissent" (*BH* 809); "Music enriches state | Of art mayhem" (*BH* 801). These semantic compactions suggest a simultaneously conservative and anarchic character to art, registering also the desire for equilibrium and tragic knowledge of the tyranny of its imposition, on the poem as on the State. Coleridge points out the dual connotation of power as *potentia*, as both potency and potential, in the state: as John Barrell writes in his introduction to *On the Constitution of Church and State*, "The notion of 'potential power' has seemed to some critics to reveal a tendency in Coleridge's thought towards anarchy, which disturbs them". Coleridge's organicism, and Hill's use of 'anarchy' in political contexts differently from in aesthetic or psychological contexts, suggests precisely the difficulty – or the unjustifiable tendentiousness – of transposing aesthetics and politics directly. However, it is the twin connotation of both 'power' and 'potential' which exercises Hill, as it exercised Coleridge, it seems, for all his avowals of the organic unity of the state (an arch-conservative position). 'Potential' equates to 'intrinsic value', that power forever latent for which Hill sees Hobbes's *Leviathan* as being an elegy. It is this elusive, perhaps phantasmal, quality to which the "hierarchist" aspires; it is a quality in the crucial sense that it cannot be quantified, and thereby subsumed into the hegemonic workings of "plutocratic anarchy".

While Hill engages with the discourse of the body politic both overtly and tacitly, this engagement is tempered by a sense of outrage at the sort of pre-Great War attitude which might with Ruskin advertise "the beneficialness of the inequality".[21] There is at times a distaste for Ruskin, but also Francis Bacon in one notable instance:

> The poor are bunglers: my people, whom I
> nonetheless honour, who bought no landmark
> other than their graves. I wish I could keep
> Baconian counsel, wish I could keep resentment
> out of my voice. (*BH* 596)

Here elegy is not employed in the service of a conservative ideal of the primacy of the past per se, but in a testimony to the brutality and injustice of such political ideas as the body politic. Similarly, the poem as an object, Yeats's closed box, as a metaphor for the perfectly proportioned state, is in Hill's later view akin to the passage spoken by the 'Man' in Act 3 Scene 4 of *Richard II*. Hill's engagement with these ideas shows his historicist bent, another instance of him struggling within and against a current of discourse which flows throughout British literature and letters; his engagement with the body politic is engagement with a major trope of British and European intellectual and literary history. "Our contemporary demand for relevance (making the past relevant to us) is in need of redirection (making us relevant to the past)",[22] observes Hill in 'Between Politics and Eternity'. His engagement with Taylor, Shakespeare, Coleridge, and Ruskin in the context of the body politic is an instance of this historicist attitude – though that is not necessarily to say that Hill rejects it entirely. The repeated appearances of Coriolanus in *Liber Illustrium Virorum* suggest an animating, agitating fascination with the body politic – along with Hobbes's *Leviathan* in the later essays – and its implications of authority and class hierarchy; though Coriolanus, the body politic, and the nostalgia of the 'Hiraeth' poems in *Oraclau | Oracles* stand for that fundamental principle of Hill's later work: metaphysical desire, a force both vital and distorting.

To extend the arguments on Coleridge, Hill, and the politics of the poem further, I wish to compare some remarks of Coleridge's with some unpublished ones of Hill's on Dante. These remarks shed light on Hill's motives in his later work, motives which distinguish this later work from what has gone before. In *Shakespeare, Ben Jonson, Beaumont and Fletcher*, Coleridge writes:

> In short, in Sophocles, the constitution of tragedy is monarchical … all the parts adapting and submitting themselves to the majesty of the heroic sceptre:- in Aristophanes, comedy, on the contrary, is poetry in its most democratic form, and it is a fundamental principle with it, rather to risk all the confusion of anarchy, than to destroy the independence and privilege of its individual constituents,- place, verse, characters, even single thoughts, conceits, and allusions, each turning on the pivot of its own free will.[23]

The language of politics, from the passage in *On the Constitution of Church and State*, is here modulated into a discussion of literature, without any need on Coleridge's part to justify, in either passage, the commonality of terms. 'Constitution' and 'monarchy' are transposable between the two contexts, without comment required from Coleridge. Hill's later poetry is broadly Aristophanean, then, by Coleridge's argument, whose description of "single thoughts, conceits, and allusions, each turning on the pivot of its own free will", sounds rather like Hill's description of a "a small intense radiance of apprehension, a miniature vortex of intuition", not to mention the obsession with will in *The Daybooks*.[24] If the central struggle of Hill's earlier mode is characterised by the attraction towards and repulsion from the notion of the dominating intelligence to which the poem is subject – as per Coleridge's remarks on the "monarchical" nature of tragedy – then his later mode is characterised by the "democratic" impulse, to the verge of "the confusion of anarchy", particularly in such books as *Speech! Speech!* and *Ludo*: a deep involvement with what he calls in one Oxford Professor of Poetry lecture the "entropy" of poetry.[25] In Coleridge's terms then, Hill's later work is characterised by its self-consciously working away from the tragic and towards the democratic, even the anarchic – in a qualified sense.

In *1599: A Year in the Life of William Shakespeare*, James Shapiro observed that:

> The meaning of the word "popularity", familiar to us today in the sense of "being admired by many", has undergone a sea-change since Shakespeare's day. In the mid-sixteenth century it was used to describe a radical form of democracy that was the opposite of tyranny. Then, in the late 1590s, a new sense of the word emerged, having to do with creating popular favour.[26]

It is interesting to think of Hill as exploring the fault-line between these two senses of 'popularity' in his later work, as a reaction to the culture of commodity in which his work takes, or does not take, its place: how the term 'elitism' itself is a courting of popular favour by hegemonic powers. As Hill puts it brilliantly, memorably, in a self-reflexive stanza in *Odi Barbare*:

> We will wing it, working through all the forms now,
> Shedding excellencies like moulting angels:
> *Nitro Glisserinski* the anarchist with
>   Nitra his daughter.   (*BH* 871)

To wing it is not just to cobble something second-rate together (though cobblers might object to that verb), it is something more akin to Keats's "viewless wings of Poesy";[27] it is to commune with something more vital altogether – what Hill called at least once the "Angel of Poetry", a sublime being quoted in truly recusant vein: "Sod off!"[28] This stanza exemplifies also Hill's two-mindedness about the anarchic, as the "anarchic and libidinous" (*BH* 610) which energises his later work, and also the "plutocratic anarchy" derived from William Morris. Nitro Glisserinski, the punningly named cipher of wanton destruction, is glimpsed here 'behind closed doors', in a tender moment, with his daughter.

There is an obsessive returning to the will, its freedoms and constraints, in the later poetry, most notably in the two collections that begin and end *The Daybooks*, *Ludo*, and *Al Tempo de' Tremuoti*. There is a turning also on the notion of anarchy, and its two connotations: the connotation most prevalent in English public discourse, that of Milton's "waste | Wide anarchy of chaos",[29] but also in the more modern political sense of an anti-hegemonic commitment to creative (or recreative) energy. Both of these senses obtain in Hill's later work, indicating the very political ambivalence which is present in Coleridge's criticism. Coleridge, like Hill, is a kind of conservative radical, committed to history and tradition and outraged by its depredations. In 'Poetry and Disproportion', Hill remarks, "[t]hose who detect in me a radical profession cannot be sure whether the radicalism implies tearing up by the roots or rediscovering the roots and carefully nurturing them. I should say that it is my narcissist belief that my critical and philosophical approach works according to both methods. I've described myself in another place as a Ruskinian Tory, adding that it is only a Ruskinian Tory these days who can be mistaken for an old-fashioned Marxist".[30] Of course, Ruskin has much more of a traditional English sense of the 'body politic', with his espousal of "the beneficialness of the inequality"[31] in the well-ordered society, than does Marx or any "old-fashioned Marxist".

In Hill's later work there is a Coleridgean assumption of the consonance between the imaginative and the political, addressed quite explicitly in an unpublished essay, 'Between Politics and Eternity', concerning Dante. Hill is more interested in *De Monarchia* than *The Divine Comedy*, and again by the Marxist Antonio Gramsci's writings on Dante's great poem than the poem itself. In this essay, Hill writes:

> I can draw no distinction between the mode in which Dante's intelligence realizes itself in the *Inferno* and the mode in which it attends to its business in the *Monarchia*. In such concinnity can be found the essential paradigm for writers of our epoch.[32]

To this example one might wish to add that of Coleridge, certainly, at least, in the similarity between his writings on church and state and those on tragedy and comedy. Hill recognises that, like Coleridge, Dante takes the "concinnity" between wordcraft and statecraft for granted. It is the bypassing of an aestheticised politics, like those of "Yeats, Pound, Eliot, McDiarmid"[33] which is exemplary in Dante (and Coleridge). It is not necessary for Dante to distort the picture to accommodate politics to aesthetics or vice versa, since the relationship between them seems self-evident. As Hill has stated, "The theory and practice of poetry is part of the civil constitution";[34] and elsewhere, "poetry written in our nation possessed and possesses a political dimension ... simply by existing".[35] Essentially, Hill is advocating for writers of the current epoch the indiscrimination between literature and politics displayed by Dante. The creative intelligence and the moral intelligence are one and the same, and the separation of them is due to a distorting cultural politics, perhaps the 'dissociation of sensibility' of our own era. In the introduction to *Leviathan*, Thomas Hobbes makes his contribution to this discourse of artistic and political "concinnity":

> For what is the "heart," but a "spring"; and the "nerves", but so many "strings"; and the "joints", but so many "wheels", giving motion to the whole body, such as was intended by the artificer? "Art" goes yet further, imitating that rationall and most excellent work of nature, "man". For by art is created that great "leviathan" called a "Commonwealth", or "State", in Latin *Civitas*, which is but an artificial man; though of greater stature and strength than the natural.[36]

Hobbes's introduction to *Leviathan* constitutes an early instance of what has been called the 'political imaginary': that is, the recognition in recent sociology and cultural theory of the fundamental role which the imagination plays in the creation of culture and society: the role of creative power in creating power. The prevailing image or metaphor of *Leviathan*, that of the bodily (Corporatist) State, seems to undermine this rhetoric of self-creation; or rather Hobbes in his introduction negotiates a place somewhere between radicalism and conservatism, as we would term them nowadays, or between creator and created – a position which the writer of poetry occupies also, however consciously.

Hill's later position is that the minute differentiations of language, evident in poetry of value, are themselves integral to the writer's own beliefs, prejudices, and opinions. "How did I so incline to this subject?

| Because aesthetics are an inclined plane", he writes in *Clavics* 33 (*BH* 823). In other words, aesthetics are all about inclination. The image of the inclined plane here seems to contradict Coleridge's proto-New Critical notion of the *lex equibilibria*, even as it seems to grate against Hill's own view of "equity":

> Poetics must here [as defined by Simone Weil as "composition on several planes at once", the same as politics] be understood as equivalent to Equity in Roman law: "*lex eterna, equity, and conscience*", mitigating the rigours of Common Law.[37]

As Hill writes in an unpublished piece entitled 'Touching Pitch', 'pitch' includes the writer's position: "pitch is to be understood, not as accidental to position but integral with it."[38] In other words, a New Critical sense of the poem as object, and of intrinsic value which to some extent implies such a position, does not exclude the writer's self, his or her inclinations and prejudices. Moreover, language is 'pitched' in a duality of senses: in Hill's sense of the connotations of words, and in the sense that it is pitched at, against, or into the "prejudicate opinions"[39] of the author herself and of society at large. Against a Thomist or even Modernist conception of the achieved artwork, Hill comes to believe in belief itself as inherent in the 'completed' artefact, and indeed questions as early as 'Poetry as "Menace" and "Atonement"' whether a literary work can ever be considered 'complete' (*CCW* 3). This perception is central to Hill's later work, and his writing through and beyond modernist conceptions of the poem as object: an overriding perception which Hill recalls in a flash at the end of that section of *Clavics*: "I would object | Mildly to seeing the object again." Hill's sense of objection (along with, perhaps, the mildness of "late wisdom") has supplanted his New Critically-influenced sense of the poetic object. Here is the underlying sense of Coleridgean *potentia*. The poem exists "Between dissatisfaction and finish" (*C* 16; *BH* 806).

Memory and civil power

> I am saying (simply)
> what is to become of memory? (*ToL* CXXXVIII)

Geoffrey Hill grew up in a society for which memory, its expressions and repressions, had the power of neurosis. Born between the wars, he was part of a generation which felt the impetus of the war-experience, its horrors and survivals, as a moral weight – a weight which his later poetry accuses his contemporary society of having quietly dropped: "Ingratitude | still gets to me, the unfairness | and waste of survival; a nation | with so many memorials but no memory" (*ToL, CCW* 261). Memory is both an act of commemoration and a function of the mind (and imagination), and has both public and private manifestations: in memory we find "a uniting of individual genius to the genius of the commonwealth" (*CCW* 531). In memorising our culture, we memorialise it. In the contemporary attenuation of memory as Hill sees it, which is also an attenuation of intelligence and imagination, there is therefore a betrayal of the dead: the dead of the world wars, the exemplary dead of cultural achievement, and in a broader sense the dead per se – those dead generations which Karl Marx described as weighing like an Alp on the brains of the living.[40] For Hill, as for Marx, the human being is inescapably historical. However, the 'dreams' of late capitalism, or "oligarchical consumerism", cannot accommodate the nightmare of history. If the civic act of commemoration is the "daily acknowledgement | of what is owed the dead" (*CCW* 275), the implication is that contemporary 'dumbing down' (if you believe in it) is of a piece with the decline of civic and historical sensibility; thus, acts of intellectual attention are acts of civil power. If "stridently post-cultural",[41] the postmodern era is 'post-memory'.

Having said that, Hill is conscious of the burdens of memory, in both the Marxian sense and in the sense of the guilt of the war-survivor. He strikes a similar note to Ivor Gurney in this respect, an essay on whom (dating back to 1984) is included in the later volume *Inventions of Value* in *Collected Critical Writings*; and so it is ironic that Gurney's 'To His Love' includes one of the most striking moments in all the English poetry of the First World War which happens to be a memorial to forgetting, as it were, an assertion of the need to forget:

> Cover him, cover him soon!
> And with thick-set

> Masses of memoried flowers –
> Hide that red wet
> Thing I must somehow forget.⁴²

But Gurney's forgetting is itself the neurotic response to an excess of memory, a turning away from the war, which was in its own way an act of civil disobedience. Gurney was writing against a culture, both a political and literary culture, for whom commemoration had become saturated with officialdom and hegemony: the "Masses of memoried flowers" are as much the masses of war-poems as they are holy masses, or patinas of official commemoration covering up the dead. Hill's historical perspective is in a sense a mirror-image of this: his own hegemony has erased memory and the commemorative, as it has erased the holy mass, and as it is erasing, in Hill's view, poetry and value.

As well as being a war poet, Gurney, like Hill, is emphatically a *post*-war poet. Hill's sense of the elegiac, which pervades his cultural politics, emanates from his sense of belonging to a post-war society – a society which has forgotten its wounds much less artfully, deliberately, and ironically than the speaker of Gurney's poem. Hill's sense of the elegiac is bound up also with his sense of the decline of intrinsic value and the post-cultural atmosphere of the postmodern. Hill's first collection, *For the Unfallen*, written during the 1950s, is a book of post-war poetry which itself struggles, in Gurney-like fashion, between remembering and forgetting, a poem such as 'Requiem for the Plantagenet Kings' being a salient example. That poem is not simply an elegy for England's lost past, an abstruse lament for a long-dead royal dynasty; within its elegiac template, as with many poems in *For the Unfallen*, the poem also barely represses the recently-passed trauma of the Second World War: "the sea | Across daubed rock evacuates its dead" (*BH* 15). The word 'evacuates' disrupts the poem's timeless rhetoric, as does 'memoried' in Gurney's poem.

While repression is a major trope in *For the Unfallen* – a repressed trope, you might say – Hill's later mode is, in psychological, formal, and rhetorical terms, driven by the "Urge to unmake | all wrought finalities, become a babbler | in the crowd's face" ('Nachwort', *BH* 601). The poems of *For the Unfallen* are indeed "wrought finalities", or at least the urge for such finality is what drives them, though an instinct that works against this is ever-present in Hill's work to some extent. However, those lines from 'Nachwort' in *A Treatise of Civil Power* stand comparison with some of Gurney's in his post-war poem 'War Books', hinging on the word 'wrought':

> Did they look for a book of wrought art's perfection,
> Who promised no reading, no praise, nor publication?[43]

It is the connection between the "wrought" and the idea of "perfection" in the poem as in the State which exercises Hill in his later work. Remarking on this in the essay on Isaac Rosenberg, Hill states: "Here Gurney indicates 'perfection', not in the sense of a working ideal for true labourers in the craft, but rather as an imposed limitation, set by an artificial consensus of tastes" (*CCW* 459). For Hill, as for Gurney, the impetus of the work away from "wrought art's perfection", modulating towards a "difficult beauty of imperfection" (*CCW* 422), registers his sense of being against the "artificial consensus" of the age, even as the nation's semantics inevitably form part of the poet's 'self'. For Hill as for Gurney, this entails writing both within and against the framework of the art, the language, and the nation.[44] "You owe me, Albion, I should have added | in Gurney's name not mine", Hill writes in *The Orchards of Syon* VIII (*BH* 358); there is a sense of affinity in Hill's later work with Gurney, ignored as a poet and a victim of the State as he was – as were, you might say, all of the soldiers of the First World War, though Gurney's sense of having been failed by his nation, to which he dedicated so much in his life and art, chimes with Hill's own sense of marginalisation and eccentricity.[45] There is a sense of solidarity with another poet of the First World War in this regard too, namely Isaac Rosenberg, as evinced in the closing remarks of Hill's essay on him:

> intelligence, such as we find in Rosenberg, is a quality that "England" has never been over-disposed to acknowledge, for it had never "delighted and inspired generations of readers". (*CCW* 423)

Gurney's and Rosenberg's relationship with 'England' may resemble Hill's own, particularly in terms of cultural hegemony and accepted taste, and especially when Philip Larkin, as representative of these forces, is brought into the picture:

> If I were to ask [Christopher] Ricks how it is that, against all the evidence his own unrivalled critical intelligence could bring to the process, he is pleased to be numbered among Larkin's advocates, I anticipate that he might answer, "Because he speaks to the human condition". (*CCW* 379)

It is fair to say that Hill sees Larkin as a representative, with Wilfred Owen, of the cultural atmosphere against which he is pitched.[46]

In 'Rhetorics of Value and Intrinsic Value', Hill writes:

> My language is in me and is me; even as I, inescapably, am a miniscule part of the general semantics of the nation; and as the nature of the State has involved itself in the nature that is most intimately mine ...
>
> I am left with no other course but to say that the great poem moves us to assent as much by the integrity of its final imperfection as by the amazing grace of its detailed perfection. (*CCW* 477)

Though I have collapsed these two short passages together, they are separated only by a few lines in the text, and are part of the same drift. 'Integrity' here is telling, implying both wholeness and probity. While wholeness, *integritas*, might imply the sort of metaphysical 'perfection' or self-completeness inherent in the distinct object (just as a Thomist *haecceitas* is implied in intrinsic value), the moral integrity of the artist leads her to reject this as a practical ideal in the work of art as in the self, even as she must acknowledge the inescapability of the desire for just such integrity. To transpose this directly to politics might imply a certain anti-utopianism, even a broad conservatism, in accepting as self-evident the imperfectability of the State and of the self; but it might also imply a foregrounding of 'anarchic' energy, or even imply a kind of violence against linguistic, civic, and existential norms.

Such an ambiguity is alluded to by Hill more than once, and is germane to his sense of the jarring internal differences that he sees in such figures as T.H. Green and W.B. Yeats as being crucial to the sense of moral self-argument:

As an Anglo-Catholic conservative I sense that I now have more in common with Gramsci, the Marxist atheist, than I have with Eliot, Charles Williams, or W.H. Auden.[47]

This counterintuitive self-appraisal is in accord with my own reading of Hill's later work. It is not that Hill leaves the likes of Eliot, Williams, and Auden behind entirely, but that there is in a figure like Gramsci much that Hill takes into his later creativity and which chimes with its cultural politics, not least the notion of hegemony, against which Hill pitches his conception of hierarchy. Where Eliot, in particular, is important to Hill's later work in that work's questioning of modernist poetics, Gramsci, for instance, is an exemplary figure within it and for it.

Hill's sympathy for and interest in Gramsci is evident in the unpublished 'Between Politics and Eternity'. In this piece Hill states that "it is Gramsci's 'Il Canto Decimo Dell' "Inferno"' which convinces" him of his affinity to the Italian Marxist.[48] Hill is drawn to moments in Gramsci's text such as the remark that "canto 10 is political in the same way as all of the *Divine Comedy*, but it is not political par excellence",[49] not to mention his insistence throughout on "letter and structure".[50] As well as these factors, it is Hill's sense of belonging to a subaltern group, or being the representative intellectual of a subaltern group, which fuels his sense of memory and the elegiac as a vital form of civil power, as it did for Gramsci. Hill's sense of being 'subaltern' – Gramsci's word, not Hill's – drives his sense of the elegiac and of civil power. In the acceptance speech for the Truman Capote Award in 2008, Hill declared:

> The overriding civic emotion of many of us today must be one of desperate fatalism. It may resemble the emotions of those survivors of Anglo-Saxon civilization during the two or three hundred years subsequent to the Norman Conquest of 1066. Indeed those terrible bankers and brokers who deemed themselves free to take *jus primae noctis* with the savings and livelihoods of ordinary people, in the years prior to 1929 and 2008, greatly resemble in their amoral self-gratification and presumption of entitlement the tribal warlords who followed the Norman conqueror. In my rage and despair, I find myself reciting this potent Victorian mythos, disputable though it must be.[51]

(This sense of "desperate fatalism" has become mainstream in the wake of the Brexit referendum, which Geoffrey Hill outlived by only a week.) Hill's sense of survival in a range of senses underlies his elegiac tendency. It is indeed the Victorian-ness of Hill's "mythos" that is in part the concern of this chapter; John Ruskin and William Morris, in particular, consider the status of art and labour under conditions of economic and hegemonic tyranny. At the end of the previous chapter I began to consider William Morris's view of the continuing isolation of the artist under the conditions of plutocracy. Morris seems to be asserting that 'genius' as we conceive it is a phenomenon arising from this increasing alienation, so that this Romantic conception is in part a recoil against the conditions of industrialisation and economic regulatory oppression:

> Thus then in considering the state of the art among us I have been driven to the conclusion that in its co-operative form it is extinct, and only exists in the conscious efforts of men of genius and talent, who themselves are injured, and thwarted, and deprived of due sympathy by the lack of co-operative art.[52]

The individual artist as injured, thwarted, and deprived of true sympathy is primarily Romantic, a figure with persistent echoes down through the nineteenth and twentieth centuries; but it can be tempting to see Hill as a figure similarly "injured, and thwarted, and deprived of due sympathy", a caricature which Hill has conjured to comic effect in such later works as *The Triumph of Love* and *Speech! Speech!* In fact, Hill's sense of "verbal power" is indeed derived in no small part from his sense of isolation and alienation, as demonstrated in the essay 'Eros in F.H. Bradley and T.S. Eliot', in which he sets out his sense of "verbal power rooted in a kind of rift between self-recognition made public (on the one hand) and public non-acceptance (on the other)" (*CCW* 562). Though one might reasonably argue that Hill has had great success as poet and critic, the objection is that the whole enterprise of literature (and increasingly the humanities in UK universities) is marginalised and belittled. A "co-operative art" would be one in which the artist is not an isolated figure, in which the 'genius' exists at the centre of the society; one in which the commonwealth included the artist and her productions at its heart. There is a distinct suggestion, however, that the very notion of genius, described by Morris and issuing from the Romantic era, is predicated upon the perceived isolation of the artist. Indeed, the very words of Emerson's apothegm – "Genius is power; talent applicability" – suggest their incommensurability, and thus the efficacy of Emerson's opposition for Romantic politics, 'genius' deriving from a Latin word for spirit and 'talent' from a Greek word meaning a measure of silver.

So, is Hill's notion of intrinsic value simply nostalgia for a Morris-like guilded England; is it even "crudely dynastic", as Hill describes Allen Tate's introduction to Robert Lowell's *The Land of Unlikeness*[53] – that is, evocative of a right-wing Conservatism, even a romantic nationalism? On various occasions Hill shows himself alive to the implications of his fascination with the intrinsic, not least in the appraisal of Tate (one of his first poetic and critical exemplars) in the lecture 'A Deep Dynastic Wound'. However, I think Hill shows the essence of his approach in a couple of places: when he says in interview that "Conservatives conserve nothing",[54] he shows himself in favour of conservation but not of modern Conservatism, which is an operative part of the plutocratic anarchy, and where he describes himself a "Ruskinian Tory" in 'Poetry and Disproportion'. As in Hill's use of the word 'radical' and its variations in Hill's later work, there are implications to Hill's poetic politics which range across ideological definitions.

However, there is something inherently elegiac about the intrinsic and intrinsic value. And since elegy is inextricably bound up with value, the elegist mourning the loss of something of enormous value, one of the pitfalls of this genre is that it can shade into a myopic lamenting for a perceived loss of value in the present: that is, praising the past simply because it is not the present. This is nostalgia. Hill, it seems, is alive to this temptation, itself a manifestation of metaphysical desire. "It is easier to say what 'intrinsic' value is in defeat than in victory. Intrinsic value, for the loser, is sealed into enduring qualities of the life that was" (*CCW* 470), he writes in 'Rhetorics of Value and Intrinsic Value'. Hill expands on this in 'Poetry and Value': "The elegiac celebration of 'intrinsic value' understands the value of being in some sense isolated from current degradation, and therefore as being inviolate, held securely within the sphere of the intransitive" (*CCW* 487). Both of these statements suggest the valorisation (as in Ruskin's 'valor') of the past simply because it is not the present. So, then, does espousal of intrinsic value entail simply an attachment to "enduring qualities" for their own sake, or are these endurances and qualities in the nature of the intrinsic? Overall, Hill demonstrates his awareness of the dangers of nostalgia in enough places to convince; and he is convincing, reminding, himself in these moments, though in typical fashion in Hill's late work there is often a Bradleian sense of fundamental ambiguity. Again, in 'Civil Polity and the Confessing State', published only, to date, in *The Warwick Review*:

> Things have been like this before and the beleaguered have always appealed, in like circumstances, to concepts such as "intrinsic value". Intrinsic value is for the defeated.[55]

As I have argued throughout, Hill's later work is powered by an awareness of, indeed a wrestling with, such longing, which exists at the heart of aesthetics, ethics, and politics. The recognition of this longing, which I have been calling in a comprehensive sense metaphysical desire, is an essential ethical revelation, essential to negotiating the "indeterminate line" which Hill argues Ruskin crosses in his consideration of intrinsic value.

In Hill's description of "elegiac celebration" in 'Poetry and Value' (*CCW* 487), there is also a Bradleian ambiguity: it is not immediately clear if intrinsic value happens to be "isolated from current degradation", or if intrinsic value is simply *that which is* "isolated from current degradation" in the individual's perception. This might well be a conscious effect in emulation of Bradley's philosophical prose, as with the assertion "We have the idea of perfection – there is no doubt as to that" which Hill discusses in 'A Postscript on Modernist Poetics', speaking of "the momentary uncertainty as to whether 'no doubt' goes with 'perfection' or with 'idea'" (*CCW* 571): this Bradleian ambiguity echoed throughout the late work, as in *Odi Barbare* XXVII, for instance: "Perfect empowerment the imperfection" (*BH* 861). In this sense, Hill is treading the "indeterminate line" of ethical temptation and discipline. However, with the statement from 'Civil Polity and the Confessing State' taken into consideration, it seems that Hill recognises the elegiac celebration of intrinsic value as one of the vital manifestations of metaphysical desire.

So, taken in this way, Hill's grappling with intrinsic value begins to look like the struggle to unite the psychological with the historical, or the "uniting of individual genius to the genius of the commonwealth" (*CCW* 531). The first statement suggests that intrinsic value is endemic to the elegiac, and vice versa, while the second nods towards "current degradation" which may or may not be specific to our own age. The crucial issue is the attitude towards nostalgia. However, as always, Hill seeks to historicise what might begin to look worryingly ahistorical, arguing that "whereas in 1690 (Locke) and 1729 (Butler) the tone [of references to intrinsic value] is optimistic or at least melioristic, by the first decade of the nineteenth century (*The Prelude*, Book XII) it is, at best, stoical" (*CCW* 486). This is a narrative of cultural decline, of the decay of the intrinsic as a credible reality, even the decline of credible reality as such: of "the value of being" (*CCW* 487).

In many of the writers Hill engages with in the matter of cultural decline, their view is similar but pertains to their *own* age. Society, culture, political life are *always* 'in decline', one might say. This is true, and to some extent Hill is lamenting the decline of the elegiac in public life and art – that is, the decline *of* this sense of decline, a sense which is somehow crucial to a sense of value and values; however, his identification of intrinsic value as the site of decline historicises it to some extent. There are similar moments in William Morris, as in 'Useful Labour Versus Useless Toil', which sound the same note of cultural decline as being within the present oligarchic consumerism: "At present all education is directed towards the end of fitting people to take their places in the hierarchy of commerce – these as masters, those as workmen. The education of the masters is more ornamental than that of the workmen, but it is commercial still; and even at the ancient universities learning is but little regarded, unless it can in the long run be made to *pay*."[56] Similarly, Hill's emphasis is on "our particular phase of oligarchical consumerism",[57] which he takes pains to point out now and again, and is not "part of the chorus of contemporary cultural lament" (*CCW* 263). In Morris's terms, the decline is from *homo faber* to *homo economicus*. There is a particular historical sense of "current degradation" running through Hill's later work, against the sense of unhistorical nostalgia:

> A poem issues from reflection, particularly but not exclusively from the common bonding of reflection and language; it is not

in itself the passing of reflective sentiment through the medium of language. The fact that my description applies only to a minority of poems written in English or any other language, and to the poetry written in Britain during the past fifty years scarcely if at all, does not shake my conviction that the description I have given of how the uncommon work moves within the common dimension of language is substantially accurate. (*CCW* 489)

This passage suggests that "current degradation", in the particular sense that Hill means, belongs to our own post-war culture, *at least* in terms of poetry. Hill's sense of cultural decline is again given a historical moment here, and issues in a critique of a lack of attention to language in the past fifty years or so, and indeed in a decline of the elegiac itself, and in "the value of being". Milton's pamphlet *A Treatise of Civil Power in Ecclesiastical Causes*, from which Hill derived the title of his 2007 collection, itself has such a political sense of the elegiac, in its appraisal of "force on one side restraining, and hire on the other side corrupting" (in Hill's terms, hegemony and patrimony): "It can be at no time, therefore, unseasonable to speak of these things; since by them the church is either in continual detriment and oppression, or in continual danger."[58] Milton (the radical) is sceptical about nostalgia. Ruskin's view of the matter, however, according to Hill in 'Poetry and Value', "is little short of the absurd" (*CCW* 487), straying too much into the realm of the "intransitive": that is, the ungraspable, the absolute itself-ness of an entity or object, about which one's nostalgia is mere sentimentality, disingenuousness, or "rant" (*CCW* 389).

In 'On Reading Crowds and Power', in *A Treatise of Civil Power*, Hill writes that "My reflexes | are words themselves rather than standard | flexures of civil power" (*BH* 575). An area of vital concern in Hill's later work is the difference between authentic and fraudulent civil power: between reflex and "standard | flexure" – the difference between sustained and honest self-attention and flexing one's muscles in the mirror. In the Oxford Professor of Poetry lecture 'Mine angry and defrauded young', Hill argues that the elegiac may be co-opted, in typical oligarchic democratic fashion, to be *the opposite* of mnemonic attention, a self-congratulating sense of 'pity' represented by the post-war cult of Wilfred Owen:

[Pity] is simultaneously a condition of empathy and an item in the machinery of social engineering.[59]

As such, the elegiac is not so much characterised by its absence, but by its travestying by oligarchic democracy: "victim-culture is a slippage from plutocratic anarchy".[60] However, in 'Language, Suffering and Silence', Hill recommends considering the notion that "the art and literature of the late twentieth century require a memorializing, a memorizing, of the dead as much as, or even more than, expressions of 'solidarity with the poor and oppressed'. Suffering is real, but 'suffering' is a sing-song, that is to say, cant" (*CCW* 405). To put this in more acutely early twenty-first-century terms, Hill's argument here is that identity politics – 'solidarity with the poor and oppressed' – is a part of the general 'cant' of postmodernity, or "plutocratic anarchy", part of the "machinery of social engineering": consensus masquerading as conscience, standard reflex masquerading as flexure. Memorialising is equated in Hill's sentence with memorising: that is, the elegiac as Hill envisages it is not a "standard flexure of civil power", but a "reflex" – that is, as much an act of self-attention as an act of civic concentration. And of course, in Hill's later work the consonance between these two positions is emphasised time and again.

Power

This notion of power is indeed more flexible, nuanced. When Hill refers to "the joyous exercise of creative power",[61] he is evoking William Morris's anti-hegemonic rhetoric, and by extension the politics of Romanticism: that is, the politics of Wordsworth and Coleridge in their first flush. Power is a word which is central to the ethos of Romanticism, which is as much a politics of the imagination as an imagining of politics, as with Coleridge's pantisocracy – and the difference between this position and the aestheticised politics of modernism is subtle, at first glance, but it is there in the way the word 'power' is used. For Coleridge, for instance, "Imagination I hold to be the living Power".[62] Wordsworth, in Book 12 of *The Prelude*, the section of that epic poem which Hill says displays a "stoical" attitude to intrinsic value, alludes to the "true power of mind". In the writings of Wordsworth and Coleridge, 'power' encapsulates the political and creative, just as it suggests both potency and potential (*potentia*) in its own etymological history, as in Wordsworth's portrait of the rural poor:

> Such meditations bred an anxious wish
> To ascertain how much of real worth,
> And genuine knowledge, and true power of mind,
> Did at this day exist in those who lived
> By bodily labour, labour far exceeding
> Their due proportion, under all the weight
> Of that injustice which upon ourselves
> By composition of society
> Ourselves entail.[63]

Though Hill gives a different extract from *The Prelude* in 'Language, Suffering and Silence', this is another instance of the "stoical" vision of intrinsic value described by Hill in 'Poetry and Value': "real worth", allied to "true power of mind", over and against the 'worth' and 'wealth' created by back-breaking tillage, imposed labour. Again, the two senses of value are in direct opposition, and the "true power of mind" in opposition to the political powerlessness of the rural labourer. Wordsworth does not here claim any success in his effort to ascertain "real worth", but rather the "anxious wish" to do so; in this sense Hill is much closer to Wordsworth than he is to Thomas Hobbes, John Locke, and Jeremy Taylor. This passage is notable too for its sense of "due proportion" amid the disproportionate circumstances of the world as it is encountered. I would suggest also that this passage is apt to Hill's view of civic attention in its reflexive action, as a reaction and a turning back upon "ourselves": "the weight | Of that injustice which upon ourselves | By composition of society | Ourselves entail", lines which constitute another vital instance of 'the political imaginary'.

There are many moments in Hill's later work in which physical labour is compared with creative labour, or "Symbolic labour", for instance *Odi Barbare* XXIV:

> What is far hence led to the den of making
>   Moves unlike wildfire; not so simple-happy

> Ploughman hammers ploughshare, his *durum dentem*
> Digging the *Georgics*. (*BH* 858)

The digging here conflates the symbolic labour of the hierarchist, or the "enabling reader", the physical labour of the farmworker, and the 'digging' of 1960s hedonistic slang. While the unjust labour of *The Prelude* is opposed to the settled land of Virgil's *Georgics*, so is the ploughman's labour opposed to the 'digging' – or enjoying – of the casual labourer, as it were. 'Enjoyment' as hedonism and as 'reaping the benefit of' are contrasted here. Hill's "*durum dentem*" condenses Virgil's *durum procudit arator vomeris obtunsi dentem* from Book 1 of the *Georgics*. The "den of making" might be the ploughman's workshop or the poet's study, but in characteristic fashion this stanza registers the dangerous attraction of equating them: the ploughman is "not so simple-happy" as he may appear in pastoral poetry, or as the poet himself perhaps. It is commonly observed, as I have mentioned in a previous chapter, that the Latin *versus* is both a ploughed furrow and the origin of our word 'verse', equating to a line of verse, its 'turn' the line-break.[64] Physical labour and creative labour have been equated at least since Virgil, then, and symbolic labour is at the heart of pastoral; it is also at the heart of Seamus Heaney's poetry, the Irish poet being a sometime foil for Hill's later work, as in *The Triumph of Love*. Indeed, the *Georgics* trope such labour as statecraft, with the settling of land serving as metaphor for the settling of *the* land, or other lands, and for the settled polity under Augustus Caesar (with that passage from *Richard II* pitched in the opposite direction). Heaney's employment of such Virgilian tropes is a latter-day instance of an aestheticised politics, no doubt, as far as Hill is concerned. Labour is a recurrent theme in the *Daybooks*, most notably in *Oraclau | Oracles*, *Odi Barbare* and *Clavics*. It is one of the key words of *Odi Barbare*, culminating, in poem LI, with:

> Ruskin past master of the keys, his sweet swart
> Labour of Zion. (*BH* 885)

Within these two lines lie the implications of the relationship between physical, imaginative, and political labour, even the Labour movement, one might add, with its origins in the Ruskinian paternalism of the

Fabian Society in the late nineteenth century, its general atmosphere of *Fors Clavigera*. Zion is utopia in Hill's later writings, with all its troubling connotations of the modern Israel and therefore, again, of a dangerously aestheticised politics: "(Terror's own concept parenthetical State | Striking the instant)" (*BH* 870). Again, though, that Wordsworthian "anxious wish" is acknowledged in Ruskin, his "sweet swart | Labour": the difference between the sweet and the swart, the benign and malign, being only that of a modulation in the vowel.

Eros, that crucial element in Hill's later approach, stands, in the terms of John Barrell's introduction to Coleridge's *On the Constitution of Church and State*, as a "potential power", disturbing to Coleridge's commentators as suggesting the anarchic energy which threatens the state's equilibrium, or its hegemony, depending on your point of view. Eros is "the becoming and endless incompletion of the world",[65] and Bradley declares in *Essays on Truth and Reality* that "the attempt to lower science and art to the rank of mere instruments springs, I urge, once more from this propensity to mistake some perverted distinction for a separate Power".[66] Bradley here opposes instrumentality to "Power", and that is indeed the thrust of Wordsworth's passage in *The Prelude* – though, as Hill claims, Wordsworth's stance is beleaguered and increasingly against the current of contemporary mores in the early nineteenth century. Wordsworth identifies, with Locke, Ruskin, Bradley, and Hill, the vexed relationship between the private recognition of this "Power" and its public manifestations; although at the same time it is held to be self-evident in Hill's later work that the imagination is as ineluctably political as politics are ineluctably imaginative. And, if "[t]he theory and practice of poetry is part of the civil constitution",[67] the fact that Britain does not have such a formally written constitution may show the Wordsworthian "anxious wish" of Hill's claim; or it may cement the importance of language's precision and vitality in such an endlessly "self-founded, self-founding" (*SC* 1; *BH* 421) ('erotic') State.

Notes

1   John Ruskin, *Fors Clavigera: Letters to the Workmen and Labourers of Great Britain*, Vol. 5 (George Allen: Orpington, 1875) p. 276.

2   Ibid., p. 287.
3   John Ruskin, *Unto This Last and Other Writings*, Clive Wilmer ed., intro., commentary, notes (Penguin: London, 1985) pp. 208–209.
4   Hill, 'Monumentality and Bidding'.
5   Samuel Taylor Coleridge, *On the Constitution of Church and State According to the Idea of Each*, John Barrell ed. and intro. (Dent: London, 1972) p. 37.
6   Ernst H. Kantorowicz, *The King's Two Bodies: A Study in Mediaeval Political Theology* (Princeton University Press: Princeton, 1957) p. 15.
7   Ibid., p. 3.
8   Hill, 'Address of Thanks to the Sponsors and Jury of the Truman Capote Award for Literary Criticism in Memory of Newton Arvin', p. 186.
9   Ibid., p. 186.
10 A debate raged in the letters pages of various literary magazines after the publication of *Tenebrae* in 1978, in which the sequence was included.
11 Hill, 'Poetry, Policing, and Public Order (1)'.
12 Coleridge, *On the Constitution of Church and State According to the Idea of Each*, p. 37.
13 Ibid., p. 10.
14 Benziger, 'Organic Unity', p. 24.
15 Hill, 'Address of Thanks to the Sponsors and Jury of the Truman Capote Award for Literary Criticism in Memory of Newton Arvin', p. 189.
16 Christopher Hill, *The World Turned Upside Down: Radical Ideas During the English Revolution* (Penguin: London, 1975).
17 William Shakespeare, *Richard II*, Andrew Gurr ed. (Cambridge University Press: Cambridge, 1984) p. 144.
18 Coleridge, *On the Constitution of Church and State*, p. 15.
19 Gottfried Leibniz, *Philosophical Writings*, G.H.R. Parkinson ed., Mary Morris and G.H.R. Parkinson trans. (Dent: London, 1973) p. 181.
20 T.S. Eliot, *On Poetry and Poets* (Faber: London, 1957) p. 110.
21 John Ruskin, *Unto This Last, The Political Economy of Art, Essays on Political Economy*, John Bryson intro. (Dent: London, 1968) p. 135.
22 Hill, 'Between Politics and Eternity', p. 12.
23 Coleridge, *Shakespeare, Ben Jonson, Beaumont and Fletcher*, p. 9.
24 Hill, '"Legal Fiction" and Legal Fiction'.
25 Hill, 'Poetry and "The Democracy of the Dead"'.

26 James Shapiro, *1599: A Year in the Life of William Shakespeare* (Faber: London, 2005) p. 144.
27 John Keats, *The Poems of John Keats*, Jack Stillinger ed. (Heinemann: London, 1978) p. 370.
28 Hill, 'Poetry Marathon 2009', www.youtube.com/watch?v=Siu MKASXJLU. Accessed 15 November 2017.
29 John Milton, *Paradise Lost*, John Leonard ed., intro., notes (Penguin: London, 2000) p. 225.
30 Geoffrey Hill, 'Poetry and Disproportion', Oxford Professor of Poetry lecture, 10 May 2011.
31 Ruskin, *Unto This Last, The Political Economy of Art*, p. 135.
32 Hill, 'Between Politics and Eternity'.
33 Ibid.
34 Hill, 'Poetry, Policing, and Public Order (1)'.
35 Geoffrey Hill, 'Poetry and "The Democracy of the Dead"'.
36 Thomas Hobbes, *Leviathan, or the Matter, Form and Power of a Commonwealth, Ecclesiastical and Civil*, Henry Morley intro. (Routledge: London, 1885) p. 11.
37 Hill, 'Civil Polity and the Confessing State', p. 11.
38 Hill, 'Touching Pitch', p. 1.
39 Ibid., p. 4.
40 Marx, *Der Achtzehnte Brumaire des Louis Bonaparte*, p. 7.
41 Hill, 'Modernism / Post-modernism', p. 28.
42 Ivor Gurney, 'To His Love', *Poetry of the First World War: An Anthology*, Tim Kendall ed. (Oxford University Press: Oxford, 2013) p. 122.
43 Ivor Gurney, *Collected Poems*, P.J. Kavanagh ed. and intro. (Carcanet: Manchester, 2004) p. 358.
44 This writing both within and against is described as 'writing *into*' by Hill in a discussion of Hopkins: "Hopkins writes *into* the language." Hill, 'What You Look Hard at Seems to Look Hard at You'.
45 Such eccentricity is probably the natural state of valuable writing, but this kind of marginalisation is itself made part of commodity culture, according to Hill. "During [the last two hundred years] licensed eccentricity has been readily granted to relatively minor literary figures of gentry status, such as Edward Fitzgerald and Walter Savage Landor in the nineteenth century and the Sitwells in the twentieth. When a magisterially eccentric work of genius, Gerard Hopkins' 'The Wreck of the Deutschland', was composed, in 1876, it was rejected by the periodical to which it was offered and did not appear in print until 1918. So-called 'literary furore', such as Booker

Prize altercations and the like, is, again, a form of indulged marginal eccentricity." Hill, 'Civil Polity and the Confessing State', pp. 7–8.
46 Geoffrey Hill, 'I Know Thee Not, Old Man, Fall to Thy Prayers', Oxford Professor of Poetry lecture, 5 May 2015.
47 Hill, 'Between Politics and Eternity', p. 28.
48 Ibid., p. 28.
49 Antonio Gramsci, *Prison Notebooks*, Vol. 2 (Columbia University Press: New York, 1996) p. 251
50 Ibid., p. 253.
51 Hill, 'Address of Thanks to the Sponsors and Jury of the Truman Capote Award for Literary Criticism in Memory of Newton Arvin', p. 186.
52 Morris, *Political Writings of William Morris*, p. 63.
53 Hill, 'A Deep Dynastic Wound'.
54 Haffenden, *Viewpoints*, p. 86.
55 Hill, 'Civil Polity and the Confessing State', p. 10.
56 Morris, *Political Writings of William Morris*, p. 101.
57 Hill, 'Poetry, Policing, and Public Order (1)'.
58 John Milton, *Milton's Prose Writings*, K.M. Burton intro. (Dent: London, 1965) p. 110.
59 Geoffrey Hill, 'Mine Angry and Defrauded Young', Oxford Professor of Poetry lecture, 5 December 2014.
60 Hill, 'Civil Polity and the Confessing State', p. 19.
61 Hill, 'A Deep Dynastic Wound'.
62 S.T. Coleridge, *Biographia Literaria, or Biographical Sketches of My Literary Life and Opinions*, George Watson ed. and intro. (Dent: London, 1965) p. 167.
63 William Wordsworth, *The Major Works, Including The Prelude*, Stephen Gill ed., intro., notes (Oxford University Press: Oxford, 1984) p. 571.
64 The sense of 'being against', or 'writing *into*', lurks in the background of *versus* too, but I have never seen it discussed.
65 Bradley, *Essays on Truth and Reality*, p. 471.
66 Ibid., pp. 471–472.
67 Hill, 'Poetry, Policing, and Public Order (1)'.

References

Works by Geoffrey Hill

Books

Broken Hierarchies: Poems 1952–2012. Kenneth Haynes ed. Oxford University Press: Oxford, 2013.
Collected Critical Writings. Oxford University Press: Oxford, 2008.
A Treatise of Civil Power. Clutag: Thame, 2005. Chapbook version.

Lectures

All Oxford Professor of Poetry lectures accessed at www.english.ox.ac.uk/professor-sir-geoffrey-hill-lectures. Accessed 1 December 2018.
'Address of Thanks to the Sponsors and Jury of the Truman Capote Award for Literary Criticism in Memory of Newton Arvin'. *Iowa Review*, 40:1, 2010.
'A Deep Dynastic Wound'. Oxford Professor of Poetry lecture, 30 April 2013.
'How Ill White Hairs Become a Fool and Jester'. Oxford Professor of Poetry lecture, 30 November 2010.
'I Know Thee Not, Old Man, Fall to Thy Prayers'. Oxford Professor of Poetry lecture, 5 May 2015.
'"Legal Fiction" and Legal Fiction'. Oxford Professor of Poetry lecture, 5 March 2013.
'Milton as Muse'. Lecture delivered at Christ's College, Cambridge, 29 October 2008.
'Mine Angry and Defrauded Young'. Oxford Professor of Poetry lecture, 5 December 2014.
'Monumentality and Bidding'. Oxford Professor of Poetry lecture, 11 March 2014.

'Poetry and "The Democracy of the Dead"'. Oxford Professor of Poetry lecture, 3 December 2012.
'Poetry and Disproportion'. Oxford Professor of Poetry lecture, 10 May 2011.
'Poetry, Policing, and Public Order (1)'. Oxford Professor of Poetry lecture, 29 November 2011.
'What You Look Hard at Seems to Look Hard at You'. Oxford Professor of Poetry lecture, 6 May 2014.

Articles

'C.H. Sisson'. *PN Review*, 39, July–August 1984.
'Civil Polity and the Confessing State'. *The Warwick Review*, 2:2, June 2008.
'Mightier and Darker'. *Times Literary Supplement*, 23 March 2016.

Unpublished pieces

'Between Politics and Eternity'. BC MS 20c, Hill/4. Brotherton Library, University of Leeds.
'Modernism / Post-modernism'. BC MS 20c, Hill/4/23, p. 22. Brotherton Library, University of Leeds.
'Noetics and Poetics'. BC MS 20c, Hill/4/17/2. Brotherton Library, University of Leeds.
'Thoughts of a Conservative Modernist'. BC MS 20c, Hill/4/22, p. 12. Brotherton Library, University of Leeds.
'Touching Pitch'. BC MS 20c, Hill/4/15, p. 4. Brotherton Library, University of Leeds.
'T.S. Eliot Memorial Lecture'. MS BC Hill/4/35, p. 25. Brotherton Library, University of Leeds.

Interviews

'The Art of Poetry: 80'. *The Paris Review*, Spring 2000.
Campbell, Jessica. *The Oxford Student*, 26 May 2011. http://oxfordstudent.com/2011/05/26/interview-geoffrey-hill-oxford-professor-of-poetry. Accessed 11 March 2015.

Haffenden, John. *Viewpoints: Poets in Conversation with John Haffenden.* Faber: London, 1981.
Rush, Christy. *The Oxford Student*, 26 May 2011. http://oxfordstudent.com/2011/05/26/interview-geoffrey-hill-oxford-professor-of-poetry. Accessed 11 March 2015.

Poetry readings

'Poetry Marathon 2009'. YouTube. www.youtube.com/watch?v=SiuMKASXJLU. Accessed 15 November 2017.

Works by other authors

Alighieri, Dante. *De Vulgari Eloquentia*. Ronald Duncan intro., A.G. Ferrers-Howell trans. Rebel Press: London, 1973.
Augustine, St. *Confessions and Enchiridion*. Albert C. Outler ed. and trans. SCM: London, 1955.
Austin, J.L. *How to Do Things With Words*. Clarendon: Oxford, 1975.
Badiou, Alain. *Being and Event*. Continuum: London, 2011.
Barth, Karl. *The Epistle to the Romans*. Edwyn C. Hoskins trans. from 6th edition. Oxford University Press: London, Oxford, and New York, 1968.
Beckett, Samuel. 'Dante… Bruno… Vico… Joyce'. *Our Exagmination Round his Factification for Incamination of Work in Progress.* Faber: London, 1972.
Beckett, Samuel. *Proust and Three Dialogues with Georges Duthuit*. John Calder: London, 1965.
Benziger, James. 'Organic Unity: Leibniz to Coleridge', *PMLA*, 66:2, 1951, pp. 24–48.
Blake, William. *The Complete Poems*. W.H. Stevenson ed. 3rd edition. Pearson: Edinburgh, 2007.
Bloom, Harold. *Kabbalah and Criticism*. Seabury: New York, 1975.
Bradley, F.H. *Essays on Truth and Reality*. Clarendon: Oxford, 1914.
Bradley, F.H. *Ethical Studies*. London: Henry. S King & Co, 1876.
Bradley, F.H. *The Principles of Logic*. Kegan and Paul: London, 1883.
Brooks, Cleanth. *The Well Wrought Urn: Studies in the Structure of Poetry.* Dennis Dobson: London, 1949.
Bryant, J.A. 'Making Peace with Disorder'. *Sewanee Review*, 97:1, 1989, pp. 153–162.
Chomsky, Noam. *Who Rules the World? Reframings.* Penguin: London, 2016.

Coleridge, Samuel Taylor. *Biographia Literaria, or Biographical Sketches of My Literary Life and Opinions*. George Watson ed. and intro. Dent: London, 1965.
Coleridge, Samuel Taylor. *Biographia Literaria: or, Biographical Sketches of My Literary Life and Opinions*, The Collected Works of Samuel Taylor Coleridge Vol. 7. James Engell and W. Jackson Bate eds. Princeton University Press: New Jersey, 1983.
Coleridge, Samuel Taylor. *Biographia Literaria: Chapters I–IV, XIV–XXII, Wordsworth, Prefaces and Essays on Poetry 1800–1815*. George Sampson ed. Cambridge University Press: Cambridge, 1920.
Coleridge, Samuel Taylor. *Biographia Literaria, Volume 1, 1817*. Scholar Press: Menston, 1971.
Coleridge, Samuel Taylor. *On the Constitution of Church and State According to the Idea of Each*. John Barrell ed. and intro. Dent: London, 1972.
Coleridge, Samuel Taylor. *Shakespeare, Ben Jonson, Beaumont and Fletcher: Notes and Lectures*. Edward Howell: Liverpool, 1874.
Dean, Tim. 'T.S. Eliot, Famous Clairvoyante'. *Gender, Desire and Sexuality in T.S. Eliot*. Cassandra Laity and Nancy K. Gish eds. Cambridge University Press: Cambridge, 2004.
Eliot, T.S. *Collected Poems 1909–1935*. Faber: London, 1936.
Eliot, T.S. *Knowledge and Experience in the Philosophy of F.H. Bradley*. Faber: London, 1964.
Eliot, T.S. *On Poetry and Poets*. Faber: London, 1957.
Eliot, T.S. *The Sacred Wood: Essays on Poetry and Criticism*. Methuen: London, 1934.
Eliot, T.S. *Selected Essays*. Faber: London, 1932.
Eliot, T.S. *Selected Prose of T.S. Eliot*. Frank Kermode ed. and intro. Faber: London, 1975.
Eliot, T.S. *The Use of Poetry and the Use of Criticism: Studies in the Relation of Criticism to Poetry in England*. Faber: London, 1964.
Empson, William. *Seven Types of Ambiguity*. Penguin: London, 1995.
Encyclopedia Britannica: 'Scottish Law'. www.britannica.com/EBchecked/topic/529712/Scottish-law. Accessed 24 February 2015.
Foucault, Michel. *Power / Knowledge: Selected Interviews and Other Writings*. Colin Gordon ed., Colin Gordon, Leo Marshall, John Mepham, and Kate Soper trans. Harvester: Sussex, 1980.
Freud, Sigmund. *Jokes and their Relation to the Unconscious*, The Penguin Freud Library, Vol. 6. Angela Richards ed., James Strachey trans. Penguin: London, 1991.
Gramsci, Antonio. *Prison Notebooks*, Vol. 2. Columbia University Press: New York, 1996.

Graves, Robert and Laura Riding. *A Survey of Modernist Poetry*. Heinemann: London, 1927.
Gurney, Ivor. *Collected Poems*. P.J. Kavanagh ed. and intro. Carcanet: Manchester, 2004.
Gurney, Ivor. 'To His Love'. *Poetry of the First World War: An Anthology*. Tim Kendall ed. Oxford University Press: Oxford, 2013.
Gurney, Ivor. *War Letters*. Midnag/Carcanet: Manchester, 1983.
Haynes, Kenneth. Letter on Hill's *Thoughts of a Conservative Modernist*. BC MS 20c, Hill/4/22. Brotherton Library, University of Leeds.
Haynes, Kenneth. Letter to Geoffrey Hill. BC MS 20c, Hill/4/22. Brotherton Library, University of Leeds.
Heidegger, Martin. *Being and Time*. John Mcquarrie and Edward Robinson trans. Blackwell: Oxford, 1967.
Hill, Christopher. *The World Turned Upside Down: Radical Ideas During the English Revolution*. Penguin: London, 1975.
Hobbes, Thomas. *Leviathan, or the Matter, Form and Power of a Commonwealth, Ecclesiastical and Civil*. Henry Morley intro. Routledge: London, 1885.
Hopkins, Gerard Manley. *Selected Prose*. Gerald Roberts ed. Oxford University Press: Oxford, 1980.
Hopkins, Gerard Manley. *The Journals and Papers of Gerard Manley Hopkins*. Humphry House ed., completed by Graham Storey. Oxford University Press: London, New York, and Toronto, 1959.
Hopkins, Gerard Manley. *The Poems of Gerard Manley Hopkins*. W.H. Gardner and N.H. MacKenzie ed. 4th edition. Oxford University Press: Oxford and New York, 1970.
Hopkins, Gerard Manley. *Poems and Prose*. W.H. Gardner selected and ed. Penguin: London, 1963.
Kant, Immanuel. *Critique of Judgement*. James Creed Meredith trans., analytical indexes. Clarendon: Oxford, 1920.
Kant, Immanuel. *Kant's Prolegomena and Metaphysical Foundations of Natural Science*. Ernest Belfort Bax trans., biography, intro. George Bell and Son: London, 1883.
Kantorowicz, Ernst H. *The King's Two Bodies: A Study in Mediaeval Political Theology*. Princeton University Press: Princeton, 1957.
Keats, John. *The Letters of John Keats, 1814–1821*, Vol. 1. Hyder Edward Rollins ed. Harvard University Press: Cambridge, MA, 1958.
Keats, John. *The Poems of John Keats*. Jack Stillinger ed. Heinemann: London, 1978.
Kendall, Tim, ed. *Poetry of the First World War: An Anthology*. Oxford University Press: Oxford, 2013.

Khlebnikov, Velimir. *The King of Time*. Charlotte Douglas ed., Paul Schmidt trans. Harvard University Press: Cambridge, MA and London, 1985.

Kierkegaard, Søren. *The Sickness Unto Death*. Howard V. Hong and Edna H. Hong ed., intro., notes. Princeton University Press: New Jersey, 1980.

Kirsch, Adam. *The Modern Element: Essays on Contemporary Poetry*. Norton: New York, 2008.

Leibniz, Gottfried. *Philosophical Writings*. G.H.R. Parkinson ed., Mary Morris and G.H.R. Parkinson trans. Dent: London, 1973.

Levinas, Emmanuel. *Totality and Infinity: An Essay on Exteriority*. Alphonso Lingis trans. Kluwer: Dordrecht, Boston, and London, 1991.

Luther, Martin. *Luther: Letters of Spiritual Counsel*. Theodore G. Tappert, ed., trans. The Library of Christian Classics, Vol. 18. SCM Press: London, 1955.

Marcel, Gabriel. *The Philosophy of Existentialism*. Citadel: New York, 1956.

Marx, Karl. *Der Achtzehnte Brumaire des Louis Bonaparte*. Berlag: Stuttgart, 1914.

Milton, John. *Areopagitica* and *Of Education*. Michael Davis ed., intro., notes. Macmillan: London, 1963.

Milton, John. *Milton on Education: The Tractate of Education, with Supplementary Extracts from Other Writings of Milton*. Oliver Morley Ainsworth ed., intro., notes. Yale University Press: New Haven, 1928.

Milton, John. *Milton's Prose Writings*. K.M. Burton intro. Dent: London, 1965.

Milton, John. *Paradise Lost*. John Leonard ed., intro., notes. Penguin: London, 2000.

Morris, William. *The Collected Works of William Morris: With Introductions by His Daughter May Morris*, Vol. 23. Longmans Green: London, 1915.

Morris, William. *Political Writings of William Morris*. A.L. Morton ed. and intro. Lawrence & Wishart: London, 1973.

Plato. *The Dialogues of Plato*, Vol. 1. B. Jowett trans. Clarendon: Oxford, 1871.

Popham, Peter. 'Geoffrey Hill Is Our Greatest Living Poet', *New Statesman*, 6 December 2012.

Potts, Robert. 'The Praise Singer', *Guardian*, 10 August 2002.

Pound, Ezra. *ABC of Reading*. Faber: London, 1951.

Pound, Ezra. *Cantos*. New Directions: New York, 1996.

Pound, Ezra. *Literary Essays of Ezra Pound*, T.S. Eliot ed. and into. Faber: London, 1954.
Ravintharan, Vidyan. 'The Spontaneity of Hopkins's Journal Prose', *Review of English Studies*, 64:267, 2013, pp. 838–856.
Ricks, Christopher. *Essays in Appreciation*. Clarendon: Oxford, 1996.
Ricks, Christopher. *Milton's Grand Style*. Oxford University Press: Oxford, 1963.
Ricks, Christopher. '*Tenebrae* and At-One-Ment'. *Geoffrey Hill: Essays on His Work*. Peter Robinson ed. Open University Press: Milton Keynes, 1987.
Robinson, Peter. 'Contemporary Poetry and Value'. *The Oxford Handbook of Contemporary British and Irish Poetry*. Peter Robinson ed. Oxford University Press: Oxford, 2013.
Ruskin, John. *Fors Clavigera: Letters to the Workmen and Labourers of Great Britain*, Vol. 5. George Allen: Orpington, 1875.
Ruskin, John. *Unto this Last: Four Essays on the First Principles of Political Economy*. George Allen: London, 1896.
Ruskin, John. *Unto This Last and Other Writings*. Clive Wilmer ed., intro., commentary, notes. Penguin: London, 1985.
Ruskin, John. *Unto This Last, The Political Economy of Art, Essays on Political Economy*. John Bryson intro. Dent: London, 1968.
Shakespeare, William. *A Midsummer Night's Dream*. Harold F. Brooks ed. Methuen: London, 1979.
Shakespeare, William. *Richard II*. Andrew Gurr ed. Cambridge University Press: Cambridge, 1984.
Shapiro, James. *1599: A Year in the Life of William Shakespeare*. Faber: London, 2005.
Sidney, Philip. *An Apology for Poetry or the Defence of Poesy*. Geoffrey Shephard ed. Nelson: London, 1965.
Sisson, C.H. *The Avoidance of Literature*. Carcanet: Manchester, 1979.
Sperling, Matthew. *Visionary Philology*. Oxford University Press: Oxford, 2014.
Starnino, Carmine. 'The Plight of the Poet-Critic', *Poetry Magazine*, May 2008.
Steiner, George. *On Difficulty and Other Essays*. Oxford University Press: New York and Melbourne, 1978.
Vaughan, Thomas. *The Works of Thomas Vaughan*. Arthur Edward Waite ed., annotated, intro. Theosophical Society: London, 1819.
Weinreb, Lloyd L. *Natural Law and Justice*. Harvard University Press: Cambridge, MA and London, 1987.
Williams, Charles. *The Descent of the Dove*. Longmans: London, New York, and Toronto, 1939.

Wordsworth, William. *The Major Works, Including The Prelude*. Stephen Gill ed., intro., notes. Oxford University Press: Oxford, 1984.

Wylie, Alex. 'Eros in Geoffrey Hill's *Scenes from Comus*', *English: The Journal of the English Association*, Autumn 2011, pp. 198–211.

Yeats, W.B. *The Major Works, Including Poems, Plays, and Critical Prose*. Ed Larrissy ed., intro., notes. Oxford University Press: Oxford, 1997.

Index

Adams, Henry
   and the "Banker's Olympus" 149
Agricola, Rodolfo 138
alchemy 77–78, 96, 97
   and indeterminacy 102
   and nostalgia 99–100
   and semiotic determinism 98
   and the Fall 103
alienation 9, 40
   and Karl Marx 40–41
American New Criticism 31
Amis, Kingsley 2
anarchical plutocracy 8
Angel of Poetry, the 154
'A Postscript on Modernist Poetics'
   33, 62–63, 79, 92, 103, 126,
   151, 165
Apostle's Creed, the 96
apprehension 16
Aristotle
   De Anima 62
Auden, Wystan Hugh 103, 162
Augustine, St. 48, 62, 90
   and *felix culpa* 89
   Hill's friction with 91
   and Kierkegaard 93
Austin, John Langshaw
   on verdictives 59–60
Averroes 68

Bacon, Francis 152
Barker, George 130

Barth, Karl 54
Beckett, Samuel
   'Dante… Bruno… Vico…
   Joyce' 92
becoming 30
being 3, 35
Belloc, Hilaire 25–26
Benziger, James 32, 148
'Between Politics and Eternity'
   152, 155, 162
Blackmur, Richard Palmer 6,
   31, 81
Blake, William 113, 134
   and hierarchy 132
Bloom, Harold
   Kabbalah and Criticism 105
Bradley, Francis Herbert 3, 21, 70,
   115, 117, 165
   and being-towards-death 30
   and eros 10, 41
   and eros in the context of
   Kierkegaard 82
   *Essays on Truth and
   Reality* 171
   and judgement 9, 93, 130
   and self-attention 43
   and Toryism 113
Bridges, Robert
   'Sonnet to G.M.H.' 106
Brooks, Cleanth 36
Bunting, Basil 66
Butler, Joseph 47

Index

Campanella, Tommaso 77
Canaan 2
Carne-Ross, Donald 37, 126
Celan, Paul 128
Chesterton, Gilbert Keith 114
Chomsky, Noam 120
   and the public intellectual 137
'Civil Polity and the Confessing State' 165
Coleridge, Samuel Taylor 78, 83, 154, 168
   and the active-passive divide 67
   Aids to Reflection 56
   and the body politic 148
   and the clerisy 131
   and "drama of reason" 139
   and "esemplastic power" 89
   and John Milton 23–25
   and "living powers" 90, 103
   and "poetic faith" 78, 95
   and "potential power" (*potentia*) 151, 157, 171
   and the primary imagination 57, 62
   On the Constitution of Church and State 144, 150, 171
   Shakespeare, Ben Jonson, Beaumont and Fletcher 153
'Common Weal, Common Woe' 84

Dante 88, 153, 155, 162
   De Vulgari Eloquentia 106
Dawkins, Richard 108
'Dividing Legacies' 1, 5, 85
de Gourmont, Rémy 130
Descartes, René 28
De Valera, Eamonn 147
Devlin, Christopher 51, 58, 62, 91
difficulty 68, 99, 124, 128
   and Kierkegaard 99
   and scrupulosity 122
   and William Butler Yeats 79
Donne, John 47, 84
   and pitch 85
Douglas, Charlotte 62
Dryden, John 23, 37
Duns Scotus 84–85

eccentricity 1, 37, 135
Eliot, Thomas Stearns 38, 60, 100, 112, 114–115, 145, 156, 162
   and F.H. Bradley 5
   and *Coriolan* 39–40, 133
   'Dante' 60
   and dissociation of sensibility 23
   and entelechy 150
   and *Four Quartets* 54
   'The Function of Criticism' 10, 73
   and hierarchy vs hegemony 61, 162
   on John Milton 24
   'London Letter' (on Marie Lloyd) 133
   and objective structures 67
   'The Perfect Critic' 27, 127, 130
   and pitch 85
   and relationship to Hill 121
   Sacred Wood, The 8, 135
   and sensuous intelligence 25
   Sweeney Agonistes 63
   and the ideal reader 127
   'Tradition and the Individual Talent' 21, 72, 113
   Use of Poetry and the Use of Criticism, The 6, 133
   Waste Land, The and *Coriolanus* 39
elitism 113, 125, 131, 154
Emerson, Ralph Waldo 7, 38, 116, 164
Empson, William 117, 123

Seven Types of Ambiguity 31, 34–35
The Structure of Complex Words 34
energy 58, 60
  linguistic 48
eros 4, 13, 14, 33, 38, 41–43, 58, 60, 106, 113, 171
  and *Scenes from Comus* 96
'Eros in F.H. Bradley and T.S. Eliot' 5, 89, 93, 106, 122, 163

Fall, the 53, 59, 83, 86
  and aesthetics 97
  and alchemy 103
felix culpa 89, 97
Fibonacci sequence 94
Fool, the 121
Foucault, Michel 119, 137, 146
Freud, Sigmund
  Jokes and Their Relation to the Unconscious 69

Gaugin's *The Vision after the Sermon* 83
Gledhill, Anne 131, 134
Gramsci, Antonio 155, 162
Graves, Robert
  on John Milton 23
  Survey of Modernist Poetry, A 31, 37, 38, 122
  and techne 31
Green, Thomas Hill 15, 47, 115, 161
Guardian, The 74, 124, 127
Gurney, Ivor 158
  on John Milton 23

Haffenden, John 51, 91
Harrison, Tony 149
Haynes, Kenneth 36, 63, 67
Heaney, Seamus 170
Hegel, Georg Wilhelm Friedrich 93

hegemony
  and value 137
Heidegger, Martin 17, 21, 29, 115, 128
  and attunement 29
  and *Gelassenheit* 30, 36, 121, 129
  and *Gerede* 134
  and thrown-ness 30
hierarchy 125
  connotations of 112
Hill, Christopher 172
Hobbes, Thomas 169
  Leviathan 70, 152, 153, 156
Hopkins, Gerard Manley 14, 21, 32, 38, 79, 97, 129
  'On the Portrait of Two Beautiful People' 106
  and Stonyhurst College 86
  'That Nature is a Heraclitean Fire and of the Comfort of the Resurrection' 80, 96
Howell, Henry 84
Hume, David
  'Of the Standard of Taste' 119

immediate context 34, 42
intrinsic value 11, 12, 35, 36, 37, 54, 113, 115, 117, 123, 125, 133, 144, 159, 166
  and elegy 164
  Hill's critique of 55
  and John Ruskin 119
  and potential 152

justice
  and writing 51–52

kabbalah 77–78, 96, 97
Kant, Immanuel
  on art as "purposiveness without a purpose" 103

Kantorowicz, Ernst Hartwig 144
Keats, John 117, 132, 154
   and negative capability 121
Khlebnikov, Velimir 62, 98
Kiefer, Anselm 9
Kierkegaard, Søren 42, 92
   and difficulty 99
   Fear and Trembling 81
   Sickness Unto Death, The 92–93
   and St. Augustine 93
Kirsch, Adam 116, 132

Laird, Nick 129
'Language, Suffering and Silence'
   39, 79, 97, 168
Larkin, Philip 2, 118, 161
Lawes, Will 49
Leibniz, Gottfried Wilhelm
   28, 115
   Monadology 151
Levinas, Emmanuel 11, 41
Locke, John 169
   Second Treatise of Civil
   Government 125
Logan, William 129
Lowell, Robert 164
Luther, Martin 90
   and *homo incurvatus in se* 85
   and natural law 54

MacDiarmid, Hugh 156
Mallarmé, Stéphane 128
Malone, Edward 124
Marcel, Gabriel 28, 115, 130
   'On the Ontological Mystery'
   35
martyrs 54
Marx, Karl 22, 155, 158
   and alienation 40–41
metaphor 78, 81, 87
   and alchemy 102

metaphorical power 95
modernist misunderstanding
   of 61
metaphysical desire 11, 35, 41
'Mightier and Darker' 1, 82, 114
Milton, John 23, 83, 100, 105,
   118, 149
   and anarchy 155
   On Education 88
   and radicalism 133
   Treatise of Civil Power in
   Ecclesiastical Causes, A 167
'Modernism / Post-modernism'
   20, 27
Morris, Mark
   and expressiveness 32
Morris, William 65, 163, 168
   and "anarchical plutocracy" 149
   'Art Under Plutocracy' 139
   'Useful Labour versus Useless
   Toil' 122, 166
Movement, the 32, 70, 72

natural justice
   and will 53
New Critical poem 5, 6, 151, 157
New Criticism 6, 31, 33, 81
nostalgia 62–63, 90–91, 100–101,
   104, 145, 164
   and alchemy 99–100
   as hiraeth 147

O'Duffy, Eoin 147
Old Testament / Torah 96,
   105, 137
ontological reader, the 126, 137
original sin 78, 89
Orwell, George
   1984 125
'Our Word Is Our Bond' 3, 58,
   60, 91

Owen, Wilfred 138, 161, 167
oxymoron 107

Paradise Lost 59
paradox 47, 106
Pater, Walter 100
Patmore, Coventry
 on Gerard Manley Hopkins 32
Pauline Christianity 77
 versus Gnosticism 89
Pavese, Cesare
 Il mestiere de vivere 131
Pearse, Patrick 147
Péguy, Charles 108
'Perplexed Persistence: The
 Exemplary Failure of T.H.
 Green' 3, 131
Petronius 135
pitch 107, 157
 and Hopkins 84
 and tone 7
Plantinga, Alvin 89
Plato
 Ion 72
plutocratic anarchy 8, 65, 137, 152,
 154, 164
poeta doctus 138
'Poetry and Disproportion' 155
'Poetry and Value' 32–33, 56,
 164, 167
'Poetry as "Menace" and
 "Atonement" 11, 18 n.29,
 66, 157
Pope, Alexander 41
Potts, Robert 122
Pound, Ezra 20, 38, 60, 72, 100,
 114, 156
 ABC of Reading 138
 Cantos 58, 60
 on John Milton 24
 and logopoeia 21, 117

prophet, the 137
Pugin, Augustus Charles 147

qlipoth 98, 114
quantum physics 94

Rabelais, Francois 90
Rahner, Karl 81
 on being 42
'Redeeming the Time' 57
reflection 56
Ricks, Christopher 50, 64, 72, 78,
 82, 142, 161
 on atonement 33
'Rhetorics of Value and Intrinsic
 Value' 125, 161, 164
Riding, Laura
 Survey of Modernist Poetry, A 31,
 37, 38, 122
Robinson, Peter 4
Rose, Gillian 74
Rosenberg, Isaac 21, 118, 138, 160
Ruskin, John 142, 155, 163
 Fors Clavigera 134, 143
 and 'illth' 149
 and intrinsic value 5, 67, 119
 and the Labour Party 170–171
 Unto this Last 65
 and value 144

Schlegel, Karl Friedrich von 148
scrupulosity 122, 123
sensuous intelligence 23,
 25–26, 138
sensuous interest 15, 85
Shakespeare, William 117, 118
 Coriolanus 38, 153
 and difficulty 122–123
 and the Fool 121
 Midsummer Night's Dream, A 17
 and natural justice 53

Othello 38
  and popularity 154
  Richard II 150, 152, 170
Shapiro, James
  1599: A Year in the Life of William Shakespeare 154
Sidney, Philip 14, 91, 96, 97, 149
Sisson, Charles Hubert 103
  on William Butler Yeats 39
Southey, Robert 57
Southwell, Robert 54, 89, 129
Stein, Gertrude 35, 36
Sperling, Matthew 90, 100
spontaneity 30
Starnino, Carmine 118
Steiner, George
  'On Difficulty' 128
structuralism 62, 98
Sun, the 124

'Tacit Pledges' 85–86, 138
Tate, Allen 20, 164
Taylor, Jeremy 149, 169
'The Absolute Reasonableness of Robert Southwell' 106
'The True Conduct of Human Judgement' 53
Thomas, Dylan 130
'Thoughts of a Conservative Modernist' 67, 114
Torah / Old Testament 96, 105, 137
'Touching Pitch' 157
'Translating Value' 6, 64, 107, 119
Trimalchio 121, 132, 135

'Unhappy Circumstances' 73

Vaughan, Thomas 102
  Anthroposophia Theomagia 98
  Lumen de Lumine 97, 102
vernacular, the
  and hierarchy 112
versus 126, 170, 174 n.64
Virgil
  Georgics, The 170
vis inertiae 67, 68, 86

Weil, Simone 80, 113, 151
Weinreb, Lloyd L. 53
Wellesley, Dorothy 79
Whitman, Walt 21, 38
'wilful' 52
Williams, Charles 81, 89, 114, 162
Wittgenstein, Ludwig 21, 134, 146
Wordsworth, William 138, 168
  and the "anxious wish" 171
  and the 'egotistical sublime' 121
  Prelude, The 170
'Word Value in F.H. Bradley and T.S. Eliot' 5
Wyndham Lewis, Percy 149

Yeats, William Butler 20, 38–39, 48, 62–63, 66, 74, 112, 114, 118, 147, 152, 156, 161
  and antinomies 21
  and difficulty 79, 126
  and Margot Ruddock 126
  and mutually repellent forces 93
  and reality and justice 53

EU authorised representative for GPSR:
Easy Access System Europe, Mustamäe tee 50,
10621 Tallinn, Estonia
gpsr.requests@easproject.com

www.ingramcontent.com/pod-product-compliance
Lightning Source LLC
Chambersburg PA
CBHW070239240426
43673CB00044B/1847